BUILDING TEAM POWER

How to Unleash the
Collaborative Genius
of Work Teams

BUILDING TEAM POWER

How to Unleash the
Collaborative Genius
of Work Teams

Thomas A. Kayser

CRM FILMS
Carlsbad, California

IRWIN
Professional Publishing
BURR RIDGE, ILLINOIS
NEW YORK, NEW YORK

Senior editor: Cynthia A. Zigmund
Project editor: Karen J. Nelson
Production manager: Jon Christopher
Interior Designer: Laurie Entringer
Cover designer: Tim Kaage
Art coordinator: Heather Burbridge
Art studio: Accurate Art
Compositor: Precision Typographers
Typeface: 11/13 Palatino
Printer: Arcata Graphics/Fairfield

Library of Congress Cataloging-in-Publication Data

Kayser, Thomas A.
    Building team power : how to unleash the collaborative genius of
work teams / Thomas A. Kayser
      p.   cm.
    Includes bibliographical references and index.
    ISBN 0-7863-0302-6
    1. Work groups. I. Title.
    HD66.K388 1994
    658.4'02—dc20   93–48207

Printed in the United States of America
1 2 3 4 5 6 7 8 9 0 AG/F 1 0 9 8 7 6 5 4

To my mentors: Dr. Alton C. Bartlett, University of South Florida; Dr. Arlyn J. Melcher, Southern Illinois University; Dr. Frank L. Simonetti, University of Akron—gentlemen who awoke and compassionately nurtured the spirit of collaboration inside of me.

Foreword

Tom Kayser's new book *Building Team Power* gets at one of the most pressing needs of business today: getting teams to work. There is a new urgency for making this happen. Yes, teams have been a part of work life since work life existed, but today I'm convinced that teams now *are* the organization. By that I mean that today's teams—especially those on the front line—are where the most important discussions, decisions, and actions are taking place.

Gone are the proclamations from above, the 700-page policy manual and the "check your brains at the door" mentality toward workers of years past. Today's organizations must move fast to collaborate and in the process find a way to come up with the right decisions more times than not. Companies need those employees who are closest to the action to be fully engaged in striving to bring their best thinking to the organization's most pressing needs. And those individuals must interact to develop even better decisions than any one employee could achieve on his or her own. As we like to say in my company, "None of us is as smart as all of us."

The team is the perfect vehicle for having the dynamic of this interaction take place. The team is where the organization's needs and employee talents can converge. With a team you can quickly bring a cross-section of perspectives to bear on issues of pressing importance to the current and future well-being of the organization. You can quickly share relevant data for determining the most appropriate action given the situation at hand.

Tom's book provides all the ingredients for making teams be the most productive possible. With it, you can harness the potential power of the team and transfer it to more competitive practices for your organization that result in greater success of your mission and objectives.

Ken Blanchard, co-author
The One Minute Manager

Preface

The symphony orchestra is routinely held up as the classic example of collaboration in action. Ninety individuals playing their instruments in perfect harmony to produce music that sends a chill down your spine. Sitting in the theater, you have the opportunity to enjoy, first-hand, the results of that collaboration. However, collaboration rarely just emerges from an orchestra, or any work group for that matter. It requires someone to orchestrate it and others to pull together and follow that lead to make collaboration a reality. Initiating, nurturing, refining, and extending collaboration throughout a work team or department takes time, understanding, and patience on the part of *everyone* involved. Yet it can be fouled up in a heartbeat by anyone with misguided intentions. The following consultant's report on ways to improve the technical efficiency and productivity of a symphony orchestra vividly illustrates my point.

> All 12 violins are playing identical notes; this is unnecessary and wasteful duplication. The violin section can be cut drastically, saving considerable labor costs. The oboe players have absolutely nothing to do for long periods of time. They just sit in their chairs. Their number should be reduced. Compositions involving the oboe must be rewritten so that the work is spread out more evenly, thus eliminating costly "peaks" and "valleys" of oboe productivity.
>
> I noted a recurring repetition of certain musical passages. What useful purpose is served by repeating on horns what has already been produced by the strings? Were all such redundant passages eliminated, the concert time (two hours) could easily be reduced to 40 minutes. This would also eliminate the need for a time-wasting intermission. Something should be done about the shocking obsolescence of equipment. The program notes informed me that the first violinist's instrument was several hundred years old. If normal depreciation schedules had been applied, the value of the instrument would have been reduced to zero, and a more modern and efficient violin could easily have been purchased.[1]

Like many people in the work-a-day world, our consultant has no understanding or appreciation of the power of collaboration. Not only didn't the consultant have any concept of the how-to's for unleashing the collaborative genius of that orchestra, in attempting to improve the orchestra's performance capability, this person was about to destroy its collaborative soul.

In any case, what does all of this have to do with you and your organization? Plenty! Why should you bother to read any further? Because what you will learn here is at the very core of organizational success for the 1990s and beyond!

THE NEED FOR THIS BOOK

After the publication and favorable reception accorded my first book, *Mining Group Gold: How to Cash in on the Collaborative Brain Power of a Group* (El Segundo, CA: Serif Publishing, 1990), and the popularity of the video based on that book (*Mining Group Gold*, CRM Films, Carlsbad, CA, 1992), I knew I was on to something that went beyond casual interest. My continuing experience as manager of organization effectiveness for Xerox, my debates with colleagues both inside and outside of Xerox, my discussions with my wife, Carol, who has worked with a number of school districts and industrial firms teaching and applying the principles of *Mining Group Gold*, along with Carol's and my review of the business literature, all validated the same thing time after time. *New and experienced managers both lack an incisive understanding of the mental maps and fundamental approaches to building team power.*

New managers most often do not have this know-how simply because of their managerial inexperience. Many experienced managers, on the other hand, lack collaborative skills and insights because they grew up in the centralized, command-and-control bureaucracy where large merit-increases, promotions, bonuses, lavish offices, and other forms of reward and recognition went to those managers who were best at dictating and directing. In those order-giving organizations, nurturing collaboration and teamwork was not a highly valued managerial behavior. Because it was looked upon as soft, weak, and a career killer, skill development in facilitating team power was squashed.

While this medieval thinking still exists in abundance today, you can no longer allow it to predominate and drive your company's culture. If your organization does not understand or believe in utilizing the power of collaboration—or dismisses it as some passing fad—you are riding into the 21st century on the same highway to failure as our orchestra consultant!

It is irrelevant whether your establishment is in the public sector or private sector, is for profit or nonprofit, or is a producer of goods or services—a paradigm of collaboration up, down, sideways, and diagonally within and across every corner of your organization is mandatory for success in the 1990s and beyond. Figuring out ways to do things right the first time, everytime; creating products and services that delight your customers and distress your competitors; forming and implementing strategies and structures to capture and hold market share; and studying and reconfiguring work processes to slice costs and improve quality are huge tasks requiring the collaborative genius of your entire organization. You cannot afford to have it any other way. However, just talking generically about the need to do a better job of initiating and nurturing organizational collaboration does not give you any clues for facilitating it.

WHAT YOU WILL GET OUT OF READING *BUILDING TEAM POWER*

This is a hands on, how-to book. It is a roll-up-your-sleeves-and-get-your-hands-dirty book. It is applications oriented all the way. Don't look for complex psychological, sociological, or group theory models here. You won't find any. *Building Team Power* extends *Mining Group Gold*. It pushes deeper into the how-to's of facilitating teamwork and collaboration within your own work group, across work groups, or in task forces, committees, problem-solving teams, executive councils, and the like. It digs into some of the crucial but tougher areas to facilitate. It is one thing to say, "We need more and better collaboration around here." It is another thing to do it. This book fills a void because it shows you how to do it in terms you can understand! Skill improvement in facilitating collaboration and teamwork is what this book is all about.

After reading *Building Team Power*, you will, I hope, pick out a few facilitation actions and get started by saying: "Hey, I can give these a try because I understand what I am supposed to do. Kayser's book taught me something."

MY APPROACH TO WRITING *BUILDING TEAM POWER*

I have tried to boil down the subject matter so it is informative, yet fun to read. I've used a personal style. That is, if I could sit down and talk with you for a day about facilitating collaboration, this is what I would say. To make the book both enjoyable and instructive, I have included anecdotes, humor, war stories, cases, and real life examples.

Also, and this is very important, *there is no requirement to read Mining Group Gold before reading Building Team Power*. While I believe they make a wonderful pair and they combine to provide an abundance of knowledge on the art of facilitation, I have taken pains to summarize points from *Mining Group Gold* whenever I wanted to draw from that material as a foundation for the new tools, concepts, and tips introduced here. As a further aid, I have cross-referenced *Mining Group Gold* at those junctures where summaries have been provided so that you can go back to the original source if you desire to do so.

THE BOOK'S FOCUS

Building Team Power moves you along your excursion to learn how to unleash the collaborative genius of work teams in four steps. These steps equate to the four sections of the book. To clarify the book's focus and acquaint you with its content and flow, this next part presents each section, along with its corresponding chapters and chapter objectives. The section headings provide the broad focus; the chapters and their objectives give the specific focus.

Section I: Stating the Case for Collaboration

Chapter 1: "The Command-and-Control Bureaucracy: An Outmoded Architecture for the 1990s and Beyond." *Objectives:* To describe the dynamic, global marketplace facing organizations in the 1990s and beyond; to outline the characteristics of the traditional command-and-control bureaucracy; to suggest how the traditional bureaucracy needs to be refined to enable quality improvement and market place success now and in the future.

Chapter 2: "Collaboration: An Organizational Necessity for the 1990s and Beyond." *Objectives:* To define collaboration; to show why collaboration is essential to organizational success today and in the future; to demonstrate the power of collaboration in action.

Section II: Setting the Foundation for Gaining the Collaborative Advantage in Your Organization

Chapter 3: "Facilitation Basics: A Few Key Concepts." *Objectives:* To define the term *facilitator*; to establish the facilitator role as an essential managerial role for the 1990s and beyond; to make clear that facilitation of any session is a shared responsibility with all attendees.

Chapter 4: "Dimensions of Collaborative Power: Understanding the Core Principles." *Objectives:* To present the four primary sources of power; to wipe away the serious misunderstandings regarding the three variables of collaborative power—authority, responsibility, and accountability; to showcase the idea that collaborative power is about sharing control, not losing control; to outline a simple facilitation pathway that ensures power sharing, not task dumping.

Chapter 5: "Purpose and Desired Outcomes: The Cornerstone of Every Facilitation Effort." *Objectives:* To define the terms *purpose* and *desired outcomes* using illustrative statements; to stress the necessity of having purpose and desired outcomes statements for every session you facilitate; to demonstrate the cornerstone role that clear purpose and desired outcomes statements play in all successful facilitation efforts.

Chapter 6: "Interpersonal Behaviors: A Shared Facilitation Responsibility among All Group Members. *Objective:* To present and discuss a set of interpersonal behaviors essential to conducting effective group sessions—group task behaviors, group maintenance behaviors, and gatekeeping processes.

Section III: Presenting the How-To's for Unleashing the Collaborative Genius of Your Work Team

Chapter 7: "Decision Making: Understanding the Range of Options." *Objectives:* To present a framework for classifying and understanding the range of decision-making options available to the work group manager or task force chairperson; to highlight the characteristics of each of the eight options; to introduce and describe five noteworthy forces that impact the selection of a particular option.

Chapter 8: "Consensus Building: Facilitating Whole-Group Support." *Objectives:* To remove widespread misunderstandings regarding the consensus process; to detail six principles that are paramount to the successful facilitation of consensus; to provide a set of tips and techniques for building consensus; to contrast the powerful process of consensus with the debilitating process of groupthink.

Chapter 9: "Conflict Management: Facilitating Five Steps to Collaborative Conflict Resolution." *Objectives:* To examine both the constructive and destructive effects of conflict on a group's performance; to present a five-step collaborative model for managing conflict; to provide the necessary how-to tips and techniques to enhance the manager's or chairperson's ability to effectively facilitate through conflict to consensus.

Chapter 10: "List Management: Facilitating Divergent and Convergent Thinking." *Objectives:* To demonstrate the vital role that orderly list management plays in successful group facilitation, to provide an integrated set of practical techniques, tips, and illustrations which will strengthen your ability to properly facilitate divergent and convergent thinking in group settings.

Chapter 11: "Analytical Tools: Facilitating Seven Structured Processes for Displaying and Analyzing Data and Information." *Objectives:* To present the techniques for constructing and using a set of tools for *displaying information graphically*—time charts, bar charts, and pie charts; to present the techniques for constructing and using a set of *graphic analytical tools* for problem solving—flow charts, cause-and-effect diagrams, Pareto analysis charts, and force field diagrams.

Chapter 12: "Group Problem Solving I: An Orientation to Systematic, Collaborative Problem Solving." *Objectives:* To provide a set of facilitation behaviors that are key to creating and maintaining collaborative problem-solving teams; to examine the pitfalls to be avoided, and the benefits to be gained, through the application of systematic, collaborative problem solving; to highlight the role of problem sensing as the precursor to problem solving.

Chapter 13: "Group Problem Solving II: Facilitating Six-Steps to Problem-solving Success." *Objectives:* To present a practical, six-step, group approach to identifying, analyzing, and solving problems in a systematic, collaborative manner; to provide the how-to's for facilitating each step of this six-step model; to demonstrate the applied power of this six-step process through a business case study.

Section IV: Integrating What's Been Learned

Chapter 14: "Human Resources Redeployment: An Integrative Case Study." *Objectives:* To use a real-life work example as a means for demonstrating the application of a variety of the facilitation tools, techniques, and processes presented throughout this book; to highlight the power of secondary facilitation in action.

IDEAS FOR MAKING THE TRANSITION TO COLLABORATIVE LEADER

The key to success in acquiring or improving your group facilitation skills is the old refrain: practice, practice, practice. There are no shortcuts. However, your skill development can be an organized endeavor using *Building Team Power* as your central resource. Your skill acquisition process involves the following steps:

> Read the book straight through to gain an overall view of each chapter and, in turn, the flow of the whole book. As you read, highlight key points that are of particular interest.

> Write a final set of notes to yourself on the Notes Worksheet at the end of each chapter.

> Choose several chapters that are the most important to you and review your highlighted points and your Notes Worksheets.

> Select several actions you want to practice to improve how you lead your work team. This is your personal action plan.

> Try out your chosen actions and assess—with the help of your team—where your efforts went well and where they did not go so well.

> Make a new plan that preserves the positive aspects of your earlier effort while reducing or eliminating the negative aspects, then try again.

With each successive cycle, you and the other group members will make progress in your ability to pull together and will soon realize that everyone on the team, not just the manager or task force chairperson, shares responsibility for successful collaboration. Along these lines of making the transition from controlling to facilitating, Fran Rees offers some reinforcing advice:

Leaders who are making the transition to a more facilitative approach will do well to remember three principles of change:

• Change takes *time*.

• Change is a *process*, not a decision.

• Change requires plenty of *experience and practice* in the new way of doing things.

Leaders seeking change must acknowledge the vast effort it takes and must not give up when it takes more time and practice than anticipated. Change is not on a switch, like a light that goes on and off, but is a process—sometimes a very long one. Leaders who effectively implement change make sure their teams have plenty of opportunities to practice new ways of doing things while they go about their day-to-day activities. . . . [Also], ask yourself what strengths, support systems, and other resources you already have that can help you make these improvements. Plan to use these strengths to your advantage when you begin to make changes.[2]

SOME FINAL THOUGHTS

As you read and reflect on *Building Team Power*, please keep the following points in mind.

> While the focus of this book is geared to the manager's perspective in facilitating his or her work team, these techniques are applicable to a variety of group situations. Any person responsible for leading any type of group session will find this material relevant and valuable.

> The points presented here are not inflexible prescriptions—cast in concrete—but rather ideas for guiding you in initiating and maintaining collaboration within your organization.

> Finally, because these are only guidelines, you are encouraged
> to initially practice the techniques and processes as described.
> However, after gaining experience and confidence in their use,
> supplement and refine this foundation in order to extend your
> skills in facilitating teamwork and collaboration.

There is a Chinese proverb that states: Even a journey of a thousand
miles must begin with the first step. After you read the Acknowledgements, let's take the first step of our journey to learn about collaboration
by moving on to Chapter 1.

Thomas A. Kayser
Pittsford, NY

NOTES

1. S. H. Simmons, *How to be the Life of the Podium* (New York: AMACOM, 1982), pp. 249–50. According to Ms. Simmons, "Leo Rosten, writing in the *Saturday Review*, originally recounted this story about an unknown wit analyzing the operations of a symphony orchestra for technical efficiency."

2. F. Rees, *How to LEAD Work Teams: Facilitation Skills* (San Diego, CA: Pfeiffer and Company, 1991), pp. 43–45.

Acknowledgments

The power of collaboration was the key ingredient that made this book a reality. The biggest collaborators were my managerial and individual contributor colleagues at the Xerox Corporation. No one is better able to challenge you to achieve excellence than Xerox people. All the tools, processes, and structures written about in this book have been battle tested by me many, many times. Over the years, every encounter with a Xerox team has been a learning experience for me, and without them, there would be no book.

I am grateful to the many hours of help my wife, Carol, gave to this project. She has worked with much of this material in service and educational settings—district superintendents and their staffs, as well as school principals and their teams. Her work helped validate that what is written here has appeal beyond business and industrial situations. Carol was my rough-draft editor and a resource helping to make content refinements throughout the book. Besides that, she crafted the multipart PTA case example that is the glue for Chapter 10.

A special debt of gratitude goes to Peter Jordan, President/CEO, and Stephanie Glidden, Founding Principal, CRM Films, for believing in my material and wanting to publish it. Thanks to Tonya Mantooth for her outstanding management of this project for CRM Films. Also, much gratitude is given to the team at Irwin Professional Publishing for their masterful collaborative effort in transforming my manuscript into this polished book: Cynthia Zygmund, Senior Editor; Karen Nelson, Project Editor; Patrick O'Hayer, Copy Editor; and Colleen Tuscher, Marketing Manager.

Finally, my thanks to a number of friends from diverse organizational settings who strengthened the content of this book with their comments: Joe Lipchek, Mead Corporation; Robert Cancasci, Denis Allemand and Associates; William Stevens, United Industries; Ronald Schleede, National Transportation Safety Board; Michael Badalich, M. J. Badalich and Associates; Dr. Jack Simonetti, University of Toledo; Donald Zrebiec, Rochester Institute of Technology; Ronald Cox, Kaset International; Jeanne Chatigny, Texaco; John Walker, Goodyear Tire and Rubber Company; and Michael Haber, XCEL Laboratories, Inc.

Contents

Section IV
INTEGRATING WHAT'S BEEN LEARNED

STATING THE CASE FOR COLLABORATION

Chapter 1

The
Command-and-Control
Bureaucracy
An Outmoded Architecture for the
1990s and Beyond

Chapter Objectives

> To describe the dynamic, global marketplace facing organizations in the 90s and beyond.

> To outline the characteristics of the traditional command-and-control bureaucracy.

> To suggest how the traditional bureaucracy needs to be refined to enable quality improvement and marketplace success now and in the future.

INTRODUCTION

It's no secret that the quality of manufacturing and service in America has been improving over the past 10 years. Still, the results are mixed and there is much room for continued improvement. An incident that happened to me on a recent business trip to Los Angeles will underscore my point.

As I reached the front of the check-in line in Rochester, New York, the airline representative asked me where I was going and I said, "Los Angeles." She asked if I was checking any bags and I replied, "Three." I also stated, "I would like one checked to LA, the second checked to Istanbul, Turkey, and the third to Auckland, New Zealand." With an icy stare and a cutting tone to her voice she slapped her hand on the counter and declared, "Impossible! We can't do that." "That's funny,"

I replied. "Last month you did it for me and I didn't even ask you to!"

We all have our favorite stories about lack of service and poor quality. In fact, baseball is no longer America's favorite pastime. Today our great pastime is recounting tales of airlines that miss schedules or lose luggage, computers that don't compute, service personnel who are rude, automobiles that don't run, and toys that break after two minutes in the hands of a five year old.

While some stories may be a bit exaggerated, they all drive home the same point. In spite of the progress that has been made, American suppliers of goods and services have a long way to go to consistently meet the requirements of their customers—all customers—whether they are around the block or around the world. One thing is clear: The hierarchical command-and-control bureaucracy is not the mechanism for consistently meeting customer requirements in a dynamic, fickle, global marketplace. The pathway to competitive success is flatter, flexible, empowered organizations emphasizing teamwork and collaboration.

UNCERTAINTY, INTERDEPENDENCE, COMPLEXITY: DEFINING THE ENVIRONMENT OF THE 90S AND BEYOND

Leaders in companies large and small, profit and nonprofit, manufacturing and service need a new vision to move their enterprises into the next century. The successful firm will rely less on centralized grand strategies, designed and dictated by senior management to the rest of the organization, and more on the collaborative abilities of managerial and employee work teams to decipher trends and react swiftly with the appropriate products or services.

In this tough new world of international competition, what reigns supreme is understanding and translating customer requirements into goods and services that give you a marketplace advantage. The old ways of doing business, including traditional organizational structures, management attitudes, and views about the role of the worker, are being challenged and reevaluated. Corporate alliances, whether joint ventures or acquisitions, are being driven by competitive pressures and strategies rather than the need for financial restructuring.

The following provides a vivid picture of the new marketplace realities.

> On the eve of the 21st century, powerful technological and political forces are converging to create a new economic order in which nations are members of a single global marketplace. Computers, satellites, and facsimile machines have already integrated the world's financial markets; when tremors hit Wall Street, London and Tokyo feel the aftershocks. More and more manufacturers are producing goods overseas, in cities whose names they can't even

pronounce. On the political front, an increasing number of both Western and communist nations are dismantling trade barriers and deregulating state-run industries—policies that pave the way for even more multinational cooperation in business. What *is* certain is that only the most agile and innovative companies will turn the opportunities ahead into gold.[1]

The dynamics of the environment for the 90s and beyond can be best characterized by this adage: The world is moving so fast these days the person who says it can't be done is generally interrupted by someone doing it. Going global is a long-term, complex process, but it's not limited to big established companies. As soon as your company steps outside its home base, to invest or sell or to source capital, technology, facilities, human resources, and/or raw materials, it is on its way to being global.

It makes no difference whether you are producing goods or services. The point is you are in a whole new ball game with a harsh new set of rules that need to be comprehended if you are to compete successfully. If your organization was progressive and highly regarded 10 years ago, you are not necessarily progressive today—nor will you be 10 years from now—unless you are able to successfully capitalize on the rampage of change to continually improve your ability to meet the demanding requirements of your customers. To put it bluntly, even if your company gets to be world-class, that achievement only allows you to compete against other world-class companies, and it won't ensure that you become "king of the hill."

A. P. Carnevale has identified six competitive standards for anyone attempting to compete in the new economy:

> Success in the new economy depends on the ability to meet the new competitive standards—to run faster in the *productivity* race while simultaneously delivering to customers the *quality, variety, customization, convenience, and timeliness* they demand. . . .
>
> A set of profound economic and social changes around the world have put consumers in the driver's seat. They are richer. They use more time making money than spending it. They demand—and new technology allows—the creation of products and services that exhibit quality, variety, customization, and convenience in a timely way at mass produced prices.[2]

In this new economy, be assured that if your organization can't make the necessary adjustments to supply what your customers require—someone else will steal your markets.

TWO CLASSIC CASES OF STOLEN MARKETS

Western Union

Sending messages and, later, wiring money not only became the cornerstones of Western Union, these services made the company an American institution. Operating revenues hit the billion-dollar mark in the early 1980s; in 1982, the stock reached a high of $54.

But how quickly those cornerstones crumbled. Western Union grossly underestimated the rapidity of the decline of Telex service, which was eclipsed by the facsimile machine, a faster, cheaper message-sending alternative that debuted in the early 1980s and whose popularity exploded in 1988. Western Union abandoned telecommunications in 1991.

Its money transfer business, although profitable, is on a slippery rope. With the advent of automated teller machines (ATMs) linked by such shared-network purveyors as Cirrus, Western Union has been reduced to catering to members of the cash economy—customers without bank accounts—and faces strong competition from American Express, whose Money Gram, introduced in 1988, offers 10-minute service to almost 50 countries. Despite financial restructuring and reorganization, the future of Western Union looks bleak.[3]

The Honda-Yamaha Motorcycle War

Honda entered the auto market in 1967 and assigned their best people to the venture. Yamaha watched. While concentrating on automobiles in the 1970s, Honda still introduced twice as many motorcycle models as Yamaha. By 1980 Honda and Yamaha shared the market, each with 35 percent.

In 1981 Yamaha took the offensive with 60 new-model introductions. Honda introduced 63. Yamaha's president vowed that his company would be No. 1 in the world within a year. Honda's President Kawashima announced that Yamaha had not only stepped on the tail of the tiger, but they had ground it into the earth.

During the next 18 months, Honda made 113 improvements and introduced 81 new models, while Yamaha introduced only 34. The following year Honda introduced 113 models to Yamaha's 37. The field inventory was flooded and prices were slashed. A 10-speed bicycle now sold for more than a motorbike.

By 1983 the war was over. Yamaha's debt to equity rose from 3:1 to 7:1. During the next year, Honda introduced 110 more models to Yamaha's 23. In 1984, Yamaha was forced to take major steps. They had to sell assets and reduce salaries to restore the company's financial health.[4]

Western Union and Yamaha had the rug pulled out from under them because they failed to adapt to the uncertain, interdependent, complex markets they faced. These two organizations were unable to measure up to Carnevale's competitive standards of productivity, quality, variety, customization, convenience, and timeliness. But Diebold (ATMs), Cirrus, American Express, and Honda could, and did, and therefore stole market share from their rivals.

THE COMMAND-AND-CONTROL BUREAUCRACY: THE OLD STRUCTURES, PROCESSES, AND ATTITUDES WON'T WORK

Characteristics of the Command-and-Control Bureaucracy

Most modern organizations are modeled after a hierarchical power distribution that was designed several thousand years ago to achieve command and control over dominions. This is often referred to, in the organization theory literature, as the traditional or bureaucratic (i.e. rational-legal) organization.

The development of the modern American corporation has its roots in the early 1900s, with the advent of Frederick Taylor's scientific management. The command-and-control hierarchy for running enterprises really took hold between 1910 and 1925 when financial and industrial giants like J. P. Morgan, Andrew Carnegie, John D. Rockefeller, Sr., Pierre S. du Pont, and Alfred P. Sloan designed and managed their companies following this model.

With some variations, most organizations in the public and private sector follow the prescription laid out roughly 80 years ago:

> A pyramid-shaped hierarchy containing narrowing layers of management as you move from the bottom to the top.

> Decision-making authority based on one's level in the pyramid hierarchy; increased position power and formal authority at each successively higher rung in the chain of command.

> Separation of decision making and implementation. Managers and staff make decisions from the top down; workers implement and provide requested information from the bottom up.

> Separation of operations from policy setting.

> An apparatus of budget, head count, planning, and other controls to manage and coordinate the various departments and divisions comprising the total organization.

> A set of rules, regulations, and policies to shape the organizational culture and resolve disputes and conflict. (Often the rules, etc., are applied uniformly across all cases to ensure consistency.)

> A division of labor at each level of the hierarchy based on functional specialization and detailed job descriptions with little rotation across functional specialties.

> No duplication of functions—tasks are handled exclusively by those assigned to them.

I must emphasize that I am not saying eradicate the command-and-control bureaucracy and bury it in some toxic waste dump 2 feet from hell. No business structure survives, pretty much intact, for 80 years without having some merits. However, the first principle of Organization Theory 101 is that optimal structures are situational. That is, they are influenced by each organization's location, market, environment, and history. The kind of structure that makes sense for a pet food manufacturer may not make sense for a video games developer or a Broadway theater.

The bureaucracy can function well in a relatively stable environment, where problems can be identified by daily or weekly reports, analyzed by staff, presented to top management for their decision, and delegated to middle managers who transmit the decisions and coordinate the implementation of the workers. If you are in a stable, slow-growth mass market, using single-purpose machinery, semiskilled workers, and producing standardized, high-volume products (e.g. chemicals, paper, lumber, electric power), the command-and-control bureaucracy can work for you. While you are *less* affected by the turbulent, global market conditions described earlier—you are not exempt from them. Those macro winds of change still will blow against your company, forcing you to refine overly restrictive policies, procedures, and control systems; to move final decision making down the hierarchy; and to search for ways to eliminate waste from your work processes.

By contrast, if you are in any of the more fast-changing markets—such as autos, office equipment, telecommunications, computers, publishing, specialty steel—then your bureaucracy needs refinement, or perhaps even an overhaul, to be a world-class competitor. The reason is straightforward. A dynamic, uncertain, interdependent, and complex market environment overloads the bureaucracy's ability to be nimble, collaborative, and fast acting.

The Illusion of Significant Change

A few hybrid structures and empowered cultures are beginning to take root today. Still, the theme of command-and-control, with all of the support functions, policies, rules, and norms to make it work, flows through the veins of most organizations today. Thus, even with the groundswell of activity that began in earnest during the mid-1980s to improve quality and productivity in America, the traditional bureaucracy still predominates because old habits die hard. Companies still hire actors dressed as General George S. Patton to give motivational speeches. The 1949 movie classic *12 O'clock High*, with Gregory Peck as a commander who whips a World War II bomber unit into shape through intimidation, is a popular executive development film even today.

The business and economic success America enjoyed during the 1980s came about because we took the structures and processes designed early in the 20th century and ran them harder. In effect, we performed organizational surgery and injected organizational "steroids." We restructured, delayered, downsized, cranked the costs out, and made efforts to pump the quality up. In essence, we took the same old organization and culture and just squeezed it, but in the overwhelming majority of instances *we didn't really transform anything.* Over and over again we subscribed to the "bird cage theory of change." It works like this. The canaries are all sitting on their perches in the bird cage. Someone reaches in and removes two canaries. The remaining canaries all flutter around the cage and come down on different perches. Voila! You have a downsized and reorganized bird cage. But nothing was actually transformed. You simply have the same canaries—albeit fewer in number—sitting on different perches in the same bird cage.

The bird cage theory of change was used often in the last decade. Thousands of managers' heads rolled, those that remained sat on different perches, and thousands of industrial workforce members were laid off, to show the world that American business was breaking away from its bloated, fat cat past. Slicing workers—and in most instances *talking about* the need to empower workers, to be more flexible, to be more risk taking, to be more innovative—was the change agenda for firms in the 1980s. However, the rigid bureaucracies, with the boss as an all seeing, all knowing, order giver, remained largely intact. This approach will be inadequate for the 1990s and beyond.

More and more organizations in the public and private sectors are coming to realize that the traditional bureaucracy has been pushed beyond its limits of effectiveness. It is an inadequate response to the new economic and market demands presented earlier in this chapter.

Steven Dichter, a principal in the New York office of McKinsey and Company, has expanded on this theme:

> [Organizational] strategies are increasingly shifting from cost-and-volume-based sources of competitive advantage to focusing on increased value to the customer. . . . The command-and-control organization is under strain. Indeed, many businesses are finding that command-and-control principles now result in competitive disadvantage.
>
> - *Cost.* Layers of management and unnecessary staff functions to communicate and control top management directives can no longer be afforded.
>
> - *Slow Response.* Standardized procedures, together with inflexible roles and responsibilities, create an organization that does not readily sense and react to changes in customer needs or technologies.
>
> - *Lack of Creativity and Initiative.* Narrowly defined tasks do not fully tap the potential of today's better educated employees.[5]

Permanent changes do need to be made, changes that refine, loosen, and reshape the bureaucracy. For many companies, wholesale changes are needed. However, you will never destroy all traces of the bureaucracy. No matter what changes you make, the fundamental vestiges of the bureaucracy will remain. Some form of hierarchy will exist. (You may have fewer layers, but there will still be a hierarchy—everyone in the total organization will not report to a single person.) People will be working in specified functions. (They may be skilled in four or five functions instead of one or two, but there is a limit to the number and variety of functions a person can be skilled in.) There will be some form of line operations and staff support. (The line operations may be built more around flexible teams working in parallel doing lots of steps in a process rather than being organized in rigid functions, and the staff support may be much smaller and have its role defined differently, but both will exist.) You are going to have some form of rules, regulations, and policies. (They may be more flexible, allowing some leeway for different situations, but they will exist to prevent anarchy.) You will also have budget, head count, or other control mechanisms. (There may be greater collaboration in setting and utilizing such mechanisms, but they will exist nevertheless.)

THE FACTS-BASED ORGANIZATION: THE TRANSFORMED BUREAUCRACY

What revisions are needed to mold a new bureaucracy and put it into fighting trim for the 1990s and beyond? If you look at recent literature, you will find that a common set of organizational characteristics have emerged. These characteristics are highly interrelated and I have summarized them using the acronym FACTS—flattened, adaptable, customer focused, team focused, and speedy.

Flattened

Flattening has been the primary effort of the late 1980s and early 1990s, as organizations stripped out unnecessary layers of the managerial hierarchy. *Unnecessary* refers to any person or function that neither makes decisions nor leads. The desired outcome is the elimination of levels whose sole purpose is to act as "mind guards"—sorting, interpreting, and censoring the information that flows between the hands-on people doing the work and senior management. Business reporter Carol Hymowitz provides additional insight:

> The old hierarchical corporation, with a pyramid-shaped management structure, allowed managers to carefully sift information before making decisions—but they decided too slowly. In today's global marketplace, what counts is speed. Companies must be able to launch new products quickly and

alter existing ones for big customers. The only solution is flatter companies in which information flows quickly from top to bottom and back up again, decisions come fast, and teamwork is the rule.[6]

However, the compression between the top and bottom that results from removing hierarchical levels has its dangers. Managers are thrust down closer to where the action is—closer to activities they do not readily know how to do or understand. The workers, on the other hand, who are used to carrying out directives, are now being asked to plan, schedule, solve problems, and make decisions. First-level managers used to implementing strategy are being asked to set it. This restructuring places a premium on something that may have been in short supply under the old system: *teamwork and collaboration up, down, and across all functions and levels of the hierarchy.*

Decision makers must also be attuned to workload as they flatten an organization:

> "The life of a manager is a lot more different now than 10 years ago," says Robert Kelley, a business professor at Carnegie Mellon University. "As companies cut layers, they haven't also cut the work, so managers are getting stretched very thin overseeing more people and jobs."[7]

Management must do a task assessment and redefine which tasks are critical in the flattened structure. Where did this task come from? How does it flow? Why do we do this task in this manner? Is it necessary? What is the benefit to the customer? If you don't cut work when you cut layers, you get nowhere.

Adaptable

Increased adaptability means eliminating or redefining any procedures, rules, regulations, or approvals that are snarling decision making and information flow or perpetuating inflexible work processes. In short, rip out and burn your red-tape! Organizational agility is essential for success in a fast-changing, highly competitive global economy.

Companies are encouraging and rewarding people to learn different knowledge and skills. This makes people a multifaceted resource and provides the organization with the ability to easily reconfigure itself. This also builds learning into the job, which in itself is a source of motivation and reward for individuals.

Another activity is to examine all job classifications and descriptions. The action of reducing and simplifying them aids organizational adaptability. For example, at some Proctor and Gamble state-of-the-art factories, all employees fall under a single category: technician. And Corning's auto pollution controls facility in Blacksburg, Virginia, is organized around five key jobs that all employees learn and perform.

In an article on the changing bureaucracy, Brian Dumaine provides additional illumination on adaptability:

> [In the adaptive organization] teams variously composed of shop-floor workers, managers, technical experts, suppliers, and customers will join together to do a job and then disband, with everyone going off to the next assignment. . . .
>
> Raymond Miles, a management professor at Berkeley, likens [the transformed bureaucracy] to a network where managers work much as switchboard operators do, coordinating the activities of employees, suppliers, customers, and joint-venture partners. . . . No matter what you call them, these designs for an organization have one thing in common: fluidity. The adaptive organization will work much the same way the big construction firms such as Bechtel, Fluor, and Brown and Root do, gathering hand-picked groups of employees and outside contractors with the right skills for each new dam, refinery, or airport.[8]

Thomas Stewart, writing in *Fortune* magazine, captures the essence of organizational adaptability with this colorful passage:

> The new flexible organization will be a powerful competitor. [McKinsey and Company principal] Douglas Smith finds a metaphor in *Terminator II*, the movie where Arnold Schwarzenegger faces a metal monster that liquifies, then hardens again in a new shape—now a man, now a machine, now a knife. Says Smith: "I call it the *Terminator II* company." How'd you like to have to compete with one of those?"[9]

Customer Focused

The driving force behind the shift away from the old bureaucracy can be summarized by two words: customer focus. Xerox Corporation's Quality Policy articulates the fusion between quality and focus on the customer.

> Xerox is a quality company. Quality is the basic business principle for Xerox. Quality means providing our external and internal customers with innovative products and services that fully satisfy their customer requirements. Quality is the job of every Xerox employee.

The Quality Policy is like the North Star: It gives everyone in Xerox a vision they can relate to, it guides their behavior, and it helps break down barriers and gets people from different functions to collaborate.

Quality function deployment is a rigorous process used by progressive companies to help internal work teams increase their focus on the external customer. The customer's voice is used to determine what the critical properties of a new product or service should be. This method leaves nothing to the imagination in determining what will satisfy customers, how the new product or service stacks up against the competition, and how internal work processes must be managed to guarantee meeting customer needs.

Being customer focused should not be taken lightly. There is a big bottom-line impact in having customers who are merely satisfied versus *highly* satisfied: Xerox Corporation found that a highly satisfied customer was six times as likely to buy again as one who was just plain satisfied, said James Heskett, a professor at the Harvard Business School.

And that translates into bigger paybacks for a company. As little as a 5 percent increase in customer retention can mean between 25 percent and 100 percent profit increases over several years according to studies cited during a Harvard case style discussion that was recently broadcast to 26 cities nationwide.[10]

Team Focused

Given the information presented under the first three organizational characteristics, it is obvious that work teams are the heart of the new organization. Companies in the 1990s are realizing that a diverse group of people—using their own creativity, innovation, judgment, intuition, and brain power—can do a better job in today's world of constant change than any set of formal procedures, methods, or controls administered by a remote, centralized management. These enlightened firms are recognizing that group learning is possible and that the group social mind is more than the sum of the individuals.

Dichter's research on behalf of the McKinsey Company is noteworthy regarding the role of teams in the new enterprise:

> The classic hierarchical structure is no longer the sole or dominant determinant of organizational relationships. Multiple performance-oriented and accountable teams are found at all levels in the organization. Within functions, members are organized in teams, cross-trained, and provided with business information to enable them to perform multiple roles and adjust quickly to varying requirements. Across functions, the formation and reformation of multidisciplinary teams to solve particular performance issues become the norm rather than the exception. As a result of this team orientation, decisions become more collaborative, due to members' possessing the skills, incentives, solution space, and information to contribute. Structures also tend to be flatter and more flexible, but a well-designed hierarchy remains.[11]

Peter Drucker, writing about the new, information-based organization, adds further insight to the team-focused perspective:

> Traditional departments will serve as guardians of standards, as centers for training and the assignment of specialists; they won't be where the work gets done. That will happen largely in task-focused teams. . . .

> In pharmaceuticals, in telecommunications, in paper making the traditional *sequence* of research, development, manufacturing and marketing is being

replaced by *synchrony:* specialists from all these functions collaborating as a team, from the inception of research to a product's establishment in the market.[12]

Speedy

The final characteristic of the refined bureaucracy for the 1990s and beyond is speed. Reducing time-to-market is critical because, as the saying goes, The early bird gets the worm. In the global economy of today, with fierce, world-class competitors lurking in every marketplace, the innovator has the edge. It goes back to Carnevale's competitive standards of providing quality, variety, customization, and convenience in a *timely* manner. Organizations that are able to meet these standards are the winners, and those that cannot become the Western Unions of the world.

According to one study of high-tech markets, products that come to market on budget but six months late earn 33 percent *less* profit over five years than products that come out on time but are 50 percent over budget.[13]

Early introduction of a product into the market gives the innovator several outstanding advantages: longer sales life, higher market share, and higher margins because of premium pricing and cost advantages from the manufacturing learning curve. Every organization must consider lost time as an irreplaceable resource. Either you put your own products out of business or your competitors will!

Rosabeth Moss Kanter enriches this discussion of speed-to-market with her penetrating viewpoint. Like the previous four principles, teams and teamwork are the foundation for success:

> Having new ideas is not enough without the ability to commercialize them before the competition does. Smaller companies unencumbered by bureaucracy can often beat their bigger rivals that are slowed by endless review committees or communication channels. . . .
>
> One important reason some companies move quickly is that they have developed teams that have total project responsibility, and every skill needed is represented on the team. . . . Ford emphasizes "chimney breaking"— eliminating the communication barriers between functional departments so that people will collaborate to accomplish a common project quickly. In addition to setting up single, integrated, cross-functional teams, Ford has located engineering and manufacturing people on the same site.[14]

What Makes the Transformed Organization Tick? The Answer: Collaboration!

If you go back and reread the information on the five characteristics defining the FACTS-based organization, you'll discover not only how tightly intertwined they are, but also that the word *collaboration* is associated with each one. In a nutshell, collaboration is the guts of the whole scheme.

Your organization's success in gaining and holding a competitive advantage in an uncertain, turbulent, complex environment will depend on how well it is able to constantly tap into the gold mine of wisdom, creativity, and innovation held in the heads of your workforce members. Being a competitive force during the 1990s and on into the 21st century means not just keeping up with the pace of change—but rather capitalizing on it to better satisfy internal and external customer requirements. *To accomplish this, your organization will have to continuously leverage the synergy and collaborative brain power of employees in many configurations, at all levels, and across all functions.* It is through these collaborations that human ingenuity and creativity are best utilized. The problems are too enormous, the pat answers too few, and the stakes too high for it to be any other way. Centralized, intellectual elitism is the surest path to organizational dry rot and an eroding customer base.

A comprehensive look at collaboration is reserved for Chapter 2.

A CLOSING SUMMARY

Clearly, the dynamic global economy will continue to increase marketplace uncertainty, complexity, and interdependence for most organizations throughout the rest of this century and into the next. However, depending on the particular sector and the goods or services produced, some organizations may face relatively stable, high-volume, mass market conditions. In these situations the traditional bureaucracy can be appropriate and work well, especially if managed with a flair for teams, teamwork, and collaboration.

By contrast, organizations constantly buffeted by shifting global markets, ever changing customer requirements, rapid technological change, quick product obsolescence, falling trade barriers, ferocious competition, and the like, will discover the traditional command-and-control bureaucracy becomes a poor fit with today's realities. These dynamic pressures overload the bureaucracy's ability to respond. Organizations facing these realities must shift from the traditional hierarchy to a new, collaborative way of doing business. Although bureaucracy elements will remain throughout the total organization, a set of consistent characteristics for a refined bureaucracy has emerged from the business and behavioral science literature. This set of new organization characteristics is based on the FACTS—flattened, adaptable, customer focused, team focused, and speedy. These characteristics are highly interrelated, but the common blood that keeps them all alive and makes them all work is *collaboration*.

Collaboration is the pathway to competitive success for any organization in the public or private sector, but it is essential for those facing turbulent markets. Facilitating collaboration at any level, within or across functions, in any type of organization, is what this book is all about. Setting the context for the study of collaboration is what Chapter 1 has been about.

NOTES WORKSHEET: DEVELOP WRITTEN
RESPONSES TO THE TWO ITEMS LISTED BELOW

What Do You Feel Are the Main Learning Points from Chapter 1?	Elaborate on Why You Feel These Points Are Key

NOTES

1. "Business Goes Global," *Best of Business Quarterly*, Winter 1989–90, p. 51.

2. A. P. Carnevale, "Put Quality to Work: Train America's Workforce," *Training and Development Journal*, November 1990, pp. 34, 36.

3. S. Costas, "Shoot the Messenger," *Investment Vision*, October/November 1991, p. 92.

4. R. B. Kennard, "From Experience: Japanese Product Development Process," *Journal of Product Innovation Management*, September 1991, p. 186. The vignette quoted from Kennard is his summary of the account of this motorcycle war taken from J. C. Abegglen and G. Stalk, Jr., *Kaisha, The Japanese Corporation* (New York: Basic Books, Inc., 1988).

5. S. F. Dichter, "The Organization of the '90s," *The McKinsey Quarterly*, no. 1 (1991), pp. 146–47.

6. C. Hymowitz, "When Firms Cut Out Middle Managers, Those at Top and Bottom Often Suffer," *The Wall Street Journal*, April 5, 1990, p. 1-B.

7. Ibid.

8. B. Dumaine, "The Bureaucracy Busters," *Fortune*, June 17, 1991, pp. 36, 42.

9. T. Stewart, "The Search for the Organization of Tomorrow," *Fortune*, May 18, 1992, p. 98.

10. Knight-Ridder Service, "Satisfied Customers Key to Bottom Line," *Times-News*, Kingsport, Tennessee, March 7, 1993.

11. Dichter, "The Organization of the '90s," pp. 148–49.

12. P. Drucker, "The Coming of the New Organization," *The Harvard Business Review*, January–February 1988, p. 47.

13. Carnevale, "Put Quality to Work," p. 37.

14. R. M. Kanter, "Navigating the '90s," *Best of Business Quarterly*, Winter 1989–90, p. 83.

Chapter 2

Collaboration
An Organizational Necessity for the 1990s and Beyond

Chapter Objectives

> To define collaboration.

> To show why collaboration is essential to organizational success today and in the future.

> To demonstrate the power of collaboration in action.

INTRODUCTION

Pat Riley, head coach of the New York Knicks, said something about hard work and practice that also rings true for collaboration. Riley said, "While hard work and practice won't guarantee you anything, without it, you can't even begin to think about successfully competing in the NBA (National Basketball Association)." So it is with collaboration. While collaboration won't guarantee anything, without initiating, maintaining, and refining it throughout your organization, you can't even begin to think about successfully competing in the turbulent, complex economic environment of the 1990s and beyond. Collaboration must be the name of your game if you are intent on becoming world-class in your marketplace.

Successfully meeting the ever increasing competitive standards of productivity, quality, variety, customization, convenience, and timely delivery of your goods or services so that you win, and hold on to, delighted customers is a formidable task. To do so means you must accept a fundamental truth: No single person—or elite senior-level staff group—in your organization can possibly have all the answers on how to capitalize on the realities of your competitive world. People must collaborate at all levels, in every nook and cranny, to develop the necessary solutions and applications that are right for your competitive situation.

If you're in a market situation that allows you to operate with a more traditional bureaucracy, *collaboration will make you better.* If you're now in the more common situation of a dynamic, global marketplace trying to make a FACTS-based (flattened, adaptable, customer focused, team focused, speedy) organization work, *collaboration is an absolute necessity.*

LESSONS FROM GEESE

For me the most revealing example of collaboration, in its most pure and genuine form, was found on a 1986 United Way campaign poster.[1] As you read this section you will appreciate the power of collaboration as never before.

The next time you see geese heading south for the winter, flying along in V formation, you might be interested to know what science has discovered about why they fly that way. Researchers have learned that as each bird flaps its wings, it creates an uplift for the bird immediately following. By flying in a V formation, the whole flock adds at least 71 percent greater flying range than if each bird flew on its own.

Whenever a goose falls out of formation, it suddenly feels the drag and resistance of trying to go it alone and quickly gets back into formation to take advantage of the lifting power of the bird in front. When the lead goose gets tired, it rotates back in the wing and another goose flies point. The geese honk from behind to encourage those upfront to keep up their speed.

Finally, when a goose gets sick, or is wounded by gunshot and falls out, two geese fall out of formation and follow it down for protection. They stay until it is able to fly or is dead, and then launch out on their own or with another formation to catch up with their original group.

As I often tell managers in my workshops, building collaboration into your organization is not too difficult. All you and your people need is as much sense as a gaggle of geese!

FRAMING A DEFINITION

The literal, sterile definition of collaboration is "to co-labor; to labor together." Robert Thomas, retired vice president of marketing for the Edmont Corporation, in a private discussion following an after-dinner speech, viewed collaboration as a primary plank in any organization effectiveness strategy. He noted: "The whole object of any organization effectiveness strategy is to engender organization-wide collaboration, on a routine basis, by figuring creative ways to get to each employee the benefit of all the knowledge and experience that each requires, from any person, anywhere in the company.''

More specifically, I have surveyed over 300 Xerox managers and individual contributors during team-building workshops by asking: ''What does collaboration mean to you?'' Although individual responses varied, five consistent themes have emerged. With this list, the theme most often mentioned is listed first, the second most popular theme is second, and so on. Collaboration means:

> Creating synergy in the production of outputs (ideas, decisions, strategies, products, services, etc.) so that the group result is greater than any individual could achieve working alone.

> Having shared goals or priorities and working together to achieve them.

> Sharing and processing information—free from hidden agendas—in the pursuit of consensus.

> Setting aside one's ego to expand the human potential of others.

> Relying on each other for advice and counsel.

This list is a good one because it presents examples of what collaboration looks like and feels like in a variety of forms.

Gauging the level of collaboration in your department or work team is not difficult using the Stevens formula. Bill Stevens, a good friend who also is president and CEO of United Industries, passed along this gem: ''For me, the bottom line measure of collaboration is the ratio of *we's* to *I's* that I hear in my interactions with people throughout the various departments of United Industries.'' The Stevens formula provides a simple, on-going means for sensing the degree of collaboration within your work unit. If you get the feeling that you are hearing more *we's* than *I's*, you have at least one indication that collaboration is alive in your organization.

Let's summarize the information presented so far into a definition to serve as a common point of reference for the remainder of this book. *Collaboration is a joint effort between two or more people, free from hidden agendas, to produce an output in response to a common goal or shared priority. Often this output is greater than what any of the individuals could have produced working alone.*

COLLABORATION: THE ROAD OVER WHICH ORGANIZATIONAL SUCCESS RIDES

David Kearns, speaking about the realities of the global marketplace, said it best in 1990 when he was still chairman and CEO of Xerox: ''We're engaged in a race without a finish line. Our competitors are world-class and they are not standing still. As we improve so do they.'' Kearns's statement reminds everyone of the specter of *kaisen*. *Kaisen* is a Japanese word and it is at the root of their quality movement. *Kaisen* means gradual, unending improvement, doing little things better, setting and achieving ever higher standards. In the spirit of *kaisen,* the awesome challenge confronting all businesses is the same. What must we do to continuously raise ''our bar of excellence'' for productivity and customer satisfaction at a faster rate than any of our competitors?

I can assure you, to do this well is going to require that collaboration in your organization be a way of life. When asked about collaboration, your employees need to reply: ''It's no big deal. It's just the way we work around here. It's the only way.'' You cannot afford any other outlook. Employees cannot be allowed to walk around for years, months, or even days with gold nuggets of wisdom locked in their head because no one cares what they think, no one believes they have any good ideas, no one bothers to take the time to listen and understand what they think. What resource in your organization could possibly be more valuable than the collaborative brain power of all your employees, regardless of their position?

Fortune magazine stated the case for collaboration in ''An American Vision for the 1990s'':

> Successful companies will constantly learn and adapt, restructuring radically if necessary. That means more than cost-cutting, a lot more. It means delivering on the promise of participatory management, allowing employees a say in how the organization is designed, how work is assigned, how they are compensated. The latest studies of business show that providing workers with a sense of participation increases productivity far more than incentive pay. Turning employees loose to figure out the best way to do a job can lead to double-digit surges in output.[2]

The Case for Collaboration

The cornerstone of building a collaborative culture is teaching your people how to make collaboration happen—how to facilitate it. That's what the remaining chapters of this book will teach you. Also, collaboration cannot be practiced by only one segment of our organization—it has to be everywhere. It has to flow up, down, sideways, and diagonally, both inside and across every function.

What you are really doing as you build collaboration is obliterating the internally competitive and destructive win/lose, attack/defend, us/them conflicts that are standard operating procedure inside so many of today's organizations. Your enemies are not within your organizational boundaries. They are outside your boundaries. Your enemies are your external competitors and they are formidable. They are after your people and your market share. Spending any time and energy erecting walls and defending turf in noncollaboration, political gamesmanship, and destructive conflict is deadly. It will bring your company to its knees.

Jack Welch, CEO of General Electric, has some provocative thoughts on this subject:

> The winners of the [1990s] will be those who can develop a culture that allows them to move faster, communicate more clearly, and involve everyone in a focused effort to serve ever more demanding customers. To move toward that winning culture we've got to create what we call a "boundaryless" company. We no longer have the time to climb over barriers between functions like engineering and marketing, or between people—hourly, salaried, management, and the like. Geographic barriers must evaporate. . . . The lines between the company and its vendors and customers must be blurred into a smooth, fluid process with no other objective than satisfying the customer and winning the marketplace. . . . We have to undo a 100-year-old concept and convince our managers that their role is not to control people and stay "on top" of things, but rather to guide, energize, and excite.[3]

Barriers, both real and perceived, complex and simple, will come tumbling down under the onslaught of collaborative thinking. When this happens, the white space between the boxes on the organization chart begins to diminish. The frozen chain of command, where the top tells the middle what to do to the bottom, begins to thaw and melt. The informal organization, consisting of alliances between people and the power relationships that actually get the work done, is recognized, freed up, and nurtured by providing the resources it needs.

Forced by relentless competition from the Japanese and the Ford Motor Company, GM is carrying out a grand collaboration experiment at its Saturn manufacturing plant in Spring Hill, Tennessee. It's a far cry from the infamous, "humans are just interchangeable cogs with the mechanical parts of the assembly-line" mentality and the adversarial, explosive union–management relations that ruled the Lordstown, Ohio, Vega plant in the 1970s.

> Saturn's best hope is that it represents a profound change in the way GM manages its people. . . . The labor agreement establishes some 165 work teams, which have been given more power than assembly-line workers anywhere else in GM or at any Japanese plant. They are allowed to interview and approve new hires for their teams (average size: 10 workers). They are given wide responsibility to decide how to run their own areas; when workers see a problem on the assembly line, they can pull on a blue handle and shut down the entire line. They are even given budget responsibility. One team in Saturn's final-assembly area voted to reject some proposed pneumatic car-assembly equipment and went to another supplier to buy electronic gear its members believed was safer.[4]

While it will take some years before we know whether America can compete head-on with the Japanese in automaking, the evidence as of early 1994 looks promising. However, in the meantime, there can be no question about the sincerity of GM's intent, given its commitment to launch the Saturn venture—$3.5 billion and eight years.

Steelcase, the Grand Rapids, Michigan, manufacturer of office furniture, has become a benchmark company for overcoming the barriers that traditionally divide and isolate functional departments from one another.

> This move [to eliminate functional barriers] was taken so seriously that the company spent $111 million to build a new 575,000-square-foot building called the Corporate Development Center. This center has brought together the design, engineering, and marketing staffs in a new way. Instead of a separate department for each function, business management groups were created for each product line. An engineer's office is located next to the designer's office next to a marketing person's office. There is no boss for each group, but only a team leader to facilitate progress. The idea was to speed development time and encourage employees to assume accountability for the product. . . .
>
> Product development time has been cut in half. Instead of a several-year process, it now takes a year and a half to go from the point of identifying a need to the point of shipping. [The] goal is to shorten that to 10 months.[5]

Steelcase provides an example of a genuine transformation as opposed to the old "birdcage" approach to change.

Goodyear Tire and Rubber Company, from my hometown of Akron, Ohio, never would be confused with Intel or Apple Computer with respect to its organizational structure and culture. Conservative, hierarchical, staid, and controlling would be apt descriptors of Goodyear—I know because my father worked there for 45 years before retiring and I spent two summers working there during my graduate school days. But those descriptors may not fit the Goodyear of the 1990s:

> Empowering workers has paid dividends for tiremaker Goodyear, which was burdened by $3.7 billion in debt and pinched by depressed sales to the auto industry when new chairman Stanley Gault arrived [from Rubbermaid] in June 1991. Gault . . . swiftly assembled teams to complete work on languishing new products and opened his door to complaints and suggestions. Since Gault became chairman, Goodyear has rolled out flashy new tires like its deep-grooved Aquatred model. . . . "The teams at Goodyear are now telling the boss how to run things," boasts Gault. "And I must say, I'm not doing a half-bad job because of it."[6]

Rosabeth Moss Kanter provides her incisive perspective on the subject of organizational collaboration:

> Perhaps the flexibility with the highest potential payoff involves the ability to combine a company's various resources in collaborative efforts: joint marketing between divisions, for example, or a product package linking components from units that traditionally sold their wares separately, or the procure-

ment staff for one business unit helping another find a supply source for a new venture. Corporations are realizing that internal competition can cause hostility and must be replaced by internal collaboration to maximize the value of having all those groups under one roof. Thus, many companies are now—to parody a popular film title—"desperately seeking synergies."[7]

Destructive Internal Conflict: The "Attack Scorecard"

The most vivid and, I hope, long-lasting impression I can give you of the destructive in-fighting and conflict existing in organizations is exemplified by the case below. The following story, which is both humorous and sobering, was given to me by a close friend who worked at a troubled Fortune 500 organization for three years, until his mounting frustration forced him to resign. Upon joining this firm, one of my friend's first assignments was to teach a five-day management development workshop required for all first-level managers. The program had been designed internally by the company's corporate training group and had been running for about a year.

The approach advocated in the workshop was participative management, mutual problem solving, coaching and counseling, motivation through recognition, group decision making, and the like. He was enthusiastic and believed in those principles back then as fervently as he still does today. However, what he was teaching and role-modeling in the classroom was not valued and rewarded on the job. He was new to the company and wanted to conduct a high-quality, professional workshop to impress the participating managers and his own boss, so he poured his heart and soul into the task.

However, things did not go well. As he bluntly states it: "Those were the most miserable five days I have ever experienced anywhere. Every module I taught was ferociously attacked. Cynicism abounded. I was looked upon as someone who had a 'screw loose' to even speak about participation, two-way communications, helping others, trust, and recognition, let alone actually believe in these things."

After the class ended and he leaned against a table in shock, a manager approached my friend and said: "You tried hard. But what you're preaching here is 180 degrees opposite from reality. It's all bullshit! Maybe 10 percent has relevance to my job. The rest, forget it. If you don't kick-ass, intimidate, stonewall, and browbeat others in meetings, negotiations, and other interactions, you are considered soft—worse than that, you're branded a loser. And when that happens, you can kiss your career goodbye. To survive and get promoted here, you need to attack, attack, attack. You need to be one nasty competitor!"

He then handed my friend the document shown in Figure 2–1 and said: "I created this 'Attack Scorecard.' I evaluate the dynamics of every meeting I attend—including myself—using this form. Others are using

FIGURE 2–1
Attack Scorecard

		Points
Direct attack	Total surprise: nailed the person. No rebuttal from opponent.	25
Direct attack with counterattack	Opponent surprised but able to defend and counterattack; casts doubt on credibility of first attacker.	20
Retaliation attack	Player burning over attack received yesterday—needs to level the score. Ten points initially, but 20 points if sustained.	10/20
Deadly humor attack	Player destroys opponent with a humorous attack aimed directly at the opponent's stupidity and/or incompetence.	15
Organization buckshot attack	Nothing specific, just taking a swipe at another organization.	5
Sideline blue shot attack	Someone on sidelines tosses in hitherto uncommunicated observation. Nobody knows how to react.	0
Collaborative effort	One or more players from each side engage in a collaborative effort to work issues and solve problems; there is no contest. Nielsen rating of game drops off. *All players involved forfeit 50 points.*	−50

it. This is reality. The higher an opponent scores on the scorecard, the tougher, more hard-nosed, and intimidating I have to be to get my way. Collaboration is good only if it is to *my* advantage." The "Attack Scorecard" says it all. It defines an internally competitive culture that is sapping too many American organizations of their *externally competitive* vitality!

Near Death Brought on by an Internally Competitive Culture: Case Study, Part I

Xerox created and lived with its own highly autocratic, internally competitive culture from 1975 through 1982. During that same period, the disciplined, determined, collaborative Japanese ran roughshod over Xerox. By creating efficient designs and manufacturing capabilities, the Japanese were able to build their products, ship them to an American distributor, have the distributor mark them up and sell them to a retailer, who again marked them up and sold them to American consumers, *for less than what it cost Xerox to manufacture its products here in the States!* The Japanese also were able to get their products to the market in half the time it took Xerox. Confronted with such competition, Xerox saw its market share in free fall. The shocking facts are prescribed by David Kearns, Xerox CEO from 1982 to 1990: "From 1976 to 1982, Xerox's share of American copier installations dropped from an estimated 80 percent to 13 percent, a staggering decline. In 1970, Xerox held about 95 percent of the market. Japanese companies were mostly responsible for our plunge."[8]

Rework, scrap, excessive inspections, lost business, and other short-comings were estimated to cost Xerox at least 20 percent of revenues annually, a figure that in 1983 amounted to nearly $2 billion.[9] It wasn't a pretty sight.

Vigorous Health Brought on by Genuine Collaboration: Case Study, Part II

Beginning in 1982, Xerox began to fight back against the real enemy, its external competitors. Seven years later its business products and systems organization won the Malcolm Baldrige National Quality Award. Since 1989, Xerox operating companies have won national quality awards in nine difference countries—Japan, Canada, the Netherlands, France, England, Australia, Brazil, Mexico, and Belgium. Xerox became the first American company—targeted by the Japanese—to win back market share. This reversal was accomplished without any tariffs or government-mandated protection. What turned the tide was the numerous changes in policies, procedures, work processes, and structures brought about by a multitude of Xerox people who were just as determined, disciplined, and dedicated as the Japanese.

From 1985 through 1991, Xerox customer satisfaction ratings improved by 41 percent, and product costs were reduced by 30 percent despite inflation.[10] Product-to-market time was reduced by up to one-half. Xerox reduced its number of suppliers from 4,500 to 350 and increased quality over 100 times. Return on assets, which was 8 percent in the early 1980s, was up over 14 percent in 1991. Finally, in 1982, Xerox did not have a single machine rated as best in its class by the industry analysts. By 1990, Xerox machines were the best in class in all seven categories.[11]

Let's fast-forward to a major activity by the Xerox United States Marketing Group (USMG) during the summer of 1991. This story provides a fitting contrast to the internally competitive, attack culture of the mid-1970s through 1980. The case epitomizes the power of speedy, customer-focused, cross-functional, collaborative teams to make life miserable for external competitors.

A highly successful national sales blitz that focused on Xerox copier/ duplicator high-volume competitors was conducted by USMG during the week of June 10, 1991. The marketing expertise of the USMG sales force, along with the support of over 175 headquarters and area personnel, yielded significant results.

The national sales blitz, titled "The Main Event," was part of a USMG marketing program, "Knock Out '90s—The Rematch." The program was sponsored by the vice president of customer marketing and was developed by a cross-functional quality improvement team (QIT) with participation from segment marketing, product marketing, marketing information services, pricing and forecasting, sales operations planning, and market coverage/telemarketing operations. The program included collaterals (banners, posters, etc.), team training, a competitive strategy binder for each sales rep, reference resources (including a national electronic file drawer), action items, a direct mail campaign, and the "Main Event" national sales blitz.

During the "Main Event" week the following actions took place:

> Made 10,279 high-volume sales calls.

> Made 7,615 sales calls directed at high-volume competitors.

> Presented 3,347 proposals.

> Conducted 1,385 demonstrations.

> Wrote 188 trial orders.

> Received 1,345 orders.

> Scored 315 high-volume competitive knock outs.[12]

Now, the punch line. *The QIT brought the whole program to the field in just 45 days from the first planning meeting!* No "Attack Scorecards" here. Months later, due to the momentum generated, Xerox was still deriving positive results from the blitz.

A PICTURE IS WORTH A THOUSAND WORDS

Cashing in on the collaborative brain power of all employees in the relentless pursuit of customer satisfaction must be the essential philosophy of today's organizations. Destructive conflicts among individuals and functions fighting each other and working at selfish cross-purposes must be eliminated. If they are not, you will be on the high road to customer dissatisfaction from operating like the firm depicted in Figure 2–2.

With genuine collaboration, you dramatically increase your chances of meeting customer requirements, growing a base of satisfied customers, and building a stronger, more committed organization. In short,

FIGURE 2–2
The Sequence to Customer Dissatisfaction

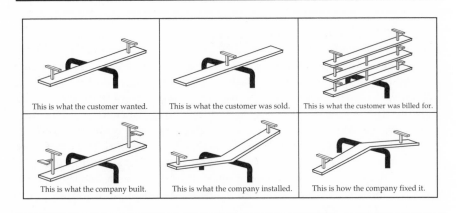

| This is what the customer wanted. | This is what the customer was sold. | This is what the customer was billed for. |
| This is what the company built. | This is what the company installed. | This is how the company fixed it. |

FIGURE 2–3
The Sequence to Customer Satisfaction

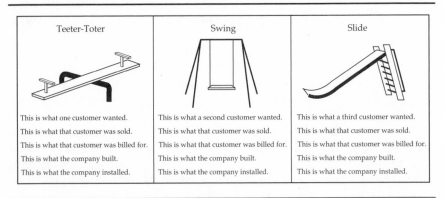

Teeter-Toter	Swing	Slide
This is what one customer wanted.	This is what a second customer wanted.	This is what a third customer wanted.
This is what that customer was sold.	This is what that customer was sold.	This is what that customer was sold.
This is what that customer was billed for.	This is what that customer was billed for.	This is what that customer was billed for.
This is what the company built.	This is what the company built.	This is what the company built.
This is what the company installed.	This is what the company installed.	This is what the company installed.

you will be able to produce customer-winning results like those high-lighted in Figure 2–3.

A CLOSING SUMMARY

Our working definition of collaboration is as follows: Collaboration is a joint effort between two or more people, free from hidden agendas, to produce an output in response to a common goal or shared priority. Often the final output is greater than what any of the individuals could have produced working alone.

Collaboration is not a pipe dream. It is not some soft, wimpy approach to doing business. Mining the gold nuggets of wisdom of your people at all levels of your organization takes some learning and know-how. It may require behavioral shifts for a large number of your people, especially managers. It is being recognized as the most effective way to cope with the turbulent, complex, and uncertain environment of the 1990s and beyond.

As Jack Welch, Stanley Gault, and Rosabeth Moss Kanter emphatically noted, and the General Motors, Steelcase, and Xerox examples graphically portrayed, the internal win/lose, us/them, political infighting that is sucking the lifeblood out of organizations must be eradicated and replaced by a culture of collaboration. It is the pathway to competitive success for the 1990s and into the 21st century. Facilitating collaboration to gain a competitive edge for your organization must be a shared responsibility among all managers and among as many individual contributors—exempt and nonexempt—as possible.

The problem is this: Thousands of books and articles talk about the requirement for collaboration. But they don't provide the most needed information of all, that is, how to create and nurture a collaborative environment in groups, how to make it happen, what specifically to do—to forge consensus, facilitate through differences, solve problems, share, and process information in a collaborative way. This book, along with my previous one, *Mining Group Gold: How to Cash In on the Collaborative Brainpower of a Group* (El Segundo, CA: Serif Publishing, 1990), presents the how-to's of facilitating collaboration. The next chapter provides a framework and some basic principles that are instrumental in successfully facilitating collaboration in groups. The following chapters get down to the specifics of collaboration.

A final thought before moving on. "Although the Boston Celtics have won 16 championships, they have never had the league's leading scorer and never have paid a player based on his individual statistics. The Celtics understand that virtually every aspect of winning basketball requires close collaboration among all players."[13]

NOTES WORKSHEET: DEVELOP WRITTEN
RESPONSES TO THE TWO ITEMS LISTED BELOW

What Do You Feel Are the Main Learning Points from Chapter 2?	Elaborate on Why You Feel These Points Are Key

NOTES

1. The reference on the United Way campaign poster read as follows: "Adapted from Barbara Stirling Willson."

2. "An American Vision for the 1990s," *Fortune*, March 26, 1990, p. 15.

3. Cited in S. P. Sherman, "Today's Leaders Look to Tomorrow," *Fortune*, March 26, 1990, p. 30.

4. S. C. Gwynne, "The Right Stuff," *Time*, October 29, 1990, p. 76.

5. K. Cahill, "The Many Faces of Empowerment," *Enterprise*, January 1993, p. 27.

6. J. Greenwald, "Is Mr. Nice Guy Back?" *Time*, January 27, 1992, p. 43.

7. R. M. Kanter, "Navigating the '90s," *Best of Business Quarterly*, Winter 1989–90, p. 84.

8. D. T. Kearns and D. A. Nadler, *Prophets in the Dark: How Xerox Reinvented Itself and Beat Back the Japanese* (New York: HarperCollins Publishers, Inc., 1992), pp. 134–35.

9. N. Rickard, "The Quest for Quality," *IE*, January 1991, p. 25.

10. "Quality Day Presentation for Customers," Xerox Corporation.

11. P. Allaire, "The New Productivity: Using Quality to Enable Our People to Create Value," speech given to the Executives' Club of Chicago, May 29, 1992. Mr. Allaire is chairman and CEO of Xerox Corporation.

12. "Today at Xerox," Xerox Corporation, July 2, 1991.

13. R. W. Keidel, "Going Beyond 'I'm O.K., You're O.K.'," *New York Times*, November 27, 1988.

SETTING THE FOUNDATION FOR GAINING THE COLLABORATIVE ADVANTAGE

Chapter 3

Facilitation Basics
A Few Key Concepts

Chapter Objectives

> To define the term *facilitator.*

> To establish the facilitator role as an essential managerial role for the 1990s and beyond.

> To make clear that facilitation of any session is a shared responsibility with all attendees.

> To demonstrate that practicing the art of excellence facilitation results in power gained, not power lost.

INTRODUCTION

Vince Lombardi, legendary coach of the Green Bay Packers during the 1960s when his teams won five National Football League championships plus Super Bowls I and II, opened every training camp the same way. After gathering all of his players together—veterans and rookies alike— he would say: "What happened last year is water over the dam. It's a new year now with new challenges. We must rededicate ourselves. We need to go back to the fundamentals; we need to start with the basics." Then, pausing to hoist a football high above his head, he would say sternly: "Gentlemen, this is a football!"

Just as Vince Lombardi took all of his players back to basics every summer, to make sure they had the fundamental knowledge to be a winning team, this chapter takes you back to the basics of facilitation to ensure that you have the fundamental knowledge necessary for successful collaboration. It also sets in place the necessary conceptual underpinnings for the rest of the book.

WHAT IS A FACILITATOR?

A facilitator is a person who helps a group free itself from internal and external obstacles or difficulties so that it may more efficiently and effectively pursue the achievement of the session's desired outcomes. The great Chinese philosopher Lao-Tse, who lived during the Chou dynasty over 2,400 years ago, developed a superb definition of the leader as facilitator when he said: "A good leader is best when people barely know that he leads. A good leader talks little but when the work is done, the aim fulfilled, all others will say, 'We did this ourselves.' "

Effective facilitation is the fuel for collaboration. Collaboration—especially within new or cross-functional groups—rarely is spontaneous. Someone needs to bring the appropriate people together, ignite a collaborative climate, and work at sustaining it. Everyone sharing in the facilitation will help maximize both the collaborative effort and the results achieved. As more and more people—especially managers—come to understand what facilitation means, internalize the philosophy, and practice quality fundamental behaviors, the payoff will be significant for your organization.

FACILITATING OTHERS: IT'S A DAY-IN, DAY-OUT, EVERYDAY ACTIVITY

As you read the upcoming chapters, please remember you do not have to be a manager to benefit from this book. As an individual contributor, if you are responsible for leading a project, spearheading a problem-solving team, heading a steering committee, expediting a task across several functions, chairing a board or commission, or providing third-party facilitation, this material still will benefit you greatly.

I have written this book from the perspective of the manager who is facilitating his or her own work group because that is where the emphasis must be placed to have facilitation take hold as a day-in, day-out, everyday activity at all organizational levels. While collaboration, as well as its facilitation, is an essential ingredient in the shift to the transformed bureaucracy, keep in mind that collaboration is a universal approach that will make any organization—even the traditional bureaucracy—stronger and more productive.

For an organizational culture to change, the facilitation how-to methods, techniques, and tips I am advocating must be an essential part of the way all managers consistently operate on a daily basis. These are not special behaviors to be used only for two hours at your weekly quality improvement team meeting, after which everyone goes back to the dictatorial, high-pressure, nonlistening, tight-control, attack/defend, hidden-agenda behaviors of business as usual. Your organization will grow stronger and be more externally formidable as it builds the collaborative advantage up, down, sideways, and diagonally within and across all levels and functions of the business.

The Role of the Manager as Facilitator

As more and more individual contributors, among both exempt and nonexempt workers, continue to move into more complex, knowledge-dependent roles in today's information age, they are becoming more technically expert than their managers. These people are closest to the customer, the product, and/or the service. Also, they are the ones walking into and out of your organization every day carrying a gold mine of wisdom about the things that count in your business—ideas on better ways of doing things internally that will improve quality and customer satisfaction. Experience tells me that employee knowledge is the most consistently underutilized resource inside most organizations.

Therefore, a primary role of any manager working in the 1990s and into the 21st century must be that of facilitator—a facilitator unleashing the collaborative genius of the organization. Thomas Stewart, in a *Fortune* article about General Electric, underscores this point:

> [GE] wrote the book on management. Now Jack Welch [GE's CEO] is rewriting it to tap into employee's brain power. . . . "We've got to take out the boss element," Welch says. By his lights, 21st century managers will forgo their old powers—to plan, organize, implement, and measure—for new duties: counseling groups, providing resources for them, helping them think for themselves. "We're going to win on our ideas," he says, "not by whips and chains."
>
> Don't get him wrong. Welch is not about to sacrifice profit on the altar of lofty sentiments. . . . Explaining the point of the exercise, Welch says, "The only ideas that count are the A ideas. There is no second place. This means we have to get everybody in the organization involved. If you do that right, the best ideas will rise to the top."[1]

To get the A ideas to rise to the top, GE has implemented a strategy involving three weapons. (1) *Work-out* is a forum where participants collaborate in taking unnecessary work out of their functions and working out mutual problems. (2) *Best practices* gets rid of the "not invented here" syndrome by finding the secret of someone else's success and spreading those good ideas from one part of GE to another. (3) *Process mapping* is the technique used in the other two processes to understand the situation being studied.

The need for people to acquire facilitation skills is well articulated in the national best seller, *Re-inventing the Corporation.*

> In the re-invented corporation, we are shifting from manager as order giver to manager as facilitator. We used to think that the manager's job was to

know all the answers. . . . The new manager ought, rather, to know the questions, to be concerned about them, and involve others in finding answers. Today's manager needs to be more of a facilitator—someone skilled in eliciting answers from others, perhaps from people who do not even know that they know. The most successful companies of the new information era are committed to the manager's new role as developer and cultivator of human potential.[2]

The facilitation of collaboration sparks a more holistic approach to problems and generates the flow of creative ideas and/or answers upward, across, and diagonally instead of just top-down. As a result, the entire organization can pull together to continually renew itself.

Jack Zenger, president of Zenger-Miller, an international training and consulting firm, speaks to the topics of teams and the manager as facilitator:

> Depending on organizational needs, teams may be permanent or temporary, functional or cross-functional, synonymous with, or auxiliary to, the activities of the natural work group, conventionally supervised, or in various degrees, self-managed. . . .
>
> Still, the well-documented vitality of teams in no way devalues the need for skilled managers. What's called for now is a different kind of manager— more strategic, more collaborative, more facilitative, and more responsive to customers, employees, and organizational imperatives.[3]

The direction described by these experts accentuates group-oriented, facilitative leadership behaviors. Increased delegation, shared decision making, empowerment, and management of cross-functional teams is not based on an autocratic model of *control*. It is grounded in a model of *teamwork, facilitation, and collaboration*.

Facilitation Is a Shared Responsibility

Although one person (the group manager, administrator, task force chairperson, team leader, or other designated individual) has the formal responsibility of being the primary facilitator for a particular group session, facilitation must be shared by everyone in attendance. All other attendees are secondary facilitators.

Whenever a group comes together to trade information, strategize, solve problems, or make decisions, every member of the group must share the responsibility for making the session as successful as possible. By recognizing that facilitation is a group function to which all members can contribute, the primary facilitator helps to develop a sense of teamwork and group cohesion. Developing a shared responsibility for facilitation ensures that all group resources will be used productively.

Dennis Kinlaw, in his book, *Team-Managed Facilitation: Critical Skills for Developing Self-Sufficient Teams*, reinforces the concept of team shared facilitation with his insightful comments:

Organizations have only just begun to discover the energy and creative power that can be generated in the interactive communication networks that are characteristics of teams. In the future that is now unfolding, organizations will not be characterized just by *having* teams. They will be characterized by *being* teams. . . .

The emphasis is on *facilitation,* not on facilitators. The reason for the emphasis is to underscore the belief that facilitation represents a set of competencies that every member of an organization can learn. . . . Organizations that translate this understanding into action and equip people with the skills for team-managed facilitation can expect to reap the benefits of team development, highly improved team meetings, and rapid strengthening of teams as self-sufficient units of performance.[4]

Let's now explore the concept of shared facilitation in more detail by examining the primary and secondary facilitation roles.

Primary facilitator. This is the primary person who focuses on the *process dynamics* of the group session as it unfolds. He or she stays keenly aware of how things are done in the session and intervenes to preserve the integrity and disciplined use of the processes described in this book. Initially the manager of the work group or the task force chairperson responsible for calling and planning the session assumes this role.

This book is written from the perspective of the *formal leader as primary facilitator.* Therefore, since the manager, chairperson, or team leader in most cases also will want to make significant contributions to the content of the discussion, he or she must verbally indicate what is happening anytime there is a switch in roles from *primary facilitator* (focused on process) to *manager* (focused on content) or back the other way. The switching of hats is for the benefit of other participants so they are not confused about the manager's changing role. (The concept of hat switching will be covered in more detail in the next section.)

As other group members acquire facilitation skills, the role of primary facilitator can be rotated among them. These people then will have to switch hats between being primary facilitators and contributing team members.

Secondary facilitators. An effective and productive group session cannot be achieved by one primary facilitator—even if it is the manager—trying to direct a pack of wild horses intent on ignoring the purpose, desired outcomes, and agenda; resisting all process discipline; making no effort to listen and understand each other; and trampling on each other to see who can dominate and control the session.

As I stated earlier, once the primary facilitator is designated, everyone else in attendance is assigned the role of secondary facilitator. The secondary facilitators share the responsibility for a productive meeting with the primary facilitator by doing two things: (1) monitoring themselves so they minimize their own disruptive behaviors and (2) intervening quickly to facilitate productivity-robbing activities as soon as they occur.

Typical examples of secondary facilitation, where a person other than the primary facilitator easily can intervene to help the group process, include:

> Alerting the group whenever it is straying from its desired outcomes.

> Stepping in to handle the disruptive behavior of another group member (side conversations, domination by one member, gate-closings, rambling, etc.).

> Gate-opening by seeking information and opinions from others, summarizing, and testing comprehension.

> Writing quickly and neatly on flipcharts.

> Providing input when the discussion has been reduced to nitpicking and there is a need to refocus on the original issue.

> Pointing out that although consensus seems to have been reached implicitly, the discussion is dragging on; suggesting that the manager (in the role of facilitator) test for consensus by going around the table.

> Relieving tension with humor or by suggesting a break.

> Monitoring time and providing regular updates on the time remaining for a particular subject.

Other actions may be needed, but these highlight how easy it is to help out with the facilitation activity. None of these actions require training to make them work. All that is required is the genuine desire on your part: (1) to have secondary facilitation be a standard operating principle of your group sessions, (2) to share your expectations on having everyone be secondary facilitators, (3) to define and clarify the specific secondary facilitation activities you believe need to be performed—see previous list, (4) to discuss these activities with your team to get their commitment, and (5) to positively recognize the people who perform secondary facilitation throughout the course of a meeting. The message bears repeating: Everyone shares responsibility for creating a productive group session.

Switching Hats

Initially, most people are ineffective at being, simultaneously, a primary facilitator and a full participant in the ongoing content discussion. Experience shows that if the primary facilitator actively participates in the content of the meeting without knowledge of the hat switching process, he or she invariably gets swept up in the debate, discussion, analysis, or disagreement, and forgets about the facilitation. While some people can do both jobs quite effectively without this technique, they are the exception rather than the rule.

If the manager, committee chairperson, or administrator is the primary facilitator for a group and, as usually happens, is unable to move naturally between the dual roles of group facilitator and full group participant, then these roles need to be consciously split up.

The reason for mentally separating the two roles is to emphasize and preserve the integrity of the facilitation process. By thinking in terms of "wearing two hats" and by switching them as required throughout the meeting, you will not forget about the facilitation role whenever you enter the discussion as a group participant.

As primary facilitator, your chief concern must be *facilitation* (helping the group free itself from internal obstacles or difficulties so that it can more efficiently and effectively pursue its desired outcomes) and not *content* (getting enmeshed in the task-related dialogue and activities).

Obviously, when facilitating your own group, you may want to contribute your perspectives and ideas to the ongoing dialogue and activities. When this occurs, you need to signal that you are stepping out of the facilitator role and into the role of group participant. Your inputs should be shared with the group and processed in line with the approach being utilized. When you are finished, announce that you are returning to the primary facilitator role and proceed with assisting the group process until the next occasion arises where personal input seems appropriate. Here is an example.

> At this point, I'd like to slip on my manager's hat and provide my perspective on the overtime issue. First of all, . . .

> Those are the main points I wanted to provide right now, especially the idea of flextime. Putting my facilitator's hat back on, I've noticed that Ben and Jeri have been quiet throughout this discussion. What are your views on the overtime problem?

Please remember, being primary facilitator in no way removes you from participating in meeting content. However, it is imperative that you distinguish your facilitation role from your group member (content) role each time these roles change during a group session. Also, from the group members' points of view, if it is unclear whether the primary facilitator is operating from the facilitator role or the active group member (content) role, secondary facilitation requires that the discussion be stopped momentarily with a performance check to ask the primary facilitator, "I'm not certain which role you're operating from at this point. Would you please clarify which hat you are wearing?"

Role splitting may seem awkward as I describe it here, but I can assure you that in the reality of the meeting process, it is a simple, smooth action. Moreover, role splitting delivers a significant two-pronged payback. It ensures the integrity of the facilitation process, and at the same time it provides a means for the primary facilitator to actively furnish his or her personal inputs regarding the issues at hand.

A CLOSING SUMMARY

A facilitator is a person who helps a group free itself from internal and external obstacles or difficulties so it may more efficiently and effectively pursue the achievement of the session's desired outcomes. To be most effective, the facilitation of collaboration must be role-modeled by managers at all organizational levels as a day-in, day-out everyday activity. It is not something done just once a week at a special problem-solving meeting and then forgotten the rest of the time until the next meeting.

The facilitation of a group session is not the sole responsibility of the primary facilitator, with everyone else merely in attendance to be facilitated. The model advocated in this book requires the establishment of one person as the primary facilitator (focusing on group process) with all other attendees designated as secondary facilitators to help with the facilitation and ensure that a productive session occurs.

As a primary facilitator, you will likely have a need to participate in the content of the discussion. When this occurs, you should signal that you are stepping out of the facilitator role and into the role of group participant. Your inputs should be shared with the group and processed in line with the approach being utilized. Once you are finished, you need to say that you are "switching hats" back to the primary facilitator role. Then proceed with assisting the group process until the next occasion when personal input becomes appropriate.

NOTES WORKSHEET: DEVELOP WRITTEN
RESPONSES TO THE TWO ITEMS LISTED BELOW

What Do You Feel Are the Main Learning Points from Chapter 3?	Elaborate on Why You Feel These Points Are Key

NOTES

1. T. Stewart, "GE Keep Those Ideas Coming," *Fortune*, August 12, 1991, p. 41.

2. J. Naisbitt and P. Aburdene, *Re-inventing the Corporation* (New York: Warner Books, 1985), pp. 52–53.

3. J. H. Zenger, B. Musselwhite, K. Hurson, and G. Perrin, "Leadership in a Team Environment," *Training and Development Journal*, October 1991, p. 48.

4. D. Kinlaw, *Team-Managed Facilitation: Critical Skills for Developing Self-Sufficient Teams* (San Diego, CA: Pfeiffer and Company, 1993), pp. 131–32.

Chapter 4

Dimensions of Collaborative Power
Understanding the Core Principles

Chapter Objectives

> To present the four primary sources from which you can draw power.

> To wipe away the serious misunderstandings regarding the three variables of collaborative power—authority, responsibility, and accountability.

> To showcase the idea that collaborative power is about sharing control, not losing control.

> To outline a simple facilitation pathway that ensures power sharing, not task dumping.

INTRODUCTION

During the summer between my junior and senior years in college, I worked in the warehouse of a small, family-owned manufacturing firm. The president and owner of this company—we called him "King Ironfist"—was the most *unempowering* manager I have ever known.

The supervisor of the warehouse often characterized the president's managerial style as "being to the right of Genghis Khan." Not only did he run an exceedingly tight ship, he was the epitome of the "hip shooter." King Ironfist dominated and cut off the sharing of important data by other people, he often sacrificed thought for action, he constantly overwhelmed his employees with a feeling of emergency, he was impatient, he delegated nothing, he wouldn't listen, and he prided himself in how quickly he could size up a situation and render a snap decision. The company was struggling financially, but because his last name was on the outside of the building in three-foot-high block letters, the president had his way.

Then one day, it all exploded in his face. King Ironfist came into the warehouse. He saw a college student lounging against a pallet of boxes reading the newspaper and raced up to him. "Hey kid," the president yelled, "how much money do you make a week?" "Two hundred dollars," was the reply. King Ironfist reached into his wallet, pulled out $200, and said angrily: "Here's two hundred dollars, hit the road. I don't ever want to see you back here again!"

We all watched this in horror. Next, King Ironfist grabbed the warehouse supervisor and asked, none too politely, "When in the hell did you hire that lazy bum?"

"I didn't," retorted the supervisor. "He works for Glenwood Freight and he was just waiting for us to finish confirming the bill of materials!"

After King Ironfist stormed off, all of us in the warehouse crew laughed until our sides ached. Reflecting back on that incident, however, I see it in a completely different light—a very gray and disturbing light. King Ironfist had created such a demoralized and demotivated culture throughout all departments that when news of the incident spread, everyone was exhilarated over his screw up. Employees' taking delight in their president's failures is not the mark of a competitive company.

How much more effective the outcome would have been had the president trusted and shared power with the warehouse supervisor. In that case, King Ironfist would not have been concerned with what he saw because he would have known that his empowered and trusted warehouse supervisor would not be allowing one of his crew to goof off. Or if he did perceive a problem, he could have had a 30-second private discussion with the supervisor—the person closest to the action—and quickly discovered the realities of the situation. In either case, a terribly embarrassing event could have been avoided and $200 saved.

As you will see in Chapter 6, there are times and places where one of the four autocratic decision-making methods is necessary and appropriate; in those instances, it is important to use that method. However, the autocratic mentality, along with its corresponding policies, procedures, and structure, cannot be allowed to dominate your way of doing business.

As Chapters 1 and 2 have emphasized, and as subsequent chapters will reinforce, organizations whose structure is a rigid pyramid and whose culture is dominated by centralized decision making lack the culture required for success today and in the future. Chapter 4 provides the framework for understanding the dimensions of collaborative power, and the remaining 10 chapters will teach you the techniques for facilitating collaboration on the basis of shared control.

THE FOUR SOURCES OF POWER: UNDERSTANDING THE BASICS

Before delving into the core principles of collaborative power, let's review the four sources from which you can draw power.

Legitimate (Position) Power

Legitimate power comes directly from your position in the hierarchy. It is formally defined in a written job description which outlines the authorities, rights, duties, and responsibilities of the position. If not formally defined, position power is derived from the culture of the organization.

Legitimate power is not tied to you as a person; it is tied to the position you occupy. The higher you are in the formal organization structure, the more position power you have; the lower you are, the less position power you have. For example, if you are promoted from supervisor to area manager, you will inherit the greater legitimate power attached to the area manager position. The person who replaces you in the supervisory job will be accorded a smaller amount of legitimate power due to the lower ranking of that position.

Moving up the organizational hierarchy not only earns you greater formal authority to render decisions of consequence, it also strengthens your ability to ensure the implementation of those decisions. Decision implementation often is managed through the judicious use of *reward power* and *punishment power*. These two power sources are subsets of, and tightly linked to, your overall position power. The higher your level in the hierarchy, the greater your power to reward and punish. Punishment is a strong word and can mean the extreme action of firing or demoting someone. But more often than not, the specter of punishment comes in the form of withheld rewards (e.g. three of the four people on your team receive pay raises in the 6 to 8 percent range; the fourth person receives nothing).

Organizational conflict often occurs over legitimate power, such as when people on equal or lower levels in the formal structure do not accept the authority and influence of someone attempting to exercise his or her position power.

Expert Power

Expert power is not directly linked to your position in the formal organization. It is derived from the type and level of knowledge, skills, and/or abilities you possess. Market researchers, information systems experts, technologists, legal eagles, organization effectiveness experts, scientists, accountants, environmental health and safety gurus, for example, all can have a great deal of expert power.

For example, Carlos is an information systems expert. In a meeting comprising his manager's manager plus six other executives, Carlos may in fact have the greatest amount of power because he is the only one with sufficient knowledge of the system's operation and potential for improvement.

Charismatic Power

Charismatic power is based on a particular person's attractiveness to other people. A person embodying charismatic power may or may not have legitimate power. If the individual has both, that person's charismatic power often is more than enough to get action from others in the accomplishment of goals and objectives. Said differently, charismatic people don't always need to rely on their position authority to achieve desired outcomes.

Joe Wilson, the driving force behind changing the sleepy Haloid Company into the Xerox Corporation, was such a person. Even though he held tremendous formal power derived from his CEO position, examples of the power of his charisma in shifting the paradigm of a small, undistinguished manufacturer of photographic paper to one that would create a $50 billion to $75 billion industry are still legendary 25 years later.

On the other hand, Mahatma Ghandi and Martin Luther King had little legitimate power, but to their many followers they had a large degree of charismatic power. Sports figures, rock musicians, T.V. and movie stars—for better or worse—at any point in time, can exert a tremendous amount of charismatic power over our adolescent population.

Political Power

Political power is grounded in the old adage, It's not what you know; it's who you know. Deriving power from high level personal connections, from access to information limited to most other people in positions of authority, and from understanding how to bend the formal rules, regulations, and policies to your advantage cannot be overlooked. Often political power is used as the springboard to achieving position power.

AUTHORITY, RESPONSIBILITY, AND ACCOUNTABILITY: THE VARIABLES OF COLLABORATIVE POWER

Now, with an understanding of the different sources of power, comes the bottomline learning point. *Of the four types of power you can acquire, the sum and substance of sharing power—of empowering others—resides soley in the area of position power.* Empowerment is activated by the desire to push formal decision-making authority lower in the organization, closer to the action of customer and supplier interface. *Delegation* of formal authority is what shared power is all about.

While the other three sources of power are real and cannot be ignored, they are not avenues for directly empowering others. I cannot delegate my expertise, my charisma, or my political power to you since each of these is uniquely personal to me. I certainly can draw from my charisma, my expertise, or my personal power bases to help you achieve some end you otherwise would not be able to achieve, but I cannot directly pass these power sources to you.

By contrast, delegation, or sharing position power, is operationalized through three root variables that interact as a dynamic system. However, the positive synergy created when they mesh properly can be quickly destroyed when the power to delegate is misused.

Each variable can be stated as a principle of shared power. Assume you are a manager holding position power within the formal organization.

Principle 1. You can delegate authority to others lower in the organization and thus share power with them.

Principle 2. You cannot delegate responsibility to others lower in the organization; however, you can assign responsibility and, in doing so, create a joint responsibility with them.

Principle 3. Each person delegated formal authority and assigned responsibility is accountable to you for the results of their specific actions.

An Example

If you, a manager, assign responsibility for achieving a particular budget target to one of your people, Debbie, and also delegate the appropriate formal authority to her so she truly can take charge and control her expenses, you have created a joint responsibility with Debbie and can hold her accountable for her results. Thus, if Debbie, through her own budget mismanagement or your mismanagement of her in this task, ends the year 25 percent overspent, which in turn forces you to come in over budget, your manager is still going to hold you responsible and accountable for the overspending in your budget. Your manager will "ding" you, not Debbie. If Debbie finishes the year on target, or better than planned, you both can take pride in fulfilling a joint responsibility.

Two Key Learning Points

Make sure delegated authority is commensurate with assigned responsibility so a joint responsibility is forged. You can empower Debbie by assigning her the responsibility to achieve a particular budget target. At the same time, you must delegate some of your budget authority to her so she is empowered to decide how expenses should be managed as the year unfolds.

When someone is sharing power and creating joint responsibilities with another person or group of people, sufficient formal authority must be delegated to carry out the assigned responsibility for which that person or group is being held accountable. When you don't delegate authority commensurate with responsibility, you don't empower—you don't forge a joint responsibility. It would be like assigning someone the responsibility to bake a cake but not giving them the authority to read a cookbook, purchase the needed ingredients, or heat the oven.

Make sure all accountabilities are clarified. Tied to Debbie's empowerment comes her accountability to you for the final results of her actions and decisions. In empowering Debbie, however, you cannot delegate your own assigned budget responsibilities to her or rid yourself of your own overall budget accountability to your manager. *You will always be held accountable by your own manager for your actions and the actions of your people.*

COLLABORATIVE POWER: IT IS ALL ABOUT SHARING CONTROL, NOT LOSING CONTROL

As we've seen, true power sharing through delegation means giving up what you most naturally would like to hold on to—the control via formal authority—and holding on to what you most naturally like to give up: the responsibility. Empowering individuals or groups through delegation means letting go of authority so others can get going with increased discretion, autonomy, and personal control. It means widening their authority boundaries and helping to broaden their window of independent action.

A comment that I have heard hundreds of times in my workshops and in my hallway conversations with managers goes something like this: "I don't know about this shared power stuff. How do you expect me to manage and lead my group if I have to *give up* my authority and control?" As this section heading says, collaborative power is all about sharing control, not losing control. In other words, facilitating collaborative power within and across work groups means that you trade off the ironfisted control of *making people do something* for the shared control of *helping make the process of their doing something possible!* It is important that everyone get over the restrictive mind set that says: "If I'm not in total control of the situation, then it must be out of control, because I'm the only one capable of keeping things controlled."

Power Is an Expandable Commodity

In order to nurture and facilitate collaborative power, you must never lose sight of this fact: control and power over others is *not a zero-sum situation* (i.e., for you to get something, I must give it up). Sharing control and power through genuine collaboration on decision making does not mean you lose or give up control and power. What you are doing is multiplying the power and control of the entire group—including yourself—over the issue in question. Groups have two assets that exceed those of any individual in the group: They possess more knowledge, and they can think in a greater variety of ways. Primary and secondary facilitation, practiced as described in Chapter 3, develops these potential assets so that the group realizes its full potential and produces a superior output which propels everyone's commitment and feelings of satisfaction to their zenith. To share power and control in exchange for a total increase in the effectiveness of your team is to move to a higher level of understanding about power and control. Plus, on top of everything else, you—the manager as facilitator—will derive a tremendous feeling of self-worth from helping, encouraging, and facilitating others in getting the job done collaboratively.

Thus, from a managerial standpoint, unleashing the collaborative genius of your work team does not diminish your assigned responsibilities, compromise your ability to make tough decisions when necessary, or weaken your ability to lead the group. Practicing the art of collaborative facilitation is not being soft on your people; it is not "turning the candy store over to the kids" and then sitting back while anarchy reigns. Facilitating shared power and collaboration does not reduce your ability to manage the group. The underlying reason is that as the formal leader of your group, with the assigned rights, duties, and authorities of your position, you always retain full responsibility for the group's performance and for helping it meet the demands and expectations placed upon it by the larger organization.

In fact, having actual responsibility for your group is a real asset. It accords you the power and opportunity to bring collaborative facilitation practices into your team by initiating and role-modeling the behaviors and actions advocated throughout the rest of this book.

Power Shared Is Power Returned

What goes around, comes around—this old refrain describes perfectly a critical point about power. Your efforts to facilitate shared power in the spirit of collaborative teamwork will be returned to you with dividends. James Kouzes and Barry Posner, in their superb book *The Leadership Challenge*, succinctly describe this process:

> A synergistic and cyclical process is created as you extend power and responsibility to others, and those people respond successfully. This increases their

competencies so that you can extend even further amounts of power and responsibility. This in turn has the effect of allowing you to expend more energy in other areas, which enhances your sphere of influence and brings additional resources back to your unit to be distributed among the group members.[1]

This two-way, dynamic benefit of power sharing can be summarized in a Chinese proverb: If you want one year of prosperity, grow grain. If you want 10 years of prosperity, grow trees. If you want one hundred years of prosperity, grow people.

Power Sharing Is Not Task Dumping

True delegating and power sharing never imply dumping tasks. Dumping does not empower or expand the capabilities of others. It is a frustrating, morale-depressing action of hit-and-run. Dumping tasks sounds something like this: "Here, you do this, you do that, you two figure out a response to this, and the three of you give me a list of 10 reasons why this won't work. Thanks, I'll be out of the office and unreachable for the next three days!"

Here are three action steps that will keep you far from the quagmire of task dumping while you stay on target for collaborative power sharing:

Choose an appropriate person or team for the collaborative activity you have in mind. An appropriate person or team would be one that possesses the skills most needed to do the task, or it could be a person or team that needs a growth experience that comes from direct involvement in the collaborative activity.

Discuss the proposed collaborative activity with the chosen person or team. By using these five steps, you'll create a collaborative framework that truly empowers:

> Jointly make sure the proposed delegated authority is commensurate with the proposed responsibility being assigned.

> Jointly clarify roles and all accountabilities.

> Jointly reach a common understanding on any boundary conditions.

> Jointly process options and agree on the type and number of review sessions.

> Jointly clarify and, if needed, work through any expectations anyone is holding

Move ahead. Facilitate implementation of the framework developed in the previous step. Uphold whatever your role was defined to be. Provide support when and where needed, bust barriers, offer encouragement and positive reinforcement.

POWER AND PERFORMANCE ARE ENHANCED VIA COMPLEMENTARY TEAM SKILLS

Jon Katzenbach and Douglas Smith, principals with McKinsey and Company and coauthors of *The Wisdom of Teams: Creating the High Performance Organization*, emphasize the necessity for developing complementary team skills within three key areas to expand power and performance. What they have to say is at the heart of *Building Team Power*. As you read their points, please note my comments in brackets.

Teams must develop the right mix of skills, that is, each of the complementary skills necessary to do the team's job. These team skill requirements fall into three categories:

Technical or functional expertise. It would make little sense for a group of doctors to litigate an employment discrimination case in a court of law. Yet *teams* of doctors and lawyers often try medical malpractice or personal injury cases. Similarly, product development groups that include only marketers or engineers are less likely to succeed than those with the complementary skills of both. [Utilizing the collaborative genius of cross-functional or cross-technical people is a main theme of this book.]

Problem-solving and decision-making skills. Teams must be able to identify the problems and opportunities they face, evaluate the options they have for moving forward, and then make necessary trade-offs and decisions about how to proceed. Most teams need some members with these skills to begin with although many will develop them best on the job. [Chapters 7, 8, 11, 12, and 13 of this book directly address how-to facilitation skills for these two crucial team processes.]

Interpersonal skills. Common understanding and purpose cannot arise without effective communication and constructive conflict that, in turn, depend on interpersonal skills. These include risk taking, helpful criticism, objectivity, active listening, giving the benefit of the doubt, support, and recognizing the interests of others. [Chapters 5, 6, 9, and 10 of this book give you the how-to facilitation skills for the critical team processes of collaborative interpersonal behaviors and conflict resolution.][2]

The complementary behavioral skills that you and your group members must acquire to facilitate teamwork and collaboration in the pursuit of high performance are contained right here in *Building Team Power*.

A CLOSING SUMMARY

Collaborative power is essential to maximizing team performance. While there are four sources of power—legitimate, expert, charismatic, and political—it is through the delegation of legitimate power that others lower in the organization are empowered. There are three principles of collaborative power: (1) You can delegate authority, (2) you can assign (not delegate) responsibility; and (3) the person with whom you share power is held accountable to you for results. Collaborative power is all about sharing control, not losing control. You should not fear sharing power with others because power is not a zero-sum action. Power is expandable. With shared power, what goes around, comes around. When sharing power, you must be certain you are not dumping tasks. Dumping can be prevented by choosing an appropriate person or team, fully disclosing the proposed collaborative activity, and moving ahead while providing support and positive reinforcement.

NOTES WORKSHEET: DEVELOP WRITTEN
RESPONSES TO THE TWO ITEMS LISTED BELOW

What Do You Feel Are the Main Learning Points from Chapter 4?	Elaborate on Why You Feel These Points Are Key

NOTES

1. J. M. Kouzes and B. Z. Posner, *The Leadership Challenge: How to Get Extraordinary Things Done in Organizations* (San Francisco, CA: Jossey-Bass Inc., 1987), p. 166.

2. J. R. Katzenbach and D. K. Smith, *The Wisdom of Teams: Creating the High Performance Organization* (Boston, MA: Harvard Business School Press, 1993), pp. 47–48.

Chapter 5

Purpose and Desired Outcomes
The Cornerstone of Every Facilitation Effort

Chapter Objectives

> To define the terms *purpose* and *desired outcomes* using illustrative statements.

> To stress the necessity of having purpose and desired outcome statements for every session you facilitate.

> To demonstrate the cornerstone role that clear purpose and desired outcomes statements play in all successful facilitation efforts.

INTRODUCTION

Sir Thomas Beecham, English conductor and impresario, was conducting his orchestra in a piece that called for an offstage trumpet to sound a long call. Beecham got to the point where the trumpet was to sound—but there was no trumpet call. He paused and then had the orchestra repeat the section leading up to the trumpet call. Once again, no trumpet. He threw down his baton and strode into the wings to see what happened. There was his trumpeter in a tussle with the backstage guard, who was insisting: "You can't play that damn trumpet in here—there's a concert going on."[1]

Obviously the guard did not know the purpose of the trumpeter or Beecham's wish that the trumpeter sound his call at the appointed time to make the orchestral movement a success. This lack of understanding on the part of just one member of the concert hall staff ruined the collaboration between the offstage trumpeter and the orchestral team Beecham was conducting. Nothing you will do in your role as facilitator will be more basic, or more essential, to preventing meeting breakdowns than setting and then communicating the purpose and desired outcomes of your session to all participants, every time, with no exceptions.

A clear understanding of what is to be accomplished is the cornerstone upon which all collaborative sessions rest. If you are unable or unwilling to clarify the session's purpose and desired outcomes in your own mind before bringing the participants together, you do not deserve the right to hold a team session! That's how fundamental the purpose and desired outcomes are.

By not defining the purpose and desired outcomes, you take a giant step toward failure. The session will tend to meander. Just as the trumpeter-guard tussle ruined Beecham's concert, you will find confusion, misunderstanding, and verbal sparring ruining your chances of conducting a collaborative meeting. Heated debates over why we are here and what we are trying to accomplish will abound. Group members' time and talents will be wasted, and an undercurrent of frustration and resentment will begin to build and eventually explode, leaving bitterness, cynicism, and strained relationships in its wake. Many participants will either simply withdraw or contribute at a level far beneath their true capabilities—in any case unleashing the collaborative genius of your work team will be impossible.

When a group doesn't know where it is headed, then any road will do. Except that in the realities of the world of work, these random roads often lead you to address the wrong issues or to address the right issues incorrectly.

THE SESSION'S PURPOSE

The session's purpose is defined as the reason for bringing attendees together within the four walls of the conference room.

Zeroing in on the session's purpose is not difficult. Since the fundamental purpose for bringing people together in a conference room is *to share and process information* relative to some topic, we have our lead-in for quickly and efficiently developing a purpose statement. Several examples of purpose statements are presented in the boxes below:

> *Purpose:* To share and process information relative to holding a team-building session for our staff.

> *Purpose:* To share and process information relative to raising community funds for the Park Road Grade School playground project.

> *Purpose:* To share and process information relative to the Effective Manager training program.

A purpose statement is brief and to the point—15 to 25 words, including the lead-in phrase, is about right. It is a general statement since it simply defines why the group is being called together. Be careful that desired outcomes are not being mixed in with the purpose statement. Statements beyond 25 words are a sure sign that too much detail is being included in the purpose definition.

There are two special-case purpose statements that vary slightly from the centerline process just described.

Communication sessions. Some group sessions are held only to impart one-way information to a large audience. This is strictly an information-sharing or reporting session. Information processing is not part of the plan. An example of a purpose statement for an information-sharing meeting would be the following:

> *Purpose:* To share information relative to the reorganization of the customer services department.

Staff meetings. Staff meetings, typically those in which discrete and independent agenda items are covered, have a standard purpose. Staff meetings should be held for one reason.

> *Purpose:* To share and process information relative to subjects of mutual interest and concern to the entire staff.

THE SESSION'S DESIRED OUTCOME(S)

Desired outcomes are specific statements identifying what needs to be accomplished during the time spent in the session. Said differently, the desired outcomes specify what you and the session attendees need to have achieved when you all walk out the conference room door at the meeting's conclusion. Simply defining the session's purpose, *why* the group is being brought together, is not enough. In addition to purpose, you also must give forethought to the session's bottom line—*what* must be accomplished as a result of bringing this set of individuals together.

Because of the major role that desired outcomes play in the scheme of productive meetings, four points require special emphasis.

1. Desired outcomes must be defined by you in advance of every meeting you initiate.

2. Desired outcomes must be communicated at the beginning of the session, preferably in writing—either as a handout or by writing them on a flip chart and posting them for all to see. Thus, the session attendees will have something in front of them to constantly remind them of "what we are trying to achieve in today's meeting."

3. In some cases, you will have desired outcomes that are nonnegotiable. You may say, "This is what I must get out of this session today. The desired outcomes are not open to discussion." This is fine, as long as you clarify, up-front, that today's desired outcomes are not open to modification. In other situations, you may decide to change the desired outcomes after discussion with participants. In those cases where changes are discussed and agreed to, the modified outcomes should be rewritten on flip charts and posted.

4. At any point in the session, the group can pause, reexamine stated desired outcomes, and decide either to stay with them or to make changes. For example, the original desired outcomes may have been too aggressive. One hour into the two-hour meeting it becomes obvious that the outcomes as presently stated won't be achieved. It's better to stop the discussion, redefine the outcomes so that everyone's expectations are in harmony, and move forward, accepting the fact that "we will not be able to accomplish everything we originally set out to do in today's meeting."

Let's return to the purpose statements presented earlier in this chapter and develop examples of desired outcomes for each one.

---

1. Purpose: To share and process information relative to holding a team-building session for our staff.

   Desired outcome:
   • Reach a consensus on either a go or a no-go decision regarding the proposed team-building session in September.

---

2. Purpose: To share and process information relative to raising community funds for the Park Road Grade School playground project.

Desired outcomes:
- Brainstorm a list of potential ways to raise money for the playground.
- Comb the list, eliminating duplicates and similarities.
- Rank the remaining ideas from best to worst using the six-item criteria chart developed by Forest Hill Grade School last year.

3. Purpose: To share and process information relative to the Effective Manager training program.

Desired outcomes:
- Reach consensus on the Effective Manager program budget for next year using the five assumptions agreed to at last week's meeting.
- Develop a list of risks and opportunities associated with conducting 20 three-day, Effective Manager programs next year.
- S. Hargan to select the three new Effective Manager instructors after whole group discussion of the six finalists.

The next example shows the desired outcomes that might be associated with a purpose confined to just sharing information.

4. Purpose: To share information relative to the reorganization of the customer services department.

Desired outcomes:
- Communicate to all customer services personnel the department's new mission, goals, organization structure, and corresponding managerial changes.
- Present rationale for the changes.

For a staff meeting, which typically contains a number of separate and distinct agenda topics, each independent agenda item requires its own desired outcome. The purpose shown in this example is the standard statement you can use for all staff meetings since their purpose is universal. The individual agenda items, with their associated desired outcomes, are what give each staff meeting its distinction.

5. Purpose: To share and process information on subjects of mutual interest and concern to the entire staff.

Agenda

1. Name for newsletter:
   Desired outcome:
   • Reach a consensus on a name for our plantwide newsletter.

2. Summer Vacation Coverage:
   Desired outcomes:
   • Complete the summer vacation plan, covering 5/15 through
     9/15, for all three shifts.

   • Highlight all dates where full coverage cannot be provided given
     our current head count levels. (Note: Discussion of any problem
     dates will be addressed at our next meeting.)

WHY ARE DESIRED OUTCOMES THE "CENTER OF THE UNIVERSE" WHEN IT COMES TO PLANNING AND FACILITATING COLLABORATIVE SESSIONS?

Having covered the fundamentals of desired outcomes and reviewed a
number of examples, we now turn our attention to why desired outcomes are the "center of the universe" when it comes to planning and
facilitating productive group sessions.

Desired outcomes perform four essential functions with respect to
meeting excellence, which are addressed in the following sections.

Desired Outcomes Create Common Expectations Among All Participants

Nothing will kill a meeting's productivity more quickly than having
seven participants at a conference table with seven different sets of expectations about what the session should accomplish. If members of a
group do not know and understand the desired outcomes of the session,
they will compete with one another to achieve their own respective
outcomes rather than collaborate to accomplish what is important to the
group.

With unstated or unclear desired outcomes, typical comments at a
meeting's conclusion can often be: "What a waste! If I'd known we
were just going to talk about customer reaction to our invoicing system
and ignore the real problem of how to eliminate the bugs in our new
order entry procedure, I never would have come." Or: "I didn't know

I would be making a formal presentation on the construction cost over-runs for our new pediatrics wing. I expected to give an informal briefing. I wasn't prepared, and now I look like a jerk.'' Or simply: ''What were the last three hours all about? I was confused the whole time as to what we were trying to accomplish.''

By getting desired outcomes developed, clarified, and committed to—before undertaking information sharing and processing of the agenda's subject(s)—you will lay the foundation for collaboration by virtually elim-inating problems like those quoted above.

Desired Outcomes Provide Constant Reference Points to Keep the Group Session on Track and Focused

How can you possibly be lost if you don't have a final destination? In much the same way, another question can be posed: How can you tell your group session has gotten off course if you haven't defined your desired outcomes? Of course, the answer to both questions is that you can't. However, with desired outcomes set in place, all group members have a means for monitoring and controlling the direction of the session.

Group meetings are robbed of their collaborative spirit when people ramble, when dialogue bounces from point to point without resolution, when the group is fixated on debating trivia, when the same points are repeated again and again, when members tell irrelevant and self-serving war stories, and so on. However, establishing clear desired outcomes helps you significantly to control these debilitating activities. The type of session to be conducted is determined by its desired outcomes.

For you in the role of facilitator, the key elements to successful meeting control are: (1) knowing where the group should be headed based on explicit desired outcomes, (2) monitoring where the session actually is headed relative to where it should be headed, (3) recognizing when there is a noticeable difference between the first two elements, and (4) intervening to redirect the discussion back on course. This is an on-going process requiring vigilance throughout the entire session.

By taking time to determine the session's desired outcomes, you have set down, in effect, the equivalent of compass headings. As the meeting journey unfolds and the needle begins to point in the wrong direction, as it were, you can make an adjustment. This can be done by asking questions or making statements that realign the information sharing and processing so that it focuses on acknowledged desired outcomes. For example:

> Your point about having Sue help John cover the tool room and the supplies area when Mark goes on vacation is a good one. I'll note that for our next session. However, remember our desired outcome for this meeting is just to highlight areas of exposure in this year's vacation plan. Let's stay focused on this activity.

Desired Outcomes Define the Type of Session to Be Conducted

A group session is not just a group session. There are different types, and they are held for different reasons. A group session can be held to make a decision, to share information, to solve a problem, to develop plans, to vent and clarify feelings, or to process a number of loosely related topics such as those often covered in a staff session. The kind of session to be held will be signified by its desired outcomes.

To be effective, different kinds of meetings require different kinds of structuring, processes, and roles. Depending on the desired outcomes, some meetings should be kept small, and some can be large. With some sessions, information can be processed by a whole group; with others, subgroups are a necessity. Some sessions require that certain individuals be present in order to have the meeting—without them, there is no session. The chief point is this: Desired outcomes define the type of session to be run.

Looking back at our five statements of purpose and desired outcomes, we see clearly that we are dealing with five different meeting types. Session 1 is a *decision-making meeting* to decide whether or not to hold a family group team-building activity. Session 2 is a *problem-solving meeting* exploring ways to raise money for a playground project. Session 3 is a *combination planning and decision-making meeting* revolving around the Effective Manager training program. Session 4 is an *information-sharing meeting* regarding the reorganization of the customer services department. Session 5 is a *staff meeting* covering two unrelated subjects, each with its own desired outcome.

Desired Outcomes Provide a Benchmark Against Which the Actual Outcomes Can Be Compared to Gain a Sense of the Session's Productivity

Session evaluations are more meaningful when a group can check its actual outputs against some predetermined desired level. The resultant critique can point out where the group either fell short, achieved, or exceeded the desired outcomes committed to at the beginning of the session. The main point here is simple. Establishing desired outcomes at the group session's start creates the opportunity for a meaningful assessment at its conclusion.

For these four reasons, desired outcomes are the center of the universe when it comes to planning and facilitating group sessions.

A CLOSING SUMMARY

Establishing the purpose and desired outcomes of every group session you convene is your mandatory obligation. The *purpose* of the session is the reason for bringing attendees together within the conference room. The *desired outcomes* are specific statements identifying what needs to be accomplished during the session. They are the foundation upon which everything else rests.

Four points require special emphasis regarding desired outcomes. Desired outcomes must be defined in advance of the meeting. Desired outcomes must be communicated at the beginning of the session—in writing—so that everyone has a constant reminder of what the session intends to achieve. In some instances, the desired outcomes may be nonnegotiable; in others, there may be some leeway for discussion and modification. At any point in the session, the group can pause, reexamine the stated desired outcomes, and decide to stay with them or make changes based on new information that comes up during the discussion.

Desired outcomes perform several essential functions with respect to meeting excellence.

1. Desired outcomes create common expectations among all participants.

2. Desired outcomes provide constant reference points to keep the group session on track and focused.

3. Desired outcomes define the type of session to be conducted.

4. Desired outcomes provide a benchmark against which the actual outcomes can be compared to gain a sense of the session's productivity.

If you are unwilling or unable to determine the purpose and desired outcomes of a session you are convening, you don't deserve the right to call that meeting!

NOTES WORKSHEET: DEVELOP WRITTEN
RESPONSES TO THE TWO ITEMS LISTED BELOW

What Do You Feel Are the Main Learning Points from Chapter 5?	Elaborate on Why You Feel These Points Are Key

NOTES

1. S. H. Simmons, *How to Be the Life of the Podium* (New York: Amacom, 1982), p. 130.

Chapter 6

Interpersonal Behaviors
A Shared Facilitation Responsibility Among All Group Members[1]

Chapter Objective

> To present and discuss a set of interpersonal behaviors essential to conducting effective group sessions: group task behaviors, group maintenance behaviors, and gatekeeping processes.

INTRODUCTION

Geronimo, a fierce warrior and chief of the Apaches who campaigned against the white settlers during the 1880s, was a wise and caring chief. One day his son, a handsome, athletic, but self-centered 18-year-old asked his father how he could become a man in his father's eyes.

A few days later, Geronimo received his son at the most sacred spot on the tribal burial grounds. First they spoke about the kind of life the son had lived to that point. Then Geronimo served a special tealike drink made from a recipe of herbs and spices handed down through the generations. He poured his son's cup full and kept on pouring. The drink overflowed and soaked into the ground.

After watching a bit, the son could no longer contain himself. "Father," he exclaimed, "stop pouring. The cup is overfull. No more will go in."

"Like this cup," Geronimo said, "your mind is full of your own judgments, opinions, values, beliefs, and speculations. How can I possibly teach you how to be a man until you empty your cup first?"

This simple tale serves as a fitting introduction to this chapter on interpersonal behaviors. Like Geronimo's son, our heads are full of judgments, opinions, values, beliefs, and speculations about interpersonal behaviors—ours and others. After all, since the minute we were born, we have been interacting with others. If there is one thing we can claim to be expert in, it is interpersonal behaviors. We have a lifetime of experience in this activity.

Before reading any further, do as Geronimo would ask: Empty your cup a little. Make room for some new perspectives and insights into interpersonal behaviors. Make room so you can look at these interpersonal behaviors through the eyes of a facilitator whose intent is to unleash the collective wisdom of your organization.

SETTING THE STAGE

As emphasized in Chapter 3, the manager (acting as primary facilitator) must share the responsibility for group facilitation with every other group member. An excellent starting point for shared facilitation is learning and using the interpersonal behaviors and processes for group sessions discussed in this chapter.[2] By practicing these behaviors, along with the gate-keeping processes to appropriately regulate group participation, all members can help strengthen the group's ability to share and process information.

For any group to be productive, it must give attention to task accomplishment. That is, the work of different members must be coordinated and combined so that everyone is pulling together to fulfill the expressed desired outcomes of the group session. At the same time, the group also must be mindful of the emotional and personal welfare needs of the members. If it doesn't, the group jeopardizes its ability to accomplish its task. Most seriously, if proper maintenance behaviors are not performed, the survival of the group is threatened.

Although these task and maintenance behaviors and gate-keeping processes are a shared responsibility, the primary facilitator must be especially tuned in to these behaviors and processes and do his or her best to role-model them while facilitating. While many benefits will accrue to the group that learns, understands, and routinely practices the interpersonal behaviors described in this chapter, four stand out.

Teamwork. Using the behaviors outlined here promotes an increase in each group member's capability to function in a group and is a major payoff. Lack of interactive skills among those attending a group session can carry an enormous price tag; just one person can interfere with the ability of the entire group to achieve its desired outcomes. Collaboration is an essential part of teamwork. Proper use of the interpersonal behaviors and processes fosters collaboration.

A climate of openness and trust. Another key benefit arising from effective interpersonal behavior is the development of an environment in which everyone in the group is encouraged to identify and communicate problems. Messengers bearing bad news are not shot; rather they are welcomed so that issues can be resolved as early as possible instead of keeping them covered up until they precipitate a major crisis. A positive climate is built because the gate is opened to help people enter the discussion, personal attacks are few, and differences are mediated by the group. Good listening is directly demonstrated by each person's ability to accurately test comprehensions, summarize various points of view, and build on another's idea or proposal.

A fuller understanding of the subject under discussion. An additional benefit derived from appropriate use of interpersonal behaviors and processes is that they help ensure that debate and discussion are objective and orderly and lead to logical conclusions. Mistakes due to misunderstandings or incomplete information are minimized.

A greater commitment to the final decision. Commitment is the fourth payback from properly utilizing the behaviors associated with the task, maintenance, and process actions. Since employing these behaviors helps to involve everyone in the group's deliberation, there is a greater commitment to the final decision, along with a greater chance of a successful implementation.

Before we discuss specific behaviors, look at Figure 6–1 to familiarize yourself with the material.

THE GROUP TASK BEHAVIORS

The *task* component encompasses 10 behaviors that are all concerned with a group's efforts to define and accomplish desired outcomes. In order to enhance your understanding of the various task-oriented behaviors, a short definition, along with several examples of each behavior, is provided.

Proposing. This behavior initiates a new idea, proposition, or suggestion to spark group action. It is vital at the beginning of a session to get the group moving, and it is also indispensable when the group gets bogged down or when it needs to look at another aspect of the issue.

"I suggest we begin by reviewing last year's figures."

"Here's my idea: Let's combine Districts 1 and 2 and place responsibility for both within a new position called senior district coordinator."

FIGURE 6–1
Interpersonal Behaviors and Processes for Effective Group Sessions

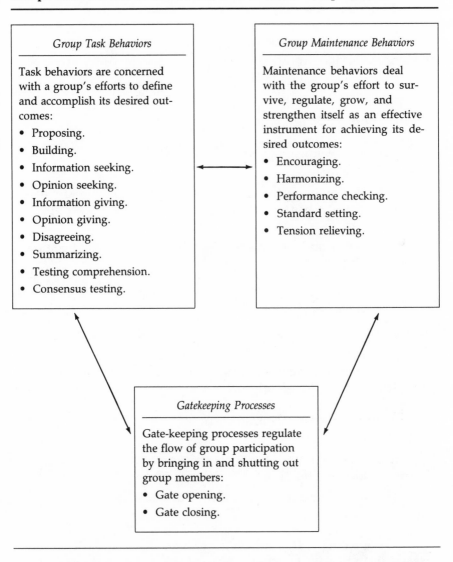

Group Task Behaviors

Task behaviors are concerned with a group's efforts to define and accomplish its desired outcomes:
- Proposing.
- Building.
- Information seeking.
- Opinion seeking.
- Information giving.
- Opinion giving.
- Disagreeing.
- Summarizing.
- Testing comprehension.
- Consensus testing.

Group Maintenance Behaviors

Maintenance behaviors deal with the group's effort to survive, regulate, grow, and strengthen itself as an effective instrument for achieving its desired outcomes:
- Encouraging.
- Harmonizing.
- Performance checking.
- Standard setting.
- Tension relieving.

Gatekeeping Processes

Gate-keeping processes regulate the flow of group participation by bringing in and shutting out group members:
- Gate opening.
- Gate closing.

Building.   This behavior takes a group member's proposal, suggestion, or idea and extends, develops, or expands it to enhance its value.

(A build on the first suggestion above) ''Then we could compare them with this year's figures and have Chad explain the variances.''

(A build on the second proposal above) ''Good. That would also allow us to promote Vandenberg to senior district coordinator for a two-year developmental assignment which will better prepare her for the assistant superintendent position."

Information seeking.   This behavior solicits facts, data, experiences, or clarification from others.

"How many 100 percent attendance days did we have in our middle school last year?"

"Who approved Perun's expense report?"

Opinion seeking.   This behavior solicits values, beliefs, or sentiments from others.

"David, what are your thoughts on having the building administrators deliver the half-day Disciplinary Procedures Workshop to their own staffs?"

"Roberta, what do you think will happen to the College Relations Program when Harlow leaves?"

Information giving.   This behavior offers facts, data, experiences, or clarification to others.

"Our inspection cost alone on those engines is $43 per unit."

"When I worked at Sajar Plastics, our six janitors were responsible for meeting with vendors, testing their products, and determining which cleaning supplies to purchase."

Opinion giving.   This behavior offers values, beliefs, or sentiments to others.

"I say let's go with it! Brillson is a strict prescription-only drug; those doctors that don't feel it's safe don't have to prescribe it."

"I don't believe that relocation of the Finance group will increase their morale one iota."

Disagreeing.   This behavior provides direct opposition to, or raises doubts and objections about, an issue (*not* the person who presents it).

Note: Technically, disagreeing occurs as a form of information giving or opinion giving; however, since it is such a powerful force—the key to a group's critical thinking—disagreeing is shown here as a distinct task behavior so that the reader's awareness of its value is heightened.

"I don't buy into Eckert's proposal because it requires a number of my people, who already are putting in six to eight hours of overtime per week, to also work Sundays for the next six months."

"I cannot support having Holmes observe our team-building session since he is not a member of our immediate group."

Summarizing. This behavior reiterates the contents of previously shared dialogue in condensed form.

"Then, to review our discussion, we've agreed to order the machine, train the appropriate personnel, and evaluate the results in six weeks."

"So, in a nutshell, we've agreed that there is little advantage to reviewing the social studies curriculum this school year unless Bartlett Publishing can guarantee delivery of materials by September 1."

Testing comprehension. This behavior poses a question in order to establish whether a previous communication has been correctly understood.

"In other words, you're telling me you get nervous when you have to make repeat calls to parents about absenteeism, right?"

"So, are you saying that if I get the revisions to you by 3:00 tomorrow afternoon, you'll have my report typed by 5:00 that same day?"

Consensus testing. This behavior periodically tests whether the group has reached consensus or whether more discussion of the issue is required.

"Do we now have consensus that we will extend this staff meeting another hour? I'll go right around the table, Judith? . . ."

"Let's see if everyone either can agree with or can agree to support the most popular alternative—setting up the copy center next to the library. I'll start with Bart and go right across the room: Bart? . . ."

THE GROUP MAINTENANCE BEHAVIORS

The *maintenance* component incorporates five behaviors associated with the operation of the group as a group. These maintenance-oriented behaviors deal with the group's efforts to survive, regulate, grow, and strengthen itself as an effective instrument for achieving desired outcomes. A definition, plus several examples of each behavior, is given below.

Encouraging.   This behavior supports, agrees with, or recognizes the contributions of others.

"Carol and Janice, your budget presentation to the school board was incisive, well organized, and documented to the hilt. You've both proven you are ready for more difficult assignments."

"Yes, that's it! You're right, we can do it together. It's risky but I know we are capable of working out our mission, goals, and operating principles as a team."

Harmonizing.   This behavior attempts to reconcile disagreements or conflict by mediating differences between group members, pointing out the strengths of alternative solutions, or searching for common elements of agreement in opposing positions.

"I don't see this as an either/or issue. We can have both! We can take 20 percent of the budget surplus, and with matching funds from the state, we can remodel the old fire station and turn it into a centrally located day-care center; *and then* we can take the remainder of the surplus and build a larger, more up-to-date fire station."

"We are all in agreement that more privacy is necessary for the 10 of you, but permanent walls are inflexible and costly. Eight-foot dividers and soft background music should accomplish the same results. What do you think?"

Performance checking.   This behavior suspends task operations in order to examine where the group stands in relation to achieving its desired outcomes, to determine how the team members feel about the group's progress in attempting to accomplish its desired outcomes, to air feelings and conflicts, or to evaluate the session at its conclusion.

"I would like to stop our process for a few minutes. Joe, Daryl, Janeen—all three of you are certainly upset over the criteria we are generating to select a replacement for De Graff. Our group really can't move forward unless we understand what your 'pinches' are. If you'll share them with the group, I'll write them on the flip chart so that the three of you will know the rest of us truly understand where you're coming from and why."

"Performance check please! We said we would be finished with our force-field analysis by 3:30; it's now 3:20 and we have at least another 45 minutes worth of work to do. I'm frustrated and feel like quitting at 3:30. I believe we need to discuss where to go form here.

Standard setting. This behavior expresses standards for the group and applies these standards to improve the quality of the group process.

"We're getting into groupthink. If we're going to make the best possible decision, we have to increase our critical thinking and take a harder look at what potentially might happen if we go to market now versus six months from now."

"Before Beverly begins her presentation, I would like to remind everyone of our 'present, then discuss' ground rule. We will allow Beverly to complete her presentation before we discuss content. Only ask questions of clarification during the present portion."

Tension relieving. This behavior eases tensions and increases the enjoyment of group members by joking, suggesting breaks, or proposing fun approaches to group work.

"Whew, that was a tedious and difficult task! Let's take a 15-minute break and get our blood circulating again."

"Why don't we hold our next all-day staff meeting at the cabin in Webster Park and then have a picnic when we're finished?"

THE GATEKEEPING PROCESSES

Unlike the task and maintenance behaviors, the gatekeeping processes do not have content per se. Gate-opening and gate-closing can occur only in conjunction with a task or maintenance behavior. In other words, the content for the gate-opening and gate-closing processes is provided by the actual task or maintenance behavior enacted at that point.

When individuals *gate-close* each other's verbal communications, they often do so by verbally interrupting. These interruptions cannot occur in a vacuum. They occur because someone has utilized a task-oriented behavior such as proposing, giving information, giving opinions, disagreeing, and the like. They also can occur because someone has introduced a maintenance-oriented behavior such as encouraging, harmonizing, performance checking, and the like, to bring about the gate-closing. The same holds true for *gate-opening*. The only difference is that behaviors like seeking information, seeking opinions, testing comprehension, consensus testing, performance checking, and tension relieving are used for bringing in others rather than shutting them out.

Gate-opening. This process utilizes a task or maintenance behavior as a means for directly including another individual in the discussion or for increasing the individual's opportunity to contribute to the discussion.

"Jeanne, I know you don't fully agree with Lyle's proposal, so can you tell us how to modify it in order to get your buy-in?"

"Barry, we haven't heard your thoughts on changing from a seventh-and-eighth-grade middle school to one covering grades 7 through 9. What's your position?"

Gate-closing. This process uses a task or maintenance behavior as a means for directly excluding another individual from the discussion or for reducing the individual's opportunity to contribute to the discussion.

John

How do you feel about our office move, Bob?

Bob

Well, from my perspective, I'm hopeful . . .

Kathi

John, I've told you a hundred times we'll be the forgotten group in that remote location!

Kathi has gate-closed Bob to insert her opinion.

Terry

Steve, do you have the figures?

Steve

Yes, we sold 451 units in . . .

Jesse

And as always you double counted the . . .

Terry

Please, Jesse, Steve has the floor. Let's give him time to complete his review.

In the first part of the interaction above, Jesse dysfunctionally gate-closed Steve; however, in the second part, Terry productively gate-closed Jesse to restore Steve as the rightful "owner of the airwaves" so he could finish his review.

A synopsis of all task and maintenance behaviors and both gatekeeping processes is shown as a learning aid in the summary at the end of this chapter.

TIPS FOR SUCCESSFUL USE

Balance Required

In order for a group to define and accomplish its desired outcomes, a balance between the task and maintenance behaviors must be sustained. Additionally, the gatekeeping processes must be employed at times to bring in individuals who are quiet and to shut out, in a productive way, individuals who are dysfunctionally interrupting and/or dominating the group session.

There is no right or wrong answer regarding the proper mix, on a percentage basis, among the task, maintenance, and gatekeeping components. All are important. Some group sessions benefit from emphasizing certain behaviors over others. However, the best balance will vary depending on the different circumstances surrounding the particular agenda item, issue, or problem to be solved.

Stop Task, Invoke Performance Checking

Another noteworthy point regarding use of task-oriented and maintenance-oriented behaviors is that at any time during a group session—especially when the task is difficult and complex—the group may be forced to do a performance check and confront group maintenance problems. Quite often this entails working through the feelings stage of the "feelings, facts, solutions" sequence to group productivity.

The central idea, however, is that the effective group stops its task-oriented process, calls attention to specific group process problems, and takes action to reduce or eliminate these stumbling blocks. After this is done, the group can refocus—often with greater unity—on the task behaviors and move forward with the *facts* and *solutions* stages. The work group manager and all group members must share the responsibility for recognizing the need, and for taking the initiative, to call for a performance check.

Moderation Is the Key

Finally, moderation is critical to successfully performing any of the described behaviors and processes. Their strength and utility are significantly impaired if they are used too much or too little, or used to thwart the group from reaching its desired outcomes.

THE MANAGER'S CRUCIAL ROLE

Attaining a reflexive (unconscious) ability to use these group behaviors takes time and patience since, in many cases, the manager and the team members will be required to practice behaviors that are new and/or awkward. The discussion that follows outlines key steps for instilling excellent interactive skills in any work group.

Role-Modeling

The degree of success a group will have in routinely performing behaviors associated with task, maintenance, and gatekeeping functions will depend to a large extent on the work group manager (or, with respect to committees, task forces, etc., the designated chairperson).

As the person with formal authority, you will be watched by the other members of your group. They will take their behavioral cues from you. Therefore, you need to take the initiative and role-model to the best of your ability the various appropriate behaviors at every opportunity. There is a good reason for you to initiate the use of the behaviors via personal action: It legitimizes these behaviors for everyone else in the group. I've used the following story many times in workshops to impress upon managers the single most important factor leading to success in role-modeling the interpersonal behaviors and processes.

In the city of Baghdad lived Hakeem, the Wise One. Many people went to him for counsel, which he gave freely to all, asking nothing in return. There came to him a young man who had spent much but received little. The young man said: "Tell me, Oh Wise One, what shall I do to get the most for which I spend?"

Hakeem answered, "A thing that is bought or sold has no value unless it contains that which cannot be bought or sold. Look for the priceless ingredient."

"But what is this priceless ingredient?" asked the young man.

The Wise One answered him: "My son, the priceless ingredient of every transaction in the marketplace is the honor and integrity of the person who sells it. Consider his name before you buy."

How well the behaviors are performed is not as critical as the "priceless ingredient"—the honesty and integrity inherent in their performance. In working with teams at all organizational levels, my personal experience validates the following principle over and over: Team members will invariably respond more positively and with greater openness to the manager (or any group member, for that matter) who makes unpolished but sincere attempts to practice the interpersonal behaviors, as opposed to the manager who mechanically performs them well, but does so with an aura of hidden agendas, double meanings, and self-serving manipulations.

Encouraging

Besides making a genuine effort to role-model, it is also imperative that you utilize the maintenance behavior of encouraging and stimulate all members to use the interpersonal behaviors and processes with sensitivity and authenticity. Each effort that a group member makes to carry out some of the more troublesome behaviors, like summarizing, disagreeing without getting personal, testing comprehension, standard setting, tension relieving, and productive gate-closing, must be recognized immediately with positive feedback.

The recognition does not need to be given with a lot of fanfare. Giving simple, straightforward acknowledgements throughout the group session is all that is required.

"Thank you, Earl, that was a crisp summary of some complex issues."

"That was a difficult topic to reach consensus on, but we were able to disagree without getting personal—that was a big plus."

"Ellen, your testing of comprehension on those two key items short-circuited a major misunderstanding that was developing between us. Nice going."

"You're right, we did agree as a group to spend 10 minutes at the end of each session reviewing our group processes. Thanks for reminding us."

"Good point, we certainly could use a break now."

Unsuccessful attempts by group members to enact the behaviors and processes should not be punished; rather, they should be used as a learning experience. This point can be illustrated by the following example.

Assume the group is confused and an individual attempts to summarize the various issues in order to clarify the situation and reduce confusion; however, the person's summary takes an inordinate amount of time, is convoluted, and does nothing to reduce the confusion. At times such as this, you have a tremendous opportunity to "make lemonade out of lemons."

Thank the individual for making an attempt to help reduce confusion, highlight at least one point from the person's comments, and then ask if anyone else has other thoughts on the subject being discussed.

"Dave, thanks for trying to help us highlight the main issues concerning our sales strategy. Your point about the impending reorganization is critical. Does anyone else have other thoughts that would help summarize the key issues?"

Coaching

Remember the priceless ingredient: The honesty and integrity of the interaction are more important than the skill in doing it. Nevertheless, to help the person do a better job of summarizing next time, a little private postsession coaching would be valuable. The basic process is very simple and nonthreatening. At the first appropriate one-on-one opportunity, you should help the individual review what he or she did, what the results were, and what might be done differently next time. Above all, the group member should be urged to try out the summarizing behavior again—and again!

As a group matures, or if some group members have already refined their abilities to effectively utilize the task and maintenance behaviors and the gatekeeping processes, the responsibility for practicing these behaviors must be shared. You should not be expected to do it alone!

LIGHTENING THINGS UP

What follows are several classic interactions that I have witnessed over the years where a variety of the interpersonal behaviors were used quite humorously.

In one lively discussion I was participating in, Mary started to speak but, after saying only two words, was gate-closed by Ken. Actually they both started to speak at the same time and Mary stopped. Ken noticed what had happened and, after pausing for a second or two, recovered beautifully. Looking directly at Mary, he replied in the sincerest tone, "Not to gate-close you Mary, but let me build on what you were about to say!" It took five minutes for the laughter to die down.

At a project team meeting, Art, a new member of the team, was extremely vocal. He had opinions about everything. Some of his ideas were good, but many others bordered on babbling. I could see that Bill, the project team leader, was getting irritated. Finally, at one point, Bill, in a firm but friendly tone of voice, said, "Art, I'd like to bring you in; you've been silent for two minutes." Art was about to respond, but before he could say anything, Bill continued, "However, we are out of time on this topic." Everyone had a good laugh. Art got the message. Then, at the meeting's conclusion, Bill held a short coaching and counseling session with Art to iron out expectations regarding Art's behavior at future meetings.

This next classic occurred at a senior-level, cross-functional task-force session that I was facilitating. It is a perfect example of the maintenance behavior of tension-relieving. The task-force was trying to decide whether a particular part should be manufactured at the Webster, New York, manufacturing facility or be produced offshore in the Pacific Basin. This was a complex, very serious issue and the atmosphere was all business. After three hours of presentations and discussions, the task force chairman announced: "Well, we finally have defined two specific alternatives. Now, before I do the consensus testing, I'd like to summarize. What you've told me is, Alternative 1 will lead to despair and utter hopelessness, and Alternative 2 will lead to total extinction! Members of the task force, let's pray we have the wisdom to decide correctly."

At that instant, the roof came down. The whole atmosphere lightened up, and even though consensus was not achieved immediately, the group was sparked to a greater effort. At the next session, the task force members all agreed on a win/win course of action.

The following interaction is a prime example of seeking and giving information. Rochester, New York, winters are nasty. In mid-February, a manager received a fax from one of her direct reports: "Stuck in Hawaii for several days due to a tropical storm. What should I do?" The manager sent a return fax: "Start vacation as of yesterday."

This final episode was related to me by a manager attending one of my workshops, and it's a terrific example of testing comprehension. The president of a company addressed the employees of the plant:

> I know all of you are worried about your jobs now that we have restructured and installed all of our robots. I can understand that you are quite concerned that these robots will eliminate your jobs. Well, I'm happy to say, that won't happen. This company values its human resources. Not only will no one be let go, but you will only have to come to work on Thursdays. Think of it! You will only have to work on Thursday to receive a full week's pay!

From the back of the room an employee asked, "You mean *every* Thursday?"

For your convenience, all 15 interpersonal behaviors and the two gatekeeping processes are reviewed in the closing summary, followed by the Notes Worksheet.

A CLOSING SUMMARY

Interpersonal Behaviors

Behavior	Definition	Example
Group Task Behaviors		
• Proposing.	Initiating a new idea, proposition, or suggestion to spark group action.	"Let's start by introducing ourselves."
• Building.	Taking a group member's proposal, suggestion, or idea, and then extending, developing, or expanding it to enhance its value.	(Build on the proposal above.) "And then tell one wild or crazy thing we've done in the last 12 months."
• Information seeking.	Soliciting facts, data, experiences, or clarification from others.	"What would it cost to ship this package first-class?"

• Information giving.	Offering facts, data, experiences, or clarification to others.	"It will cost $6.75 to go first class."
• Opinion seeking.	Soliciting values, beliefs, or sentiments from others.	"What do you think about Shurgot's chances of winning the election?"
• Opinion giving.	Offering values, beliefs, or sentiments to others.	"Unless Shurgot takes a more liberal view on tax reform, I don't think he has any chance of winning."
• Disagreeing.	Providing direct opposition to, or raising doubts about, an issue not the person.	"No way, we'll have to find an area other than travel to cut expenses."
• Summarizing.	Reiterating the content of previously shared dialogue in condensed form.	"So, what we'll do then is take legal action, take it before May, and issue a writ in the chairman's name."
• Testing comprehension.	Posing a question in order to establish whether a previous communication has been correctly understood.	"Are you saying that I can use the yearly dividends from my policy to increase the death benefit on my wife's policy?"
• Consensus testing.	Periodically testing whether the group has reached consensus or whether more discussion of the issue is required.	"Alternative six seems to be everyone's favorite; let's see if we have consensus. Ed? . . ."

Group Maintenance Behaviors

• Encouraging.	Supporting, agreeing with, or recognizing the contributions of others.	"Excellent point, Wayland, I wish I had thought of it."
• Harmonizing.	Reconciling disagreements and conflict by mediating differences between group members, pointing out the strengths of alternative solutions, or searching for common elements of agreement in opposing positions.	"Ed's proposal costs us $50,000 but could be completed within four weeks. Don's idea costs us $45,000 but would take six weeks to complete. Since both are within budget and schedule constraints, we really can't lose with either one."

• Performance checking.	Suspending task operations to tend to internal group processes.	"We're definitely confused. Let's stop for a moment and reaffirm what this decision *is* and *is not* about."
• Standard setting.	Expressing standards for the group and applying these standards to improve the quality of the group's process.	"From now on, all staff meetings begin at 8:00 AM sharp."
• Tension relieving.	Easing tensions and increasing the enjoyment of group members by joking, suggesting breaks, or proposing fun approaches to work.	"This meeting has gone on long enough in this conference room. Let's finish it over margaritas at the Red Onion."

Interpersonal Processes

Process	Definition	Example
Gate-keeping		
• Gate-opening.	Utilizing a task or maintenance behavior to include another person in the discussion.	"Ashley, you've been quiet; in what other areas might we cut costs?"
• Gate-closing.	Utilizing a task or maintenance behavior to exclude another person from the discussion.	**Sandi:** You turn left at the first light . . . **Duke:** Naw, go to the third light, hang a left and then . . . Duke has gate-closed Sandi.

1. Tips for successful use.
   > Balance is required.

   > Stop task; invoke performance checking.

   > Moderation is the key.

2. Integrating interpersonal behaviors and processing into the group is the manager's crucial role:
   > Role-modeling.

   > Encouraging.

   > Coaching.

NOTES WORKSHEET: DEVELOP WRITTEN
RESPONSES TO THE TWO ITEMS LISTED BELOW

What Do You Feel Are the Main Learning Points from Chapter 6?	Elaborate on Why You Feel These Points Are Key

NOTES

1. This chapter is reprinted from my first book, *Mining Group Gold: How to Cash in on the Collaborative Brain Power of a Group* (El Segundo, CA: Serif Publishing), pp. 83–102, © 1990 by Thomas A. Kayser. Without an understanding of the basic interpersonal skills that are the crux of successful facilitation, much of the learning value of the forthcoming chapters would be lost. Reference and examples from this chapter will be used often throughout the rest of the book. If you have already read *Mining Group Gold*, Chapter 6 will be a worthwhile review for you.

2. The interpersonal behaviors and processes model presented in this chapter draws from the following research: K. D. Benne and P. Sheats, "Functional Roles of Group Members," *Journal of Social Issues* 4, no. 2, (1948), pp. 42–47; R. F. Bales, "A Set of Categories for the Analysis of Small Group Interaction," *American Sociological Review* 15 (1950), pp. 257–63; R. Likert, *New Patterns of Management* (New York: McGraw-Hill, 1965), pp. 162–77; J. K. Brilhart, *Effective Group Discussion* (Dubuque, IA: William C. Brown Publishers, 1967); A. G. Athos and R. E. Coffey, *Behavior in Organizations: A Multidimensional View* (Englewood Cliffs, NJ: Prentice-Hall, 1968), pp. 115–27; N. Rackham, P. Honey, and C. Colbert, *Developing Interactive Skills* (Guidsborough, Northampton, England: Wellers Publishing, 1971); D. W. Johnson and F. P. Johnson, *Joining Together: Group Theory and Group Skills* (Englewood Cliffs, NJ: Prentice-Hall, 1975), pp. 18–30, 40–42; L. P. Bradford, *Making Meetings Work* (La Jolla, CA: University Associates, 1976), pp. 35–46; P. S. Goodman and E. J. Conlon, "Observation of Meetings," in S. E. Seashore et al., eds., *Assessing Organizational Change: A Guide to Methods, Measures, and Practices* (New York: John Wiley & Sons, 1983), pp. 353–67; W. G. Dyer, *Strategies for Managing Change* (Reading, MA: Addison-Wesley, 1984), pp. 127–33; "Building a Team through Effective Meetings," *Trainer's Workshop: A Publication of the American Management Association* 1, no. 5 (November 1986), pp. 22–33; and E. H. Schein, *Process Consultation: Its Role in Organizational Development*, vol. I (Reading, MA: Addison-Wesley, 1988), pp. 49–56.

SECTION

III

PRESENTING THE HOW-TO'S FOR UNLEASHING THE COLLABORATIVE GENIUS OF YOUR WORK TEAM

Chapter 7

Decision Making
Understanding the Range of Options

Chapter Objectives

> To present a framework for classifying and understanding the range of decision-making options available to the work group manager or task force chairperson.

> To highlight the characteristics of each of the eight options.

> To introduce and describe five noteworthy forces that impact the selection of a particular option.

INTRODUCTION

One of my mentors, Dr. Frank Simonetti, chairman emeritus of the department of management at the University of Akron, defined the realities of decision making for his students by reciting this little rhyme. I've never forgotten it:

> You can and you can't,
> You shall and you shan't;
> You will and you won't;
> You'll be damned if you do,
> And you'll be damned if you don't.

While you may not always be "damned if you do" and "damned if you don't," for complex decisions it often seems that way. Moreover, when facing what seems like a tough or unpopular no-win situation, people often retreat from making *any* decision.

This chapter will pinpoint eight decision options available to you in a decision-making situation. However, it is important to note that a frequently used decision method is the one just mentioned—"decision by not deciding" or "decision by default." R. K. Mosvick and R. B. Nelson elaborate on this point:

Dr. Marcus Alexis, former chairman of the Interstate Commerce Commission, estimates that as many as 50 percent of the important organizational decisions end up being decision by default. Experienced managers are all too familiar with this phenomenon. They have observed too many potentially good decisions become strangled by indecision, consigned to some bureaucratic limbo, or overtaken in one brilliant move by a competitor. Decision by default continues to thrive as one of a number of irrational decision methods too vast to catalogue here. It is best seen as a sharp reminder to all that a decision by a nondecision is still a decision.[1]

The eight decision-making options to be covered in this chapter are all *proactive* options. The decision avoidance approach was mentioned here simply to acknowledge its existence. It is obviously not a desirable option since it really is decision abdication. Indeed, decision by nondecision means you are surrendering decision-making influence to ''the four winds,'' ''chance,'' ''fate,'' ''the system,'' or ''the powers that be.''

UNDERSTANDING THE EIGHT BASIC DECISION-MAKING OPTIONS

Before moving on to consider the eight proactive options, you are cautioned to keep one important point in mind. *Do not judge one method as being better than another.* Each of the eight decision alternatives presented here has its time and place. Each can produce positive as well as negative consequences depending on how it is applied within the context of a particular situation.

Figure 7-1 depicts a simple framework for classifying the eight rational decision options available to you. As you move from left to right on the diagram, the first division is made according to the two basic decision-making approaches—*autocratic and shared.*

Next, these broad classifications are refined to reveal the two decision types within each. The autocratic approach contains the *pure autocratic* (PA) type and the *consultative autocratic* (CA) type. For the shared approach, there is the *partial group* (PG) type and the *whole group* (WG) type.

Finally, our classification sets forth the specific decision-making alternatives within each type. There are eight options in all. The *full bore* and the *human filing cabinet* options are the subdivisions of the pure autocratic decision type, and the *processing information with people separately* and the *processing information with people in a group* alternatives are the components of the CA classification. The *less than half decide* and the *more than half decide* methods are the choices within the partial group approach, and the *consensus* and *unanimity of consent* practices are the components of the whole group designation. Each of the eight options will be described more fully below.

The four *autocratic* options which follow are available to you whenever

FIGURE 7–1
A Method of Classifying Decision-Making Options

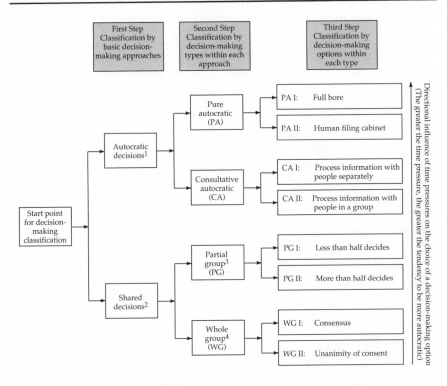

[1]The autocratic decisions classification contains four decision options in which the authority to make the final decision rests with *one individual.*

[2]The shared decisions classification contains four decision options in which the authority to make the final decision rests with *more than one individual.*

[3]The PG I and PG II options, in which part of the group makes a decision for the whole group, always carry the burden of being win/lose unless carefully facilitated.

[4]The WG I and WG II options, whereby the entire group reaches a joint decision fully supported by all members, are win/win.

you hold final decision-making authority regarding the issue being processed. If you are a chairperson, committee leader, or task force manager or are in some other leadership position, *but without final decision-making authority,* you will not be able to use these four autocratic methods. Instead, you will have to facilitate decisions using one of the four alternatives from within the *shared* categories.

Pure Autocratic (PA I): Going Full Bore

A baseball umpire working the game behind home plate is the perfect example of the pure autocrat. As Bill Klem, a National League umpire from the 1920s through the mid 1940s so eloquently put it regarding balls and strikes, "They ain't nothing until I call 'em."

With the pure autocratic approach, the manager or some other person with final decision-making authority simply makes a decision and announces it to others. For example: "The next staff meeting will be held Wednesday at 10:00 AM in Building 129, Room 100." Or: "I'll take responsibility for writing the memo to Lipchek explaining our $3,500 cost overrun." Or: "I want a full analysis of the problem on my desk by Tuesday morning so I can best defend our interests in the policy meeting that afternoon."

A group can have a PA I decision transpire and not even know it because it is so subtle. This occurs when someone, without any discussion, acts immediately on his or her own proposal and the group goes along with it (often referred to as a self-authorized decision).

For example, you could say: "I propose we use round-robin brainstorming and build a list of potential solutions to our waste-removal problem. I'll even be the scribe." Then, going up to the flip chart and holding the marker reader to write, you say, "Teri, what ideas do you have for solving the waste-removal problem?" Teri gives an idea, and the group is off and running on a round-robin brainstorming session.

Pure Autocratic II (PA II): The Human Filing Cabinet

You use this option to obtain information from other individuals *without sharing the problem or need for the information*—hence, using the people as human filing cabinets.

For example, regarding a budget cut for your department, you would speak to an employee privately and might say, "Marty, I would like you to get me a copy of your unit's spending for the last 12 months, itemized by budget account numbers." After doing this with all your direct reports, you would process the data alone, determine which accounts are to be cut by what amount from each unit's budget, and announce the revised budgets to your staff.

Consultative Autocratic I (CA I): Processing Information with People Separately

You use this option to *share the problem with individuals one-on-one* and solicit their responses.

For example, regarding switchboard coverage during lunchtime, you could say: "Holley, I'm asking all the secretaries for ideas to help me fix this nagging switchboard problem once and for all. What thoughts do you have on how to maintain switchboard coverage during lunchtime?" After talking with all the secretaries one-on-one and gathering their individual responses, you would process the information alone, decide how the switchboard will be covered, and announce the plan to the secretaries.

Consultative Autocratic II (CA II): Processing Information with People in a Group

You employ this method *to share and process the problem with others in a group, but retain final decision-making power.*

For example, bringing all your direct reports together, you might say: "I would like your ideas, thoughts, and feelings about slipping our schedule another two weeks. After we consider the evidence, both pro and con, I will announce my decision at tomorrow's operations review meeting." Then, after obtaining, processing, and considering the group's input, you would make a decision and announce it at the ops review the next day.

Stanley Kramer's experience in making his 1963 classic movie, *It's a Mad, Mad, Mad, Mad World,* illustrates the consultative autocrat in action. The movie was a comedy on a grand scale and featured a multitude of world-famous comedians, including Buster Keaton, Joe E. Brown, Milton Berle, Sid Caesar, Jerry Lewis, Buddy Hackett, and Jonathan Winters. When asked how he maintained control over these rather egotistical performers, each wanting to do his own shtick, Kramer admitted that during the first week of rehearsals, it was a staring contest between the comedians and the serious-minded producer-director (himself). Then Kramer held a de-shticking session. He gave the comedians the freedom to make contributions about routines, setups, and even script changes, and he told them he would listen and discuss proposals with the people involved. But he would have the final say as to what changes were actually made. Kramer noted that once everyone understood and accepted the process, "we were in business."

Partial Group I (PG I): Less then Half Decide

Using this alternative allows you to share the problem with the group and facilitate a discussion to process information about the issue. At some point, *a decision is made by less than half of the group for the whole group.* PG I can be a very constructive decision-making approach when it becomes apparent, either before or during the discussion, that a group of individuals—comprising less than half of the group—possesses the knowledge, skills, and expertise to make a quality decision that the entire group can support. Realizing this, the majority defers final decision-making authority to the minority group.

However, PG I can be filled with pitfalls that turn it into a nonconstructive, politically explosive win/lose process. One example of using the process in this way is "railroading," wherein a coalition composed of less than half of the people present emerges. Then, because of their rank, influence, expert knowledge, charisma, political power, verbal skills, or some other factor, they are able to drive the final decision in their favor even though the members of the majority do not support it.

Partial Group II (PG II): More than Half Decide

Using the majority rule option allows you to share the problem with the group and facilitate a period of open discussion. At the conclusion of the discussion period *you poll everyone and if a majority share the same opinion, the decision passes.* More formally, at the end of the discussion period you would state clear-cut alternatives and solicit votes in favor, votes against, and abstentions, with the outcome determined by majority rule. However, while voting may seem straightforward, you should be aware of some potential snares before facilitating this process.

First, you and the group need to agree on the definition of *majority* before the vote is taken. Do you mean a simple majority, with 51 percent concurrence required to carry the decision? Or do you mean a two-thirds majority, with 67 percent needed before the decision passes?

Second, voting plays up differences among members and makes taking sides unavoidable. Voting tends to split the group into opposing factions, which encourages members to pay more attention to the arguments of people on their side than to actively listen to the arguments of the opposition.

Third, decisions made by the voting process may turn out to be poorly implemented because of the internal win/lose atmosphere that is created. E. H. Schein points out that

> [a person advocating the minority position] often feels that the voting has created two camps within the group, that these camps are now in win/lose competition, that his camp lost the first round but it is just a matter of time until it can regroup, pick up some support, and win the next time a vote comes up. In other words, voting creates coalitions, and the preoccupation of the losing coalition is not how to implement what the majority wants but how to win the next battle.[2]

Fourth, a portion of the group's members may feel dissatisfied with a decision even though they participated heavily in the discussion. While their participation might have been high, their dissatisfaction stems from lack of influence. N. R. F. Maier comments:

> The research results clearly show that each participant's satisfaction with group discussions is related to whether he had the opportunity to influence the outcome as much as he wished. Thus satisfaction depends more on a person's felt influence than on how much he talked at the meeting. Fre-

quently members feel that if they had had more time, they could have changed the outcome.[3]

For voting to have any chance of being a constructive process, all members must be given time to understand and assess the situation, as well as be provided an opportunity to exert real influence on it. If this is done, the minority coalition will have a far greater sense of obligation to go along with the majority decision. Incidentally, the fourth point (covering the role of personal influence versus participation in decision satisfaction) applies just as forcefully to the whole-group options—consensus and unanimity of consent.

Whole Group I (WG I): Consensus

Exercising the consensus option lets you share the problem with the group first and then facilitate the group members in processing information to *reach a solution each member can either fully agree with or, at least, agree to support.*

Two points are critical relative to facilitating consensus. First, in the role of facilitator, you must channel the group's thinking by asking again and again, How can we accomplish our stated desired outcome(s)? This is invaluable in maintaining the necessary collaborative effort. Second, the common "us versus them" polarization that frequently occurs in group deliberations, producing win/lose or lose/lose outcomes, must be countered by your constant reminders that the group members need to focus on defeating the problem rather than defeating each other.

A vivid example of group members' achieving consensus despite the issue's difficulty is the presidential commission, headed by former Secretary of State William Rogers, that investigated the space shuttle tragedy of January 28, 1986. Among other things, this 12-member commission uncovered many issues relative to NASA's role in the *Challenger* explosion. In writing their final report—a grinding task—11 members of the commission were reluctant to assign personal blame to specific NASA officials even though they were quite willing to strongly denounce the agency's "flawed" process. This caused the 12th member, a physicist, a great deal of alarm and he pushed hard for stronger language. He wanted to call some of NASA's managers "stupid," something the other members would not support, and the group stalled. Then, after more dialogue, the commission resolved the matter by reaching consensus by allowing the dissenting member to record his own views in an appendix.

The commission had developed a win/win outcome. The physicist got his views into the report, but they could not be interpreted by readers as representing the view of the entire commission.

Because of its impact on group processes and its role as a key facilitation tool, consensus and its ramifications will be treated in much greater detail in Chapter 8.

Whole Group II (WG II): Unanimity of Consent

This is the ultimate in decision making. To achieve unanimity of consent, *all group members must agree with a given course of action.* For the majority of situations, consensus will be more than adequate for making whole-group decisions that everyone is committed to implementing.

It is interesting to note, however, that sometimes in seeking consensus, a group actually winds up with unanimity of consent. This occurs when the manager discovers in going around the table testing for consensus that all group members agree with the proposed course of action, as opposed to having some state agreement and others state support. Unanimity as a by-product of consensus is fine, but because of the length of time it typically takes to achieve unanimity, it should be reserved only for the group's most critical decisions.

FORCES IMPACTING THE CHOICE OF A DECISION OPTION

Which decision option is best? As mentioned earlier, each has its time and place; they all can produce positive as well as negative consequences for group operations. What may be a well-timed and effective decision-making choice in one situation may, under different conditions, be an ill-timed and ineffective option. While any number of factors can affect a decision method's success or failure, Figure 7–2 highlights a few that are especially pervasive and influential.

Decision Quality and Decision Acceptance Requirements

These two factors represent a framework first developed and studied by N. R. F. Maier.[4] He defined *decision quality* as the *objective fitness of a decision;* in other words, *the purely objective or impersonal attributes which indicate that one solution is superior to an alternative solution.* For example, the payback of machine X is 10.5 months less than machine Y. Maier defined *decision acceptance* as the *commitment and emotional support of those who must execute the decision.* With acceptance, individuals and groups are willing to put in extra time and effort to make the decision work. They believe in what needs to be done and won't settle for less than achievement of the objective.

A striking example of total commitment and emotional support to a decision involves Arnold Schwarzenegger and the making of the block-buster movie *Terminator 2.*

> B. J. Rack [co-producer of the picture] emphatically declares during an interview, "Arnold is totally committed to this project."
> To underscore the point, Rack tells a Christmas tale: "It's December 23 and everyone's made their holiday plans and got their tickets, and of course

FIGURE 7-2
Five Forces Affecting Decision Selection

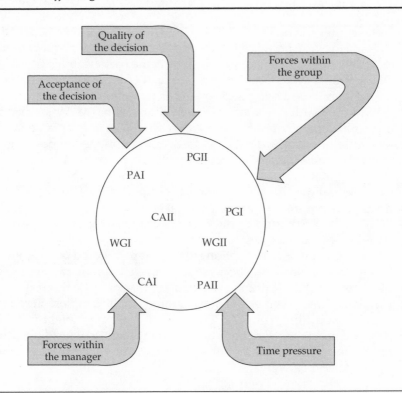

we run into trouble on this incredibly difficult scene at the steel mill." James Cameron [the director] came to his co-producer and told her, "You've got to ask Arnold to work an extra day." Obviously the actor is not too thrilled at the news. "C'mon B. J., I made all these plans," he tells her.

"So I'm preparing my how-much-do-we-have-to-pay-to-get-your-full-attention speech," says Rack, "and Arnold just looks at me and says, 'Is this really important?' and I say, 'Yeah, it's *really* important.' So he says, 'Okay,' and walks into the other room and I'm just sitting there talking to a friend and I hear him talking to his assistant and he says, 'Okay, I want you to call Bruce Willis and tell him he and Demi can't take the jet to Utah because the schedule is screwed up. And then I want you to call my production company and tell them the Christmas party tonight is cancelled, and then I want you to call the Shrivers and tell them that the big Christmas party we were throwing tomorrow night is off, and then get on the phone to George Bush and tell him the Goodwill tour to Saudi Arabia has gotta be postponed. . .' "[5]

Now that's commitment! In spite of the huge financial rewards Schwarzenegger was to receive for doing the movie, he made many personal sacrifices to comply with Cameron's decision to do the steel mill scene over again. Without commitment to the project, Schwarzenegger, as the star, could have walked off the set and said, "Goodbye, we'll do the retake after the holidays." The production would have had to shut down until the noncommitted star was either "bribed" with more money to redo the scene the next day or until he came back from his Christmas holidays. Don't ever underestimate the value of acceptance and emotional support in powering decision implementation excellence.

Regarding the quality and acceptance dimensions, Maier studied the four possible combinations of these two dimensions using an either/or classification. Let's now review what decision options are best aligned with each of these quality-acceptance combinations.

Neither quality nor acceptance is important.   This type of decision is made from among alternatives that are equally good from a quality point of view; furthermore, the final choice makes little difference to those who have to execute it.

Any of the eight decision options in this chapter would be appropriate in this instance. However, because the pure autocratic methods—(PA I) full bore and (PA II) human filing cabinet—would be the least time-consuming, either could be the most favored. In the simplest situations, one could even flip a coin. An example of a decision event in which quality and acceptance are both unimportant might be deciding where to hold a meeting, given a choice of three conference rooms equally comfortable and convenient for all attendees.

Quality is important, acceptance is not.   Such decisions do not require emotional commitment from the people who must execute them. Decisions about where the company buys its raw materials, the rate at which to expand facilities, or how much the firm charges for its products are examples. The success of decisions like these depends on careful analysis of the facts, figures, pros, cons, trade-offs, and the like, and a decision by the manager.

In a situation where the quality of the decision is the main ingredient and the requirement for acceptance is relatively low, the final decision has to rest with the person responsible for the activity. However, since other individuals may have specialized knowledge and technical information critical to making a high-quality decision, the person in charge must be capable of drawing upon this expertise by consulting with the specialists either individually or in a group before rendering a decision. Hence the consultative autocratic approaches (CA I and/or CA II) would be the most suitable decision options.

Acceptance is important, quality is not.   This condition exists when there are a variety of possible outcomes with insignificant differences in quality. In this case, winning the emotional support of all people affected by the outcome is paramount. A few examples would be: deciding which four people in a group of six should work overtime; selecting who, from a sales staff of nine, gets to go to the national trade show; or determining which 3 administrators from a team of 10 will receive the new personal computers. Often these decisions *involve* a good deal of *emotion* as well as the issue of *fairness*.

This issue of fairness is a somewhat nebulous one—we don't learn much from the saying What's fair is fair. I've used five guidelines with managerial groups to get them through some sticky encounters where a scarce and highly desired resource (e.g., money, head count, space, location, perks) had to be apportioned among a group of people. The approach used was not to get the group members to agree on the allocation results per se, but rather to get them to agree on a fair method for making the allocation.

A fair method is any structured process that guides the allocation of scarce resources in a manner that assures the commitment and emotional support to the final outcome by all involved. To create a fair process, you and all other group members need to collaborate in making certain your process meets these five guidelines.

> It shows no evidence of favoritism.

> It does not permit the promotion of self-interest.

> It has some mechanism that allows the process to be reviewed and modified, whenever and wherever needed, to keep it fair.

> It is morally, ethically, and legally correct.

> It allows all people affected by the process to have their concerns represented during its creation.

Since these high-acceptance situations have no best or correct solution, the fair, effective choice is the one most desirable to the people involved. Use of the whole-group decision options of consensus (WG I) or, in an extreme case, unanimity of consent (WG II) would be the most fitting here. Alternatively, an open group discussion followed by a majority vote (PG II) might be advantageous, depending on the situation and the group's maturity.

Quality and acceptance are both important.   In many situations, the quality of the decision and its acceptance are working in tandem. Examples include the redistribution of workload among the members of a staff following a workforce reduction, a change in the way products are designed (e.g., going from drafting boards to computer-aided design), or the institution of Total Quality in an organization. Maier states: ''These problems frequently involve: (1) conflicts in interests (real or apparent) between managers and workers; (2) use of expert opinion; and (3) complex patterns of variables that create issues of fairness."[6]

In striving to optimize both the quality and acceptance dimensions, you will face your most difficult facilitation challenge. The whole-group decision options of consensus (WG I) or unanimity of consent (WG II) are the ones required here. In the role of primary facilitator helping the group reach a consensus, or unanimity of consent if that is the goal, you are attempting to do two things: (1) draw on the group's knowledge, skills, and expertise to optimize the decision's quality and simultaneously (2) gain the group's full commitment to the final outcome. This is no small task; however, learning and practicing the skills taught throughout this book—especially Chapters 8 and 9—will lessen the facilitation burden significantly.

Time Pressure

Time pressure is one of the greatest stresses that any manager feels. As the vertical arrow in Figure 7–1 shows, when urgency figures in decision making, the decision process is likely to shift from a more time-consuming option to a less time-consuming one. For example, time pressures may force a shift from the more time-consuming consensus process (WG I) to the less time-consuming voting, with the majority's "carrying the day" (PG II). Time pressures may cause you to change from being a consultative autocrat processing information with the group (CA II) to being a pure autocrat using people only as human filing cabinets (PA II).

Still, selecting a decision option solely on the basis of expeditiousness overlooks two other crucial factors: (1) the time required for those affected to develop an understanding of, and commitment to, the decision, and (2) the time to execute the decision once it's made.

Obviously, as the manager of your unit, with full authority and responsibility for its performance, you can make decisions much more quickly in the autocratic mode than in the whole-group mode. When employing either of the two whole-group approaches, you are actually building commitment along the road to the final decision. On the other hand, concurrent commitment-building most likely is not taking place if you select the autocratic choices. Once you make an autocratic decision, often additional time must be spent persuading the implementers to "get on board" if commitment is essential. Thereafter, more time must be spent checking to ensure proper implementation.

On the subject of time pressure, M. Sashkin and W. C. Morris astutely note that

> the participative decision approach, where the leader shares authority with all group members, may often be more efficient than a purely leader-determined decision. . . . Both the time required to reach a decision or solution in a problem-solving group, and the time needed to implement the decision, depend on the part played by group members in the decision-making process. . . .

Although the shared leadership approach may increase the time initially required to arrive at a decision, it drastically reduces the time needed to develop the degree of commitment that ensures effective and rapid implementation.[7]

The relationship between time pressure and the choice of a decision option is rooted in urgency. If the immediate need for a decision is driving you, you are very likely to decide to use one of the four autocratic options or the majority vote (PG II) despite the fact that it may generate additional time pressures when the decision needs to be carried out. On the flip side, due to the need for acceptance, you and your group may decide to go for consensus (WG I) despite time pressures. In doing so, however, everyone realizes that if consensus cannot be achieved, you will have to resort to a majority vote (PG II) or fall back to a consultative autocratic mode (CA II) to obtain a decision within the time constraints.

Forces within the Group

Thinking about the group's composition will influence the selection of a decision-making option. Figure 7–3 summarizes the typical forces that would drive a manager to select an autocratic option, as well as the forces that would move a manager to choose a shared-decision approach—consensus in particular.

With respect to the last item listed under shared decisions, in a comparison of 20 long-established committees and 20 ad hoc groups created for a specific problem, J. Hall and M. A. Williams found that the veteran units were superior in their ability to process information accurately and to handle conflicts among members. The newly formed groups spent too much energy avoiding controversy, fearing it would spoil their groups' efficiency.[8]

Forces within the Manager

Finally, the manager—as a person—is a prime element in the selection of a decision-making option. The manager's technical knowledge of the issue combined with his or her personal values, beliefs, and philosophy about managerial practices will influence how a decision is made in a given situation.

Figure 7–4 summarizes the typical forces inside the manager that would influence one to choose an autocratic option and those forces that would lead to the selection of a shared option—especially consensus.

PULLING IT TOGETHER: SOME GENERALIZATIONS ABOUT THE CHOICE OF A DECISION OPTION

As pointed out in the previous section, there are no hard and fast rules to be followed that will "light up the sky" with a message stating un-

FIGURE 7–3
Major Forces within the Group Impacting the Choice of a Decision-Making Option

Forces Driving toward Autocratic Decision	Forces Driving toward Shared Decision— Especially Consensus
• Need for a high-quality decision (PA or CA options are capable of providing a high-quality decision).	• Need for a high-quality decision (PG or WG options are capable of providing a high-quality decision).
• Team members have diverse viewpoints regarding the best solution (use CA options to collect and process these viewpoints and then the manager makes decision).	• Team members have diverse viewpoints regarding the best solution (use PG or WG options to collect and process these viewpoints and make decision).
• There are externally imposed limitations on the manager or group such that the decision is pretty much fait accompli.	• Effective implementation is deemed impossible with low team acceptance.
• Crisis/time crunch.	• If one person makes the decision, the team will not accept it.
• The time needed to involve group members would not be justified by the advantages gained from involvement.	• The team views the problem as significant and interesting and thus worth their time and effort.
• Team members' needs/goals are not in sync with those of the organization.	• Team members understand and identify with the goals of the organization.
• Team members are not qualified to make a shared decision.	• Team members have the requisite knowledge, skills, abilities needed to work through the problem and make a shared decision.
• Team members tried, but were unable to make the decision themselves.	
• Team members will support whatever the manager decides to do.	• The team members thirst for active collaboration in shared decision making.
	• The team members have had experience in working together and in making shared decisions on various tasks.

equivocally, "Given these circumstances, this is *the* decision style to employ." The sheer number of variables involved and their complex interactions makes this a fantasy.[9] However, by identifying and defining each situation in terms of the five major forces that both research studies and experience deem crucial, you are able to acquire keen insight into the appropriateness of electing certain decision approaches over others.

Relative to the ideas developed in this chapter, several implications stand out.

> First, you have a deck of eight decision-making cards from which to select a particular decision option. This provides a great deal of latitude when choosing a decision style.

FIGURE 7–4
Major Forces within the Manager Impacting the Choice of a Decision-Making Option

Internal Forces Driving Manager toward Autocratic Decision	Internal Forces Driving Manager toward Shared Decision
• The manager doesn't possess sufficient information to make a quality decision (use PA II or the CA options to get the info, but decision power remains with manager).	• The manager does not possess sufficient information to make a quality decision (use PG or WG to get the info and make the decision).
• The manager's mind is made up and he or she is not open to being influenced.	• The manager has been successful using this approach in the past.
• The manager's own leadership inclinations are skewed to the autocratic options.	• The manager's own personality and values are socially oriented.
• The manager, after considering the group's knowledge and competence, believes that it is not qualified to make a final decision.	• The manager doesn't want to come across as dictatorial or be perceived as heavy-handed.
• Uncertainty makes the manager feel insecure, bringing a desire for predictability and stability (holding on to decision-making power is a way to create this environment).	• The manager has no preconceived notion of what the best course of action might be and believes that the best answer will come from the synergy of collaboration.

> Second, in order to improve the chances of selecting an appropriate option, you need to understand the role of the five major forces and how each affects the way your hand is played. As treated here, the major forces you need to consider are: the *quality* and *acceptance* ramifications of the decision, the inherent *time pressures*, the *forces residing within the group*, and *personal forces within yourself.*

For example, if the group members have useful information, if their acceptance is critical, if you do not have all of the knowledge and expertise to make a high-quality decision alone, if you feel secure facilitating a group decision, and if time pressures are moderate, then utilizing the whole group option of consensus (WG I) would be appropriate. However, if opposite conditions exist, then one of the autocratic approaches would be effective.

> Third, most people do not want—or need—to be involved in every decision, especially those toward which they are indiffer-

ent. When they do contribute, however, they want those contributions to be taken seriously.

> Fourth, trade-offs among aspects of the five forces will be the rule, not the exception. Consider a situation where the group members have useful information, their acceptance of the final decision is critical, and you do not have all the knowledge and expertise to make a high-quality decision alone. Now add your own insecurity in facilitating a group decision, as well as severe time pressures, and a trade-off must be made. You will have to decide if the time pressures and your own insecurities outweigh the other aspects of the decision situation. If they do, choosing one of the consultative autocratic options (CA I or CA II) could be an appropriate way to go; if they do not, selecting the partial group option of majority vote (PG II) may be a workable option. Moreover, consensus (WG I) might be chosen in spite of your insecurities and attendant time pressures because group acceptance is paramount.

> Fifth, being flexible and using a variety of decision options is vital in successful decision making. The flexible manager is one who maintains a high batting average in accurately assessing the forces impacting the choice of a decision option and, based on the results of the assessment, is willing to make a sincere effort to behave accordingly. Because of circumstances, you may have to go with an option you are less comfortable with than some other alternative. In those cases, the experience you gain in working with the less-favored option will outweigh your feelings of discomfort.

A CLOSING SUMMARY

The eight alternatives presented in this chapter are all viable, legitimate, and useful ways to make a decision. The danger in reading a chapter such as this is making value judgments about various options in the array and deeming some to be better or more mannerly than others. However, doing so is a mistake. Each decision option has its appropriate time and place, and each can produce positive as well as negative consequences depending on how it is applied within the context of a particular situation.

Figure 7–1 depicts a simple framework for categorizing eight decision-making options. Since so much time in group sessions is spent making decisions, it is imperative that any person acting as primary facilitator be familiar with the full set of decision alternatives. Effective facilitation requires being totally familiar with the range of decision methods available to a group, being steeped in how the five major forces impact the choice of a decision option, and understanding the mechanics, strengths, and drawbacks of each decision method. As such, the information in this chapter is the foundation upon which other facilitation skills are built.

The main points detailed in this chapter are summarized here for easy reference.

The eight basic decision-making options.

1. Pure autocratic I (PA I): the full bore method.
2. Pure autocratic II (PA II): the human filing cabinet method.
3. Consultative autocratic I (CA I): processing information with people separately.
4. Consultative autocratic II (CA II): processing information in a group.
5. Partial group I (PG I): less than half decide.
6. Partial group II (PG II): more than half decide.
7. Whole group I (WG I): consensus.
8. Whole group II (WG II): unanimity of consent.

Forces impacting the choice of a decision option.

1. Quality of the decision.
2. Acceptance of the decision.
3. Time pressures.
4. Forces within the group.
5. Personal forces within the manager.

NOTES WORKSHEET: DEVELOP WRITTEN
RESPONSES TO THE TWO ITEMS LISTED BELOW

What Do You Feel Are the Main Learning Points from Chapter 7?	Elaborate on Why You Feel These Points Are Key

NOTES

1. R. K. Mosvick and R. B. Nelson, *We've Got to Start Meeting Like This* (Glenview, IL: Scott, Foresman and Company, 1987), pp. 49–50.

2. E. H. Schein, *Process Consultation*, Vol. 1, *Its Role in Organizational Development*, 2nd ed. (Reading, MA: Addison-Wesley Publishing Company, 1988), pp. 72–73.

3. N. R. F. Maier, *Problem-Solving Discussions and Conferences* (New York: McGraw-Hill Book Co., 1963), pp. 146–47.

4. Ibid., pp. 1–19.

5. I. Blair, "The $100 Million Man?" *US*, June 27, 1991, p. 33.

6. N.R.F. Maier, *Psychology in Industrial Organizations*, 5th ed. (Boston: Houghton Mifflin Co., 1982), p. 172.

7. M. Sashkin and W. C. Morris, *Organizaitonal Behavior: Concepts and Experiences* (Reston, VA: Reston Publishing Company, Inc., 1984), pp. 189–90.

8. J. Hall and M. A. Williams, "A Comparison of Decision-Making Performances in Established and Ad Hoc Groups," *Journal of Personality and Social Psychology* 3 (1966), pp. 214–22.

9. See V. Vroom and P. W. Yetton, *Leadership and Decision-Making* (Pittsburgh: University of Pittsburgh Press, 1973). Vroom and Yetton have created a formal procedure that prescribes which decision styles best suit what situations. They developed a simple decision tree limited to seven yes/no answers to questions the manager asks to define the decision problem. With a specific decision defined, the model indicates the appropriate level of participation required to make a quality decision. While far from being all inclusive, as well as being somewhat rigid in application, the model is a useful mechanism for bringing into focus the amount of employee participation, given the variables of a particular situation.

Chapter 8

Consensus Building
Facilitating Whole-Group Support

Chapter Objectives

> To remove widespread misunderstandings regarding the consensus process.

> To detail six principles that are paramount to the successful facilitation of consensus.

> To provide a set of tips and techniques for building consensus.

> To contrast the powerful process of consensus building with the debilitating process of groupthink.

INTRODUCTION

Will Rogers, American actor and humorist, once remarked, "If all the politicians in the United States were laid end to end, they wouldn't reach a consensus." What is this decision-making process we call consensus? The word is derived from *sensus*, meaning a mental process, not from *census*, meaning counting. Thus it refers to minds coming together.

Consensus decision making is not a superficial, candy-coated, let's-all-be-nice-to-each-other-and-agree process. It takes work, but *it works*. While consensus, like the seven other decision options, has its drawbacks (too time-consuming is the classic argument), when consensus is fully comprehended and well facilitated, group members will feel that they personally contributed to the decision. The reward for your facilitation effort is that group members will have a greater ownership in the outcome, greater feelings of group unity, and a higher commitment to carrying out the decision.

With respect to consensus versus unanimity of consent, while unanimity is rarely required as a decision option, the approach to generating it is the same as for building consensus. The difference is that unanimity takes even longer to achieve, since full agreement among all group members is the desired outcome. In the vast majority of cases, consensus will be more than sufficient for making whole group decisions.

Before proceeding with a complete explanation of consensus, please remain mindful of the following points.

> From the previous chapter, we know that eight options are available when we want to make a decision.

> Consensus (Whole Group I) is one of them.

> Consensus is not appropriate for every situation and every decision; it should *never be considered* the *only* way or the *best* way to make decisions.

> Consensus should be used for *major elements* of a decision, not the many specifics. Problem definition, assumptions about the situation, criteria for evaluating solutions, the choice of a final solution, and setting priorities are a few examples of major decision elements.

> Used inappropriately, consensus is a frustrating and time-consuming process that can create hostile, unyielding, and polarized cliques that prevent the group from reaching any decision.

> Used appropriately, consensus is a vibrant and energizing process that builds joint ownership, enthusiasm, and unified commitment to action.

CONSENSUS IN PERSPECTIVE: PRINCIPLES FOR EFFECTIVE IMPLEMENTATION

Despite the recent publicity and emphasis given to consensus under the banners of high-performance workteams, quality improvement teams, self-managed workteams, problem-solving teams, and the like, the consensus decision process continues to be misunderstood and misused. The six principles that follow are intended to correct the misunderstandings and to provide a road map for properly facilitating the consensus process.

Always Think of Consensus as Win/Win, Not Compromise

The essence of consensus is win/win. In a decision-making situation, win/win indicates the development of a solution that does not dilute any strong convictions or needs of individual group members. Consensus, then, is a cooperative effort to find a sound solution acceptable to everyone, rather than a competitive struggle in which an unacceptable solution is forced on others.

Compromise, on the other hand, is a solution that "splits the difference," "strikes an average," or "meets everyone halfway." Compromise generally produces an outcome that does not meet the needs or convictions of all the people involved. It is a partial solution that often leaves group members unenthusiastic.

The following story portrays the contrast between win/win and compromise.

> Janice and Lenny are a married couple. It is breakfast time. A bowl of fruit containing one orange is on the kitchen table. Janice and Lenny both reach for it at the same time. Janice says, "Well, I can see we both want that orange." Lenny agrees, so they argue over it for a minute, then decide to split it. Janice cuts the orange in half and gives Lenny his piece. Lenny peels his half, eats the fruit, and puts the peel down the garbage disposal. Janice peels her half, throws the fruit down the disposal, and keeps her half of the peel for the marmalade she'll be making that afternoon.

The outcome of this interaction was a compromise: Each person had his or her needs partially met. Had the two spent more time understanding each other's interests, they could have developed a much better solution. Instead of half an orange for each, and thus settling for 50 percent of what each desired, Lenny could have had his needs fully met by getting 100 percent of the fruit and Janice could have had her needs totally met by receiving 100 percent of the peel. This would have been win/win, since each person's needs would have been fully satisfied.

Win/win alternatives seldom are obvious to the group members attempting to decide a course of action. In order to uncover one, all members must be willing to search for a particular solution that does not compromise anyone's strong convictions or interests and that everyone can embrace. Your goal in the role of primary facilitator is to move the information processing to the point where: (1) all the positions being advocated by group members are known and understood by the entire group and (2) each member feels he or she has had sufficient opportunity to influence the final outcome. When the group reaches this stage, the work group manager, employing the maintenance behavior of consensus testing, can check whether the group members have converged on a course of action acceptable to all or whether more discussion and searching for alternatives are required. Let's look at two actual cases that illustrate the attainment of win/win outcomes.

The controversial furs.   During the week before the 1987 Miss USA Pageant, Bob Barker, the host of the pageant and an outspoken animal rights activist, discovered that the backdrop for the swimsuit competition would be a ski resort and that each of the semifinalists was initially to appear on stage wearing a fur coat. Barker felt it would be hypocritical for him to be directly involved in an event that so blatantly violated his animal rights concerns. He threatened to quit his job as host if the semifi-nalists wore fur coats. The show's sponsors said the scene was locked in, with insufficient time to rework it. After five days of intense discussion, Barker and the show's sponsors reached a consensus to garb the contes-tants in synthetic pelts—something that Barker was quick to point out to viewers at the beginning of the swimsuit competition.

This illustrates win/win. The solution developed did not compromise Barker's strong animal rights convictions and, at the same time, met the sponsor's requirement to leave the scene intact, saving time and money.

The fire stations and the day care centers. This excellent exam-ple of consensus in action has been summarized from M. Doyle and D. Straus's *How to Make Meetings Work.* They described a city of 100,000 in the West, an old city undergoing rejuvenation. The population was growing and new construction had started; however, this prosperity was the source of a major problem.

The city had accumulated a $3 million surplus, and two well-organized and vocal coalitions were vying for these funds. Coalition 1 included homeowners and members of the firefighters' union who were con-cerned that the city had only an AA fire insurance rating due to its aging fire equipment and facilities. If the city used the surplus to modernize its equipment, it would be able to get an AAA rating, homeowners' insurance rates would decrease, and the city would attract additional federal funds for housing. Coalition 2 comprised various women's groups publicizing the city's lack of adequate day care centers. The $3 million could be used to rectify this deficiency, they argued.

Both sides agreed that there was not enough money to finance new day care centers *and* new fire stations and fire fighting equipment. Also, three members of the city council were up for reelection at year-end and they knew that taking either position would meet strong opposition.

Facing this predicament, the city council urged both parties to work with representatives of the relevant city departments, state and federal agencies, and experts from the insurance companies. They did and they developed a win/win solution.

Part of the $3 million was used to convert the five outdated fire stations into day care centers. The day care centers thus would be able to operate on matching funds from state and local agencies. The bulk of the $3 million city budget surplus was then used to construct three regional fire stations and supply each with the latest fire fighting equipment, allowing the three stations to serve the city more efficiently than the old setup. This resulted in an AAA insurance rating.[1]

Both coalitions got a win. The city got new fire stations and new equipment without having to remodel the old buildings, homeowners were pleased with the AAA insurance rating, and day care advocates got inexpensive, well-located facilities and the funds to operate them.

Bottom line, if a group can reach consensus, the effort will be worthwhile, since there will be no disgruntled minority refusing to support, or coerced into supporting, the group action. The search for consensus places a premium on trying to understand the other person, rather than arguing or forcing that individual into submission.

At Key Decision Points, Combat the Illusion of Consensus—Explicitly Test for It

The *illusion of consensus* is the most common trap to snare the unwary facilitator. The trap comes in two forms: the *silence trap* and the *hubbub trap*.

The silence trap.   The purchasing team manager says:

"Let's see how we stand. Does anyone have an issue with buying the part from Melcher Manufacturing? [Silence from group members.] Good, it looks like we have consensus; I'll call Melcher tomorrow and place the order."

In this episode, the manager takes the group's silence to mean consent. If no one spoke up against the proposal, then everyone must be for it, he assumes. But many times group members who are not fully committed to the course of action hold back their comments because they assume that everyone else's silence implies agreement or support, and they are reluctant to disrupt the "unity" of the group.

The hubbub trap.   The store owner says:

"Is everyone OK with the plan to open up an hour earlier on Tuesdays and Thursdays and to close two hours earlier on Sunday?"

Two group members remain silent while the other five erupt in simultaneous chatter:

"Yes." "Great.". . . "I love it" . . . "Aw right.". . . "Best decision we ever made."

The store owner says:

"Fine, I see we have an enthusiastic consensus. We can make the changes starting the first week of next month."

This situation is more subtle than the previous one. Here, two silent members have not indicated their position. Are they for or against the change-in-hours plan? The manager can't know for certain unless she asks them. What she does know is that there is a vocal groundswell of enthusiastic agreement from the group. Unfortunately, this hubbub of confirmation from the majority masks the silence of the other two people, and the manager, reinforced by the chorus of support, declares that consensus has been achieved.

In both of these examples, the manager has fallen victim to the illusion of consensus. *Silence does not mean consent!* Maybe all of the silent members involved in each of the two situations were genuinely on-board and committed to the decisions just made; on the other hand, maybe they were not. By accepting silence as consent or by missing a few silent members in the hubbub of affirmation, neither manager knows for certain if genuine consensus has been attained. They both have assumed it—a very dangerous course that could produce bad consequences down the road during or after implementation of the decision.

Therefore, don't equate silence with consent. Find out what the silent, thoughtful people are thinking. The quiet ones are often harboring valuable ideas or insights that are contrary to the consensus being shaped. As a "miner of group gold," the only way for you to *avoid* being seduced by the illusion of consensus is to *explicitly check for it* by using the task behavior of consensus testing. This means going around the table asking each person one-by-one the following question:

"Do you *agree with* the proposed course of action, *or* if you do not agree with it, *will you support* the proposed course of action?"

If each group member responds that he or she either agrees with or, at a minimum, agrees to support the alternative under consideration, a consensus has been cultivated. If one or more members can neither agree with nor support the action in question, consensus has not been achieved and the information processing and search for acceptable solutions must continue. If, after the trip around the table, consensus has not been attained, the manager should go back to each of the dissenting members and ask them to elaborate on what they would add, subtract, or otherwise modify in the alternative being considered so that changes might be made to win their support.

In attempting to build a consensus within your own group, you must keep in mind a point fundamental to any consensus-building effort. Individuals who do not agree with the majority position quite often still will support it if three conditions have been met: (1) they have had sufficient opportunity to present their viewpoints to the group, (2) they are sure their views have been heard and understood, and (3) they can see that the group considered their views in formulating the final decision. Therefore, the most straightforward method for determining if all members either agree with or will support a course of action is to ask them directly.

Stamp Out the Declaration "I Can Live with It"

In the role of process consultant working with many different work groups throughout Xerox, I became keenly aware of a very subtle, but crucial, difference in the way groups practiced the consensus process. The difference was use or nonuse of the statement *"I can live with it."*

Groups that routinely used and accepted the I-can-live-with-it pronouncement to signify support for a given proposal were observed to reach nominal consensus—consensus in name only. Their nominal consensus was hollow and lacked substance because the vital ingredient—genuine commitment to the final outcome by all group members—was lacking.

By verifying observations with meeting participants in a variety of organizational settings, I made several discoveries:

> First, the true message of the I-can-live-with-it declaration is ambiguous. Sometimes it is used as a sincere statement of genuine support for the alternative being considered. More often than not, however, the phrase is used to give an impression of full support, while in reality, the true message being communicated is "I can live with the rest of you going off and implementing this decision, but don't count on me for much help in carrying it out because I'm not committed to what the rest of you want to do." Used inauthentically, the I-can-live-with-it statement can be a means for terminating the consensus process without really committing to the course of action being decided.

> Second, in a majority of cases, groups that make a decision based on nominal consensus are forced to confront a greater degree of destructive conflict, uncooperativeness, finger pointing, and misunderstandings among group members during the implementation phase than are groups that work out an honest consensus.

> Third, groups that build a genuine consensus are able to do so in part because they virtually outlaw the I-can-live-with-it declaration from all of their consensus deliberations. The only acceptable affirmations for indicating consensus are *"I agree with* the course of action" or *"I will support* the course of action." Groups that were observed welding true consensus abided by a rule that was crystal clear: If a group member was unable to state agreement with or support of the alternative under consideration, he or she was considered not on-board, and consensus had not been achieved. It was that simple.

The major implication of these findings is that "I can live with it" has no place in the consensus process. The statement is ambiguous and does not indicate a genuine buy-in to the proposal being deliberated. Frequently it is used as a cop-out, allowing group members to give the impression of being fully behind a particular proposal when, in fact, they are not. It produces nominal consensus that does not stand up through the many implementation challenges the group members invariably must face. Finally, it is used as a ploy by some group members to give an illusion of consensus in order to move on to another subject. If several members use the phrase, they can give the false impression that consensus has been achieved when it hasn't. Through this subtle manipulation, the dissenting members can close off the discussion prematurely without making a bona fide commitment to the final decision.

Develop Shared Values regarding Consensus Decision Making

In order to put the consensus decision-making process in proper perspective and to enhance its effectiveness, all task-oriented groups—whether permanent or temporary—need to take some time to decide what consensus means to them and how consensus will operate within their group. As illustrated by the previous example, consensus will not be a win/win process unless all members agree on what it means and how it functions within their group.

As part of a three-day team-building session, I had the opportunity to facilitate a group comprising the president and the 11 vice presidents of Xerox's Business Products and Systems Group (BP&SG) while they determined how consensus decision making would operate within their team. The discussion was intense, lasting for three-and-a-half hours before the senior staff achieved unanimity of consent on their process. Their efforts produced the following document:

**Business Products and Systems Group Senior Staff
Shared Values Regarding Consensus
Decision Making***

Whenever we, the BP&SG Senior Staff, have decided to make a decision by consensus, and I cannot agree with the course of action being advocated by the majority, I still can state that "I will support" the preferred course of action (meaning do my very best to ensure a successful implementation) if none of my deep concerns have been violated and the integrity of the consensus process has been preserved. Preserving the integrity of the process means that free and open debate and discussion of the issues were maintained and my needs were understood and considered as the preferred course of action evolved. Stating "I will support" puts me fully on-board and makes me a part of the consensus.

Canandaigua Lake
Canandaigua, NY

*Consensus is only one form of decision making; this process only applies to consensus.

Each executive signed the document and its principles became integrated into the senior staff's everyday way of working together.

This management team's approach to consensus is presented here because it is more than just the shared values of a high-level executive team. It is an outstanding definition of how consensus decision making should operate on a consistent basis in any group. Let's examine the power behind these words. The executives defined *support* to ensure that anytime one of them says "I will support" a particular course of action, that person is fully aware of the obligation he or she has to the staff. At the same time, all the other staff members are certain of what that obligation is. Also, the senior staff's shared values put a premium on maintaining the integrity of the process. The final decision may not reflect the exact wishes of each executive, but if it does not violate the deep concerns of anyone, the decision still can be willingly supported by those not in complete agreement with it. Andrew Grove, CEO of Intel, in his book *High Output Management,* nicely addresses the subject of "how can I support something I don't agree with?"

> Many people have trouble supporting a decision with which they do not agree, but that they need to do so is simply inevitable. Even when we all have the same facts and we all have the same interests of an organization in mind, we tend to have honest, strongly felt, real differences of opinion. No matter how much time we may spend trying to forge agreement, we just won't be able to get it on many issues. But an organization does not live by its members' agreeing with one another at all times about everything. It lives instead by people committing to support the decisions and moves of the business. All a manager can expect is that the commitment to support is honestly present, and this is something he can and must get from everyone.[2]

It pays to spend the necessary time to develop shared values around the issue of "How do we want consensus to operate within our work group?" Once this framework is in place, disruptive friction, misunderstandings, and hedging of commitments ("I can live with it") will be greatly reduced as the team focuses on win/win collaborative outcomes.

Determine in Advance the Fallback Decision Option if Consensus Cannot Be Reached

Most decisions must be made by a deadline, and generating consensus does take time. Therefore, do not impose unrealistic time limits that doom the consensus effort before it begins. Group members quickly will see through this manipulation. If tasks repeatedly have time frames too short to allow the necessary debate, discussion, analysis, understanding, and buy-in relative to issues and proposed solutions, the members soon will become frustrated with the process of consensus and curtail its use as a legitimate decision-making option.

Still, there will be occasions when the time frames are realistic, when all members of the team will work diligently to preserve the integrity of the consensus process, when everyone will pour their hearts and souls into the search for a win/win alternative, and yet be unable to bring about a consensus. That is, the group will be unable to uncover a course of action that all members either can agree with or can support.

In such cases, when a *decision is due*, there are only three legitimate options. As pointed out in Chapter 7, there is a fourth option of decision by default; that is, doing nothing and letting nature take its course. While real, it is not considered a legitimate option here because it is decision abdication, decision avoidance. Let's highlight the three legitimate fallback options available to a group when consensus cannot be reached.

> The work group manager, or the person with final decision-making authority in other types of hierarchical groups, can act as a consultative autocrat by making the final decision, but doing so in light of all the sharing and processing of information that has transpired up to that point (the Consultative Autocratic II option).

> A vote can be held, having the majority opinion determine the final outcome (the Partial Group II option).

> A majority and minority position can be written and the issue passed to a higher authority for resolution.

However, it is important to point out that in situations involving various boards, councils, committees, and task forces, the fallback position is limited to either the second or third alternatives. In other words, in meetings where the group session leader lacks final decision-making authority, the only available alternatives to consensus are majority vote or escalation of the decision to a higher authority. In councils, committees, and so on, the leader often lacks the option of halting the information processing and providing the decision because the authority and responsibility for making the decision are fully shared with the other group members and cannot be taken back.

Employing the Consultative Autocratic II option.   After striving to achieve consensus, but being compelled by circumstances to shift to the Consultative Autocratic II option, the most effective process for you to employ would be: (1) summarize the different positions and interests of the team members (to demonstrate your understanding of all the positions and interests being advocated), (2) take all of those positions and interests into account, (3) make the final decision, (4) announce it, and (5) report the rationale for the decision back to the whole team.

If a genuine effort by everyone fails to result in consensus, reverting to the consultative autocratic method should not be considered a facilitation flop. At least the group understands the issues, knows who stands where and why, and sees the difficulty of making the decision. Also, as a result of attempting to build a consensus, you have been the recipient of valuable information, new ideas, and maybe even a solution that was not apparent at the beginning of the dialogue. Finally, research and experience have shown that group members tend to be more understanding and accepting of a decision made by the manager if they are first allowed meaningful involvement. In other words, most of the time you will find little is lost in terms of group commitment when the Consultative Autocratic II option is chosen after a genuine effort to facilitate consensus.

Employing the Partial Group II option.   Using the second option, majority vote, the team leader or the chairperson of a committee, council, task force, and the like, calls for a vote to arrive at the final decision. While PG II is a simple method for obtaining a decision when time has run out for consensus, it is not the perfect alternative. Majority vote by its nature produces win/lose decisions. For example, in a group of 12 people unable to reach consensus—8 advocating position A and 4 backing position B—a vote merely produces a decision that was already obvious: position A *wins* over position B eight to four.

Voting can be a suitable strategic option when a group meets over time; members sometimes vote on the winning side and sometimes on the losing side and the alternatives voted on are reasonably acceptable to all. However, if certain people continually lose, and if they view such losses as personal defeats, then majority rule to resolve time-constrained consensus decisions can eventually destroy the team.

Elevation to a higher authority.   Sometimes this situation arises: After an open, honest effort, consensus cannot be reached; the group session leader does not have the authority to make an autocratic decision; and since it produces winners and losers, voting is not seen by the group as an acceptable decision-making option. Under these conditions the only way to get a final decision is to elevate it to a person who does have the requisite authority.

Routinely moving decision making up the chain of command is not a preferred method. It should be used only after every means to a win/win consensus solution has been exhausted. However, if elevation is the only recourse, both the majority and minority positions must be written clearly, concisely, and without attacks on each other, so that the higher-level decision-maker can most fairly assess the data and make the decision.

The salient point is that anytime a group sets out to make a decision by consensus, the fallback (contingency) option—Consultative Autocratic II, voting, or elevation to a higher authority—needs to be determined before information processing begins. I have found that once a contingency option is predetermined, team members are quite motivated to reach consensus in order to avoid resorting to a less-preferred backup option. Also, since all team members understand the fall-back position's ramifications in advance if it must be used, surprises are eliminated, as is any resentment over how the final decision ultimately was made.

Use Consensus as the Process for Selecting a Decision Option

Using consensus up front to determine how the group should proceed in making a decision is a significant missed opportunity within most family groups. Irrespective of which one of the eight options is singled out, using the consensus process as the method for making the selection will produce understanding, enthusiasm, and commitment to the chosen option. Also, because time is taken at the outset to reach consensus on the appropriate decision method for the task and situation, the rationale for choosing a particular option is clear to everyone. This virtually eliminates any residual mistrust or desire to undermine the group process.

A few illustrations will help clarify the process advocated here. For example, the team may decide, by consensus, to resolve a particular issue by having you discuss it with relevant parties individually, and then make the final call by yourself (the Consultative Autocratic I option). Or, through consensus, the team may decide to hold a whole group discussion for 90 minutes to analyze the information and make several recommendations to you; then, after considering the recommendations, you choose one as the final decision (the Consultative Autocratic II option). In another situation, the group may decide by consensus that the best way to resolve a problem is through consensus (the Whole Group I option). Finally, the group may reach consensus that you are in the best position to make the decision and therefore turn it over to you to make alone without discussion (the Pure Autocratic I option).

There is, however, no need to use consensus to select a decision-making procedure for every decision the group faces. In many cases the group will be comfortable with the method you decide to use or the one that emerges as the group digs into the task at hand. However, for complex issues requiring a unified commitment to the process for resolution, it is wise to use consensus to select a decision-making option before the information sharing and processing begin.

THE REALITIES OF FORGING CONSENSUS: SOME TIPS AND TECHNIQUES

The journey to consensus is rarely straight or smooth. Therefore, when the group has trouble converging on a win/win solution, the manager or chairperson will be able to keep the group moving toward consensus and away from tangents, confusion, and destructive conflict by drawing from the set of tips and techniques presented here.

Encourage Flexibility: Exploding the Mind-Set that It Has to Be All or Nothing

One of the most important techniques for advancing consensus is for you to relentlessly encourage flexibility. Proposed ideas and options are not always mutually exclusive, although at first they may appear to be. Proposals should be treated as a pool of information to be taken apart, examined, modified, extended, and reconfigured in the pursuit of an outcome that everyone can either agree with or agree to support. The power of flexibility in facilitating consensus is underscored by Doyle and Straus.

> Don't assume that you have to choose a single alternative. Sometimes several alternatives can work together. It does not always have to be either Plan A or Plan B, but both A *and* B: price cuts *and* salary reductions, high-rise *and* low-rise buildings, cleaning the house *and* going to the movies. Don't force your group to choose between two or more compatible and feasible alternatives. . . . Encourage people to surface and keep voicing their concerns until their fears have been dealt with. They are doing the group a valuable service by pointing out shortcomings of the solution; in the end the quality of the final solution will be higher. . . . Build on success: "Look at how many points we agree on." Encourage flexibility. Keep dancing around the problem. Try different approaches.[3]

The main point is this: Rather than viewing the decision process as a method for determining winners and losers, you, in the role of facilitator, must remind and encourage the group members always to look for ways to include part or all of every good alternative in the final decision. If most of the group is homing in on alternative 2, you should be alert to ask the question: "How can we incorporate the best features of alternatives 1, 3, and 4 into our final decision as well?" If the group members see pieces of their own ideas in the final solution, they will be willing to support it even if it was not their preferred outcome. Also, combining ideas consistently improves overall decision quality.

Start with the Alternative Having the Least Opposition: Generating Momentum—When No Alternative Stands Out

Imagine that a group has brainstormed a list of potential solutions to an identified problem. Weighted voting was used to reduce the original list of possible alternatives to the significant few. These remaining few were then openly examined, taken apart, moved around, refined, and combined into a reconfigured list of solutions in the search for a win/ win solution. Nevertheless, the group discovers it is stalled in its effort to achieve consensus. What to do?

For example, if the group members are divided among three reconfigured options and no one is able to propose a new alternative, you can keep the consensus process from grinding to a frustrating halt by identifying the least objectionable proposal and using it as the new base for generating consensus. This technique—*negative voting*—can be used to identify the least-opposed alternative.

Using this method, you would point to the first alternative on the flip chart and ask the group: "How many people *cannot support* alternative 1?" Let's say that out of a group of seven (including yourself) four hands are raised. This number would be written next to alternative 1. Then the same question would be asked of alternative 2; let's assume six hands go up. With alternative 3 only two hands are raised. Because it received the fewest votes, option 3 then is checked as the option of least opposition and becomes the base for building consensus.

You would then concentrate on facilitating a full understanding of why the two dissenting members opposed the third alternative. Their points would be recorded on the flip chart. Next, drawing from the tools and techniques presented throughout this book, you would facilitate a whole-group discussion to produce modifications that would satisfy one or both of the opponents. As an illustration, you might say:

> Dorothy has stated that she is against option 3 because she would have to use the 8080 work station and she doesn't feel she has the skill to keep up with the heavy work volume. Does anyone have a proposal for overcoming this barrier? . . . Okay, Diane has volunteered to work with you for two weeks to ensure you are properly trained in mastering the 8080. Dorothy, given Diane's offer, if she starts training you a week from today, would you then be able to support alternative 3 as it now stands? . . . Okay, great! Daphne, I know you had an issue with alternative 3 as originally stated; how do you feel about it now?

Thus, the process would continue. Given that no alternative is an overwhelming favorite, by starting with the alternative of least opposition, you begin the consensus-seeking process with a favorable chance for success.

Use the Swiss Cheese Approach: Gaining Momentum When Differences Are Numerous and/or Complex

Consensus grows out of collaboration. As long as individuals or coalitions are attacking each other and talking about differences rather than attempting to collaborate, the possibility of forging consensus around a particular solution is virtually nonexistent. Group members often resist a joint search for options and the mutual creation of a win/win solution because the number of identified differences overwhelms them. Moreover, the complexity of the differences (politics, values, economics, timing, past history, etc.) may shatter the group members' confidence that consensus is possible. In this situation, the manager should bring the "Swiss cheese" technique into play.

The Swiss cheese technique suggests that the total problem is like a huge slab of cheese—overwhelming. However, by taking several bites and thereby putting a few holes in the slab, the problem does not seem so oppressive. Whenever the group resists making a collaborative attack on the identified issues, you must pick one issue the group members agree is important and focus everyone's attention and energy on this single problem—bite 1. In rallying the group, you should ask the members: (1) *to be optimistic that this single problem can be resolved,* and (2) *not to get hung up on devisive, destructive arguments.* Once this first collaborative bite is taken, the second and third collaborative bites can be taken in the same manner. Then, with three bites out, the group will have gained momentum by operating as a collaborative unit. The original set of problems will not seem so overwhelming, plus a can-do spirit will have been generated.

An interesting application of the Swiss cheese method involved Professor John Dunlop of Harvard University while he was working with two maritime unions. His reflections are summarized below.

Neither union was strong enough on its own, both were in financial trouble, and each hated the other's guts. But the leaders of both unions realized that somehow they had to get their unions to agree to a merger just for the sake of survival.

Dunlop backed off hitting the merger issue straight on. The complexity of the situation was enormous. Instead, he asked the two unions to be optimistic and assume that all the problems would be resolved. He acknowledged that it could take a month or more, but asked them to imagine they were near the end of the proceedings and the only thing that remained was to find a name for the new organization. (Note: This is the single-issue focus.) The people said OK but made it clear that they were certain they could not agree on any of this. It was too complex. Dunlop affirmed that he understood and accepted their feelings but asked them to pretend they had agreed on all the other issues because they were tired of the fighting and arguing. He then precisely refocused their attention and energies by restating: "Let's pretend we have agreed and we just need to think of a name for the merged organization." At that point, he wrote "U.S. of A." on a flip chart, which stood for United Seafarers of America.

This was a very patriotic collection of people on both sides—the kind that wear American flags on their lapels. Needless to say, they loved the proposed name. Dunlop said that they got involved and started talking about subsets and issues within the U.S. of A. Also, because the name did not draw from the name of either union, it became a magnetic rallying point for everyone.

Dunlop emphasized that getting the two unions to agree enthusiastically on one topic broke the ice and got them working on the real issues they had been adamantly resisting before.[4]

Utilize a Committee from the Whole Group: Creating Consensus within a Small Group to Be Used as a Springboard to Consensus within the Whole Group

If a large group (say, 10 or more) is bedeviled in its attempt to reach a consensus, another tactic for generating positive thrust is to set up a small committee to wrestle with the problem at hand. Key point: When striving for consensus, it is not imperative that all group members be encumbered with all aspects of the problem all of the time. As the adage goes, Too many cooks can spoil the broth.

Break the large meeting into a small one by assigning the problem to a committee. Because it is smaller, the committee members will be more intimate and possibly more informal. Advantages of the committee approach are that members more easily can be heard and understood; additional research can be undertaken; more facts, data, and advice can be solicited from people outside the whole group; and committee members may relax, be more open, and be more tolerant of others' behaviors and viewpoints due to the committee's small size.

The committee that is formed should contain an equal number of individuals representing each opinion. Keep the committee as small as possible. The committee's assignment is to take all of the information generated by the whole group, draw from it, and achieve a consensus on amendments, modifications, resolutions, and/or new proposals. The committee is given a clear deadline for accomplishing its task. This deadline could be anywhere from 24 hours to several weeks, depending on the complexity of the problem.

When presented back to the whole group, the committee's new ideas can get the rest of the group off the dime by offering fresh perspectives or, better yet, possibly the solution that accommodates everyone's interests. In any event, the whole group now has the opportunity to process, modify, prioritize, and select alternatives that have already been thrashed through and given the stamp of consensus by all the committee members. New energy and ideas are injected into a group that previously was stalled. The committee has provided food for thought and the whole group can use it as a springboard to full group consensus. Experience has shown that the committee technique has a high rate of success in stimulating consensus within a larger group.

In those instances when neither the committee nor the whole group can accomplish consensus, majority vote, executive decision, or elevating the problem to a higher level will have to be used.

Take Breaks: Calling Time Out to Reflect, to Regroup

Breaks are a useful tool. Calling for a break, for a few minutes or a day or two until another session is convened, serves a number of purposes in the facilitation of consensus. It gives members time to be alone, to reflect, to reconsider positions, interests, roles, and behaviors. When tempers begin to flare and positions start to harden, breaks allow people to cool off and become more rational. Finally, breaks can be used by group members, including the manager or chairperson, to "work issues offline." Session members can meet in small groups and resolve differences among themselves. When a behind-the-scenes resolution is worked out and then conveyed to the rest of the group, often a roadblock is eliminated and the whole group is revitalized in its search for a win/win outcome.

Make Use of Straw Votes throughout Deliberations: Maintaining an On-Going Sense of the Consensus

Trying to facilitate a consensus without being attuned to the ebb and flow of who stands where as the proposing, counterproposing, and building take place is facilitating blind. Periodic straw voting to maintain a sense of the consensus is critical because it highlights who does and who does not support a particular decision as currently formulated. Objections then can be sorted out so that the group can unite in eliminating them.

Avery, Auvine, Streibel, and Weiss make several noteworthy points regarding straw voting:

Straw voting is an informal, nonbinding show of hands to test the number of people in a group who agree with or support a particular decision. . . . First, in extremely large groups, it is often difficult to tell whether a long, drawn-out discussion represents serious disagreement, or if participants are merely raising all the issues and expressing opinions. A straw vote may be used to estimate how close the group is to consensus, and whether it is time to start struggling to finalize a decision, or whether much more discussion is necessary. Secondly, in large groups, many people do not have a turn to speak. A straw vote is a way for silent people to express their opinions and feel that they are being given a chance to have input.[5]

Should you decide to use a series of straw voting activities over the full course of deliberations to achieve consensus, the following message must be communicated loud and clear: *The straw vote is not a movement to majority rule.* It is merely a means for gauging how close the group is to consensus, and for identifying the most serious objections for further discussion.

Seek a Conditional Consensus if the Group Is Polarized: Getting Support to Try a Particular Option for a Certain Period of Time

Commonly, the consensus effort grinds to a halt with several options still open and members arguing their rationale for a particular option—but without any hard facts, figures, or past history to substantiate their arguments. When this occurs, the angle of the facilitation effort can be shifted from shooting for full consensus to going for conditional consensus. Conditional consensus is willingness on the part of group members to give a particular solution a trial run. In some instances, depending on the specifics involved, it may be possible to give several proposed solutions trial runs simultaneously. In any case, conditional consensus represents support to move forward, try out different options, gather data on the results of the trials, evaluate the results, and use that information as the basis for building a full consensus.

In facilitating conditional consensus, when the recalcitrant group members do agree to support the trial run of a particular course of action, it is extremely important that their expressed interests and concerns be taken into account whenever possible in setting up, conducting, and evaluating the trial event. This tactic maintains the collaborative spirit so necessary to reach full consensus later.

Recycle When Stymied: Backing Up and Trying Again

When faced with a situation in which full consensus or even conditional consensus looks bleak, you should not hesitate to stop the current discussion and recycle back to the beginning, repeating the problem-solving steps. R. Likert and J. G. Likert provide an excellent exposition on this technique:

> In essence the group says, "Since we have not reached consensus, we must not have done the problem-solving process well. Let's try again." The group starts by re-examining the statement of the problem to be sure that it is considering the real problem and that the problem is stated well and clearly. It would be well to examine the conditions that were originally thought essential to see if any of these conditions can be classified as desirable but not essential. Two steps in particular need intensive effort when trying to do a better job the second time. These are (1) searching for both additional and stronger integrative goals and requirements, and (2) seeking to create or discover an innovative solution which will meet all of the essential conditions and, consequently, be acceptable to all.[6]

Achieving consensus by recycling can be fairly rapid or quite time-consuming. In the role of facilitator, you must be flexible and patient. However, the time spent reaching consensus by this method will be worthwhile if group commitment and acceptance of the solution are crucial. Also, recycling will be most effective when all group members realize that the whole group faces serious consequences if a satisfactory solution cannot be uncovered.

Stop, Do a Process Check: Using the Group as a Resource to Determine and Resolve Its Consensus Achievement Hang-Ups

This is a technique that probes at the heart of the matter—asking those involved why consensus is not being reached and what can be done to achieve it. Wearing your facilitator's hat, you should not be the only person in the group striving to achieve the consensus. You should be getting secondary facilitation help from most, if not all, the people present. By stopping and asking for their help, you make it easier for them to present their views as to what is hanging up the group and how those hang-ups might be eliminated.

My experience is that when given the opportunity to step back together and look at why they aren't meshing, group members have keen insight. This self-examination process should be facilitated in an open, collaborative way, with conflicts and disagreements encouraged, but managed so that they stay constructive. The key is getting the members to explore ways of overcoming any identified barriers so that consensus can be achieved.

If, as often is the case, the roadblocks are not "show stoppers"—we're too tired, we need more data, we're not listening, we're confused, we're just stuck in a rut, and we're not being creative—the group can get back on track with a collaborative look at the situation. In fact, the seventh technique, seek a conditional consensus, came from this type of session.

On the other hand, if it is a problem at the core of the group's ability to function—politics, an unyielding blocker, mistrust, and so forth—you've got a deeper problem, and under these conditions, achievement of consensus may be impossible. You then can decide whether or not you want to face the deeper problem. If not, at least you know what the barrier is. You can cut your losses and stop wasting time on a situation that doesn't have the ingredients to make a consensus possible. You may be forced to move ahead without consensus by resorting to one of the techniques described next.

Make Progress without Consensus: Moving Ahead When Consensus Is Not Possible

Consensus is never a certainty. As mentioned earlier in the chapter, at times a problem will be so difficult, or the hostilities so great, that even though the manager or chairperson is an able facilitator who does all of the right things, consensus cannot be achieved within the time frame before the deadline. In such circumstances, there are several actions open to you.

> Resort to the fallback, or contingency, decision option selected in advance of the deliberations—executive decision, vote, or elevation to a higher authority. The importance of having a contingency option was well documented in the previous section.

> Lacking a preselected contingency option, figure out the fallback option in the crunch. In other words, in the heat of battle, under severe time constraints and pressures, determine how the decision will be made. If you are the manager of the group holding position authority, this means choosing either to make an executive decision, call for a vote, or send the problem to a higher authority for a decision. If you are a chairperson without position authority, quite often the only possible alternatives are the latter two. The problem with this approach is that it means playing the game of surprise, and often the chosen decision option is not readily accepted by the group.

> Suggest that since the group has not reached consensus and yet action must be taken, the group should proceed with the solution favored by the members who have the major responsibility for implementing it since it's up to them to make it work.

> Suggest that since consensus was not possible, the group should move forward with the option favored by the majority *but* with a stipulation that this alternative does not set a precedent and cannot be used as a basis for future decisions.

> Override the dysfunctional blocker. If consensus has been thwarted by a chronic objector who, *in spite of everyone's sincere efforts to understand and accommodate his or her interests*, still digs in with a "hell no, I won't go" attitude, the will of the majority should determine the decision. However, you must realize that this is a sensitive situation requiring careful facilitation.

A group manager or another person with the authority to render a final decision might say something like:

Well, in spite of our extensive discussion, consensus is not possible at this time. Since the deadline for the decision is today, I'm going to have to make the decision myself. Is there any other information that anyone wants to share with me before I decide? [Any information that is offered would be listened to and confirmed. Then the manager would make a decision that conforms to the wishes of the majority—that is, everyone but the chronic objector.]

Similarly, a task force or committee chairperson who lacks the ability to make an executive decision could say:

> Well, in spite of our extensive discussion, consensus is not possible at this time. Since the deadline for the decision is today, we are going to have to vote. Is there any information that anyone wants to share before we vote?'' [Any information that is offered would be listened to and confirmed. The vote would be held. The chronic objector would be outvoted and the wishes of the majority would prevail.]

The point is, a whole group cannot be held hostage by one unyielding person who discounts the interests and needs of others despite all genuine efforts to accommodate his or her feelings, interests, and desires.

We will close this chapter by studying groupthink. This negative process is found in misguided groups that strive for consensus at the expense of debate, constructive dissent, and critical thinking. For these groups, reaching consensus becomes more important than making a well-thought-out decision.

GROUPTHINK: CONSENSUS CARRIED TO THE EXTREME[7]

Understanding Groupthink

The groupthink malady is a product of cohesive groups, that is, groups in which members have strong, positive feelings toward one another and are highly motivated to remain a part of that group. In such cases, a sense of solidarity encourages the group members to strive for agreement and prevents them from seriously considering problems or possible consequences. Voicing objections and doubts is subordinated to fear of rocking the boat or reluctance to blow the whistle. *Groupthink is consensus in excess.* It is a style of deliberating that members use when their desire for concurrence overrides the good sense to evaluate the courses available to them. Any person facilitating a group must be on guard to prevent the powerful process of consensus from degenerating into the debilitating process of groupthink.

Five Symptoms of Groupthink

Illusion of invulnerability. The group feels invincible. It is marked by a high degree of esprit de corps, by implicit faith in its own wisdom, and by an inordinate optimism that allows group members to feel complacent about the quality of their decisions.

Whitewash of critical thinking. The group members discuss only a few solutions, ignoring other alternatives; they fail to examine the adverse consequences that could follow their preferred course of action; and they too quickly dismiss any alternatives that, on the surface, appear to be unsatisfactory. When warnings do appear, the group members engage in collective rationalization to comfort and reassure each other that the agreed-upon plan is workable or still has a high probability of succeeding.

Direct pressure. When a group member does speak out and take issue with the direction in which the group is headed, direct pressure is applied to the dissenter. He or she is reminded that the group's aim is agreement, not argument.

Negative stereotypes of the opposition. Because "they" are not at the meeting to represent themselves, the group stereotypes the "other guys" as the "bad guys." This fosters inaccurate and dangerous assumptions about the opposition as well as an "us/them" mentality.

Mindguarding. The group members make little effort to get the advice of outside experts or consultants since this might expose them to ideas and opinions contrary to their own. Hence, they guard their minds against the intrusion of perspectives and viewpoints that would disrupt their groupthink. As the old joke goes, "Don't confuse me with the facts; my mind is made up."

The Role of Facilitation in Counteracting Groupthink

For you as facilitator, it's essential to be aware of the five symptoms of groupthink because the recognition of some or all of these symptoms is a signal to combat groupthink with specific facilitation techniques. What can you do to undercut this phenomenon?

Invite experts and consultants into the group sessions. Invite outside experts and consultants to speak to the group, and ensure that what these people have to say is heard, understood, and processed by the group members. Outsiders can be a tremendous resource for critiquing the assumptions of the group as it prepares to make a decision.

Make all group members critical evaluators. Legitimize disagreement and skepticism by assigning the role of critical evaluator to every group member. Each should feel free to act as a *constructive* devil's advocate. Through words and actions, you must demonstrate that questions, reservations, and objections are welcome within the group, and that loyalty should not obstruct the expression of doubts. Drawing on the behaviors presented in Chapter 5, you can facilitate the group members in exploring all alternatives as they converge on an informed decision.

Avoid exerting too much personal influence. It is natural for you, the manager or chairperson, to come to a meeting with preconceived solutions or courses of action. In practicing the art of excellent facilitation to counteract groupthink, however, this tendency should be initially suppressed to encourage freedom of thought among all group members. This approach keeps the door open for members to explore the subject matter freely. Your views may be woven into the general group discussion as information and data are processed; if necessary, you can interject a different position to help the group see the situation from a different perspective.

Utilize the loyal opposition. Facilitate the group in seeking out, understanding, and examining the positions, interests, needs, and desires of people whose views are known to conflict with the group's preference. What does the opposition believe? Why do they hold the position(s) they do? What are the interests behind their position(s)? What are merits to their position(s)?

Inoculate against premature decisions. Double-check to determine if a decision *must* be rendered within the original time frame. If not, or if time can be extended, postponing a decision to obtain more information is far more practical than making an inferior decision that the group will regret later. Furthermore, whenever possible, schedule information processing separately from decision making to give group members a chance to mull over the alternatives. This will help prevent the group from being caught up in the heat of the moment and embracing a poorly thought out decision.

In reality, groupthink is consensus gone awry. It is a serious condition that severely limits the group's decision-making capabilities. You must be ever mindful of this condition and relentlessly facilitate it away by initiating and maintaining an open, collaborative climate, and by practicing the five techniques just covered. Doing so will infuse critical thinking as an acceptable, routine way of doing business within your work team or task force, and this, in turn, will prevent groupthink from taking hold.

A CLOSING SUMMARY

The renewed interest in and practice of consensus in the public and private sectors of countries around the world have resulted in misunderstanding and misuse of this decision-making alternative. This chapter not only identifies and corrects these misunderstandings, it provides tips and pointers to help upgrade one's skill in facilitating consensus. Consensus is win/win. It refers to a condition in which *all* members of a group can state that they either *agree with* the proposed course of action *or*, if some members do not agree with it, they *will support* the course of action being considered. Built into the consensus process is the belief that all group members have some part of the truth, and that the group will reach a better decision by putting all pieces of the truth together first.

Facilitating a group in the achievement of consensus takes effort. Time must be allowed for all group members to state their concerns and be reassured that the others around the table truly do understand their position and interests. This requires careful listening by all members. It also requires use of the *task behaviors of testing comprehension and summarizing*. The only way to know if consensus has been achieved is to employ the *task behavior of consensus testing,* verbally checking for it around the table. Silence or a few head nods do not signal consensus.

Consensus in excess is groupthink. Groupthink occurs when the group strives so hard for agreement that virtually all critical thinking is eliminated. You must constantly be aware of the small margin of error in facilitating consensus versus going overboard and facilitating groupthink. Critical thinking has its roots in differences, disagreements, and constructive conflict. These must be accepted as natural and helpful, not repressed. Critical thinking is a boon to the consensus process because with a greater array of data, information, proposals, and so forth, there is a greater chance that the group will hit upon adequate solutions. A considerable return awaits the group that invests time and effort to forge a genuine consensus. Consensus decision making typically yields high decision quality, full ownership of the decision among group members, and a high potential for successful implementation of the decision.

A summary of how-to tips and techniques for forging consensus and combatting groupthink is presented here for easy reference.

Consensus in perspective: Guidelines to effective implementation.

1. Always think of consensus as win/win, not compromise.

2. At key decision points, combat the illusion of consensus—explicitly test for it.

   > Avoid the silence trap.

   > Avoid the hubbub trap.

3. Stamp out the declaration "I can live with it."

4. Develop shared values regarding consensus decision making.

5. Determine in advance the fallback decision option if consensus cannot be reached.

6. Use consensus as the process for selecting a decision option.

The realities of forging consensus: Some tips and techniques.

1. Encourage flexibility; explode the mind-set that it has to be all or nothing.

2. Start with the alternative having the least opposition; generate momentum when no alternative stands out.

3. Use the Swiss cheese approach; gain momentum when differences are numerous and/or complex.

4. Utilize a committee from the whole group; create consensus within a small group to be used as a springboard to consensus within the whole group.

5. Take breaks; call time out to reflect, to regroup.

6. Make use of straw votes throughout deliberations; maintain an on-going sense of the consensus.

7. Seek a conditional consensus if the group is polarized; get support to try a particular option for a certain period of time.

8. Recycle when stymied; back up and try again.

9. Stop, do a process check; use the group as resource to determine and resolve its consensus achievement hangups.

10. Make progress without consensus; move ahead when consensus is not possible.

Groupthink: Consensus carried to the extreme.

1. Five symptoms of the phenomenon of groupthink:

    > Illusion of invulnerability.

    > Whitewash of critical thinking.

    > Direct pressure.

    > Negative stereotypes of the opposition.

    > Mindguarding.

2. The role of facilitation in counteracting groupthink:

    > Invite experts and consultants into the group sessions.

    > Make all group members critical evaluators.

    > Avoid exerting too much personal influence.

    > Utilize the loyal opposition.

    > Inoculate against premature decisions.

NOTES WORKSHEET: DEVELOP WRITTEN RESPONSES TO THE TWO ITEMS LISTED BELOW

What Do You Feel Are the Main Learning Points from Chapter 8?	Elaborate on Why You Feel These Points Are Key

NOTES

1. M. Doyle and D. Straus, *How to Make Meetings Work* (New York: The Berkley Publishing Group, 1976), pp. 57–58.

2. A. S. Grove, *High Output Management* (New York: Vintage Books, 1985), p. 91.

3. Doyle and Straus, *How to Make Meetings Work*, p. 244.

4. P. Petty, "Successful Negotiation Builds on Feedback, Patterns of Agreement," *Rochester Democrat and Chronicle*, February 13, 1987.

5. M. Avery, B. Auvine, B. Streibel, and L. Weiss, *Building United Judgment* (Madison, WI: The Center for Conflict Resolution, 1981), p. 99.

6. R. Likert and J. G. Likert, *New Ways of Managing Conflict* (New York: McGraw-Hill Book Company, 1976), p. 150.

7. For an extensive discussion of how important government committees made poor decisions as a result of their unyielding desire to avoid controversy within their groups, see I. L. Janis, *Victims of Groupthink* (Boston: Houghton Mifflin Book Company, 1972). Also see the excellent documentary film *Groupthink* (Carlsbad, CA: CRM Films, 1991). Videocassette.

Chapter 9

Conflict Management
Facilitating Five Steps to Collaborative Conflict Resolution

Chapter Objectives

> To examine the constructive and destructive effects of conflict on a group's performance.

> To present a five-step collaborative model for managing conflict.

> To provide the necessary how-to tips and techniques to enhance the manager's or chairperson's ability to effectively facilitate through conflict to consensus.

INTRODUCTION

An old sea captain and his chief engineer got into a major conflict over which one of them was more important to the ship. Neither person would concede a thing to the other. Their voices grew louder, their tone more sarcastic, and their attacks more personal. Failing to agree, they resorted to a unique plan of swapping places. The chief ascended to the bridge and the captain went into the engine room. After a couple of hours the captain suddenly appeared on deck covered with oil and soot. "Chief!" he yelled, wildly waving aloft a monkey wrench. "You'll have to come down here; I can't make 'er go!" "Of course you can't," replied the Chief. "We're aground."

Destructive conflict has struck again—big egos, one-upmanship, personal attacks, foolish decisions, disastrous consequences. It doesn't have to be this way as you'll see. This chapter is an extension of the previous one. Taken together, they deal with a variety of simple but powerful approaches to enhancing the effectiveness of group interaction.

THE ESSENCE OF CONFLICT MANAGEMENT: A FEW THOUGHTS FOR SUCCESS

Anyone who does much facilitating sooner or later will have to deal with conflict. This is a normal and essential dynamic of group sessions. If all members' approaches, perspectives, and values were the same, there would be little need for group decisions at all—certainly there would be virtually no need for facilitation. The very idea of facilitation, in fact, presupposes that there will be divergent ideas, opinions, and proposals regarding the best course of action or method for solving a common problem, reaching a goal, or making a decision. The goal of the group should not be to avoid or eliminate conflict, but rather to view this diversity as a healthy and essential step in the process of working out a constructive win/win resolution to the problem at hand.

As a facilitator attempting to process discord, you have a dual responsibility. First, you must make sure that members' divergent viewpoints are brought forward and used as a wellspring of critical thinking and innovative solutions. Second, in conjunction with the first responsibility, you also must facilitate this diversity so that the conflict does not deteriorate into interpersonal strife and wreck the entire session.

Properly managing conflict requires that you never lose sight of a fundamental point: *conflict itself is neither good nor bad*. Whether conflict enhances critical thinking and productivity or undercuts it will depend on how you facilitate the differences at hand. Understanding how to handle disagreements and how to use them as an asset in group deliberations is primary knowledge for anyone putting on the facilitator's hat. Many managers and chairpersons experience their most uncomfortable moments at the helm when attempting to facilitate interpersonal differences and conflict. Frequently such situations create immense difficulty for them because they don't have the foggiest idea how to facilitate through the disharmony and help the group build a win/win solution. However, following the advice in this chapter can help to rectify that problem.

Conflict in Perspective

Conflict is a word that is used in many ways. For our purposes the following definition will be helpful.

> Conflict occurs when two or more parties discover that what each wants is incompatible with what the other wants. A want that is incompatible with another is one that interferes with, or in some manner hinders the achievement of, the second.

The parties can be individuals, groups, organizations, or nations. Their wants may range from acceptance of an idea to control of a limited resource. Our definition specifies that conflict is a condition that arises when seemingly incompatible concerns exist. It may be a temporary condition or one of long duration—a mild skirmish over a routine matter or a complex, highly charged interaction. It may result in visible, vigorous activity or internal ferment.

Conflict falls into two categories. *Substantive conflict* occurs when participants are in opposition relative to the content, or substance, of the issues under discussion. *Personal conflict* derives from the emotional clashes that occur during the struggle to resolve the issues at hand.[1] In this chapter, we will describe methods to handle substantive conflict collaboratively even in situations where feelings may arise and make management of the conflict more difficult.

When differences exist, destructive conflict may or may not be present. Differences, particularly differences in values, often lead to destructive conflict. Whether differences actually *do* lead to destructive conflict depends on the character and facilitation of the interaction process.

In essence, the challenge to you as facilitator is to encourage diversity without encouraging personal conflict—to harness the constructive power of substantive conflict without igniting its destructive power.

The Signs of Constructive Conflict

When facilitating a discussion, what cues or signals indicate fruitful friction? First, there will be high team spirit and a commitment to the desired outcome(s). The task behaviors of testing comprehension and summarizing are used by members to ensure that each other's viewpoints are understood—even though they may not be supported. Participants respond to what others are saying, not to what they think others are saying. The discussion stays on the topic and contributes to the attainment of the desired outcome(s). Finally, members see the time and energy spent discussing and modifying differing ideas and alternatives as worthwhile because it produces a result that is better than any one individual's initial proposal.

The Signs of Destructive Conflict

There are telltale indications for you that the discussion is headed toward ruinous conflict, just as there are signs of constructive controversy when it is occurring. A sure sign of destructive conflict is when members start resorting to personal attacks instead of keeping a focus on the facts and issues. Another red flag to watch for is the generation of attack/defend/counterattack spirals by group members. Other key warning signs include: the same negative statements being presented again and again by the same people, members not listening to what others are saying but reacting to what they think others are saying, members dug in with unyielding attachment to their own ideas, and—a big one—emotionally charged one-upmanship.

Intervening versus Waiting

As facilitator, your job is to pay attention not only to what is being said but also to how the group members are interacting. Wearing the facilitator's hat, you are constantly faced with making a judgment about whether to intervene or wait and let the conflict discussion proceed. This is not an easy call to make. The best advice is, monitor the constructive and destructive signs presented earlier and, if in doubt about what to do, let the discussion continue a little longer. However, if resentment starts building and people begin entrenching their positions, step forward and actively facilitate.

FIVE PRIMARY STRATEGIES FOR MANAGING CONFLICT

This section reviews five basic strategies for dealing with conflict: avoiding, smoothing, compromising, forcing, and collaborating.[2] As will be shown, each of these approaches is useful and appropriate in certain situations. After the five approaches are briefly addressed, the remainder of Chapter 9 will concentrate exclusively on the strategy of collaborating.

Avoiding: Leave Well Enough Alone

Avoiding involves retreating—either physically or mentally—from an actual or potential conflict situation. Sometimes called withdrawal, this may mean leaving the solution to fate or chance. Those employing this style simply do not address the conflict and are indifferent to each other's needs and concerns even when there is a need to take a position.

Avoiding can make sense when you need more time to collect information, enlist support, augment resources, or when there seems little chance to resolve the differences in a satisfactory way because the timing is wrong, you lack the necessary power and/or influence, or the issue is trivial (from your perspective).

Smoothing: Hey, Don't Worry! Everything is OK

Smoothing is a step up from avoiding. It is a strategy that involves minimizing differences by assuming or pretending they are unimportant. Smoothing concentrates only on similarities and agreement. It requires covering up and glossing over the actual discord by taking a posture that everything is pleasant, cooperative, and trouble free.

Smoothing is groupthink in its full-blown glory. Regarding smoothing, M. Sashkin adds:

> When all parties to a conflict openly participate in smoothing, it is often labeled "agreeing to disagree." Smoothing does not seem to work as a long-term strategy because the problems and conflicts do not really go away; often, the conflict reappears even more forcefully. But there are occasions when smoothing, or "agreeing to disagree," can be a useful temporary strategy.[3]

Smoothing may be productive when preserving harmony and sidestepping disruption are especially important or when another person has a great deal more power and is using it on you.

Compromising: Let's Split the Difference

Compromising, as noted in Chapter 8, involves searching for solutions that bring only partial satisfaction to each of the differing parties. Parties involved in compromise are mainly concerned with personally avoiding an unfavorable share of the outcome, rather than with achieving a solution beneficial to both. Compromising means settling for "half a loaf" rather than risking an all-out, win/lose struggle.

Compromise can make sense when two parties with equal power are strongly committed to mutually exclusive goals, or when each party can gain more from a split-the-difference agreement than the best alternative available if no agreement is reached. Compromise also can be used to achieve temporary settlements to complex issues, to arrive at expedient solutions under time pressure, or when the goals of the parties are moderately important but not worth the effort and time required for collaboration.

Forcing: It Will Be Done My Way

Forcing is a power-oriented approach that involves threat, pressure, and intimidation to achieve your objectives without concern for the needs and acceptance of others. This is vividly demonstrated by a letter from Queen Elizabeth I to Bishop Richard Cox in 1559:

> Proud Prelate—You know what you were before I made you what you are now. If you do not immediately comply with my request [to read the English litany in London churches], I will unfrock you by God![4]

Forcing often takes place as an open, competitive battle that produces a clear victor and a clear loser. For a group, this is rarely a productive strategy, especially if the winners must work with the losers in the future.

With forcing, the content of the conflict often becomes generalized from a specific issue to an atmosphere of bitter dispute as each party's original firmness and sense of confidence becomes exaggerated and escalates toward coercion and arrogance. The image that comes to mind is Charlie Chaplin's *The Great Dictator* where Mussolini and Hitler are in barber chairs, and each is pushing his chair a little higher in order to get "one up." Pretty soon they're both up to the ceiling yelling at each other. Forcing produces that kind of escalation.

Still, forcing can be useful in emergencies, when you know you are right, where unpopular actions must be implemented, where the organization's welfare is at stake, and when you need to protect yourself against those who take advantage of nonassertive and/or noncompetitive behavior.

Collaborating: Let's Use the Synergy of the Whole Group to Develop a Win/Win Resolution

Collaborating addresses differences directly, confronting them with synergistic problem solving. The affected parties join forces to work through their differences; they channel their energies to defeat the differences, rather than defeat each other. This is an integrative approach, in which each person enmeshed in the conflict actively seeks to satisfy his or her own goals, as well as the goals of the others. Instead of dividing up the pie as in compromising, with collaboration the parties look for ways to make the pie bigger.

Collaborating is especially useful for finding an integrative solution when both sets of goals are too important to be compromised, for merging people's insights with a variety of useful perspectives on the problem to improve the quality of the decision, or to gain commitment and acceptance through consensus.

BUILDING THE CASE FOR COLLABORATION

Now that we have reviewed the five strategies for managing conflict, we will concentrate in the remainder of this chapter on *collaborating*. There are three reasons for doing so:

1. No particular facilitation knowledge, skills, or abilities are required by the manager or chairperson to carry out the avoiding, smoothing, compromising, or forcing processes. These are rudimentary activities that discount the conflicting parties' wants, concerns, and goals. There is no need to identify issues, work through them, and develop a solution that is win/win for everyone concerned. Collaborating, on the other hand, is a higher-order process. Effectively facilitating collaboration is the most difficult of the five strategies. It requires more knowledge and skill, as well as time and commitment on the part of the family group manager or committee chairperson.

2. Collaboration is emphasized here because it is the way to build consensus.

3. Collaboration is the one means to manage conflict that has consistent positive benefits as shown in research studies.

Let's examine the research on organizational behavior since it provides a basis for inferring the relative effects of the managing-differences approaches just covered.

J. W. Lorsch and P. R. Lawrence[5] studied the use of collaborating, forcing, and smoothing in six organizations across three industries, plastics, container, and food. They concluded that managers in the two highest-performing organizations used collaborating to a significantly greater degree than did managers in either medium- or low-performing organizations. Similarly, managers in medium-performing companies used collaborating to a significantly greater extent than those in low-performing organizations. Regarding smoothing and forcing, Lorsch and Lawrence noted that while heavy reliance on collaborating is essential, a backup mode that includes some forcing and a relative absence of smoothing may be useful. They concluded that the presence of moderate forcing indicates the managers they studied were more willing to reach some decision than to avoid the problem.

G. L. Lippitt[6] presents evidence that substantiates the conclusions of Lorsch and Lawrence regarding the greater effectiveness of collaborating (win/win) over forcing (win/lose). Table 9–1 shows the results of comparing 53 case descriptions of effective conflict resolution with 53 case descriptions of ineffective resolution. Of these, 58.5 percent of the effective outcomes were achieved through collaborating as opposed to only 24.5 percent effective resolutions via forcing and 11.3 percent through compromising. The results regarding ineffective resolution are even more dramatic: 79.2 percent of the ineffective resolutions were due to forcing, while none of the ineffective outcomes were the results of collaborating! M. Sashkin and W. C. Morris, summarizing the literature, state:

> Research studies on the effects of the various strategies [for managing differences] confirm that forcing and avoiding are associated with the development of negative feelings between conflicting parties, and are also found to be associated with negative outcomes, such as decreased performance. Only collaborating is clearly related to positive outcomes in a wide range of circumstances. Bargaining [compromising] and smoothing seem to have mixed results.[7]

In a similar vein, Tom Peters, coauthor of *In Search of Excellence* and *A Passion for Excellence* and author of *Thriving on Chaos*, has been evangelical in spreading his message that to succeed in our organizational environments, both industrial and nonindustrial, we must replace antagonism with partnership. We need to begin by examining our attitudes

TABLE 9–1
Methods Associated with Effective and Ineffective Conflict Resolutions

| | Effective Resolution (N = 53) | | Ineffective Resolution (N = 53) | |
	N	Percent	N	Percent
Avoiding	0	0.0%*	5	9.4%*
Smoothing	0	0.0	1	1.9
Compromising	6	11.3	3	5.7
Forcing	13	24.5*	42	79.2*
Collaborating	31	58.5*	0	0.0*
Other (still unresolved; unable to determine how resolved; irrelevant to assignment; etc.)	3	5.7	2	3.8

*Percentage difference between groups is significant at the 0.5 level of confidence.
Adapted from G. Lippitt, *Organization Renewal* (Englewood Cliffs, NJ: Prentice-Hall, 1982), p. 152.

and embracing the belief that sharing power and working together are natural and productive, not soft and counterproductive.

D. W. Johnson and R. T. Johnson, in their comprehensive examination of cooperation and competition, draw some general conclusions from the behavioral science literature:

> Over 185 studies have compared the impact of cooperative and competitive situations on achievement. The results of these studies indicated that cooperation promoted higher individual achievement and greater group productivity than did competition.[8]

D. Tjosvold's research into the literature on cooperation, competition, and independence resulted in these conclusions:

> Five hundred studies, conducted by many types of social scientists and summarized in recent reviews (including meta analysis) . . . consistently indicate that it is through cooperative teamwork, much more than through competition or independence, that people communicate directly, put themselves in each other's shoes, support each other emotionally, discuss different points of view constructively, solve problems successfully, achieve at high levels, and feel confident and valued as persons.[9]

Before moving ahead to lay out the tools and processes for facilitating collaboration, a few points need to be stressed once more for clarity. All five strategies can be useful and are appropriate under certain conditions. Examples of appropriate use were presented during the individual review of each strategy. Also, research evidence suggests that proper application of the collaborating approach offers the greatest probability of producing results that are of the highest quality and that give the most enduring satisfaction to the parties involved. However, please keep in mind that not all conflicts are worth resolving collaboratively. Collaboration is being overemployed if seeking resolution to a conflict is tapping into energy more wisely spent in other endeavors. The remainder of this chapter will concentrate on showing how conflict can be managed in a collaborative, problem-solving way.

A COLLABORATIVE APPROACH TO MANAGING CONFLICT: FIVE STEPS TO SUCCESS

Managing disharmony, especially in a situation that is highly charged and volatile, is a major challenge for the manager or committee chairperson in the role of facilitator. There is little chance that this challenge can be avoided for very long. Nevertheless, by holding one's temper in check and utilizing the five-step process depicted in Figure 9–1, differences can be managed successfully.

An Overview of the Model

The process model for resolving conflict is composed of five steps broken into two phases: differentiation and integration. Before you can effectively resolve conflict, you must first facilitate the differentiation phase in order to understand the nature of the conflict. This entails three steps: clarifying the existing positions and associated interests, defining the areas of agreement, and then defining the areas of difference. Next, in the role of facilitator, you must facilitate the integration phase. This requires two steps: orienting the entire group to the task at hand—defeating the difference, not defeating each other—and facilitating resolution of the conflict in an open, collaborative, problem-solving manner.

The significance of the differentiation phase and the integration phase in conflict resolution is explained by R. E. Walton:

> The basic idea of the *differentiation phase* is that it usually takes some extended period of time for parties in conflict to describe the issues that divide them and to ventilate their feelings about [the issues] and each other. This differentiation phase requires that a person be allowed to state his or her views and receive some indication that these views are understood by the other principals.
>
> In the *integration phase* the parties appreciate their similarities, acknowledge their common goals, own up to positive aspects of their ambivalences, express warmth and respect, or engage in other positive actions to manage their conflict. . . . The potential for integration at any point in time is no greater than the adequacy of the differentiation already achieved. To the extent that the parties try to cut short the differentiation phase, dialogues are likely to abort or to result in solutions that are unstable.[10]

FIGURE 9-1
A Five-Step Process Model for Managing Conflict

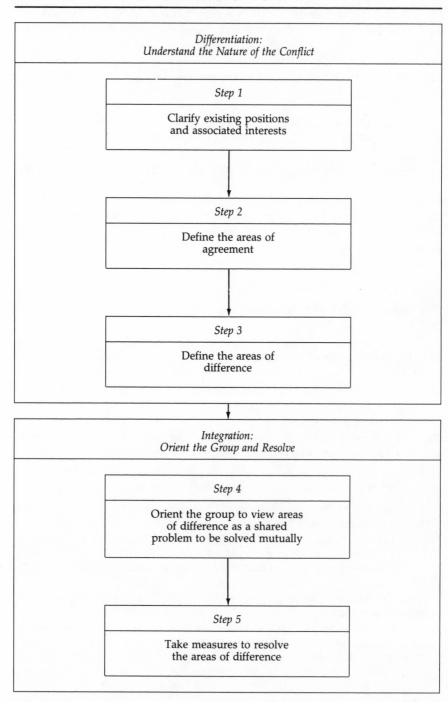

The strength of this five-step model is that it provides a straightforward set of basic guidelines, organized into two phases, that can be employed time and again in a variety of situations. It should be employed anytime the manager's hat must be swapped for the facilitator's hat to help the group constructively work through controversy and diversity.

Fundamentals: The Bedrock for Facilitating the Conflict-Managing Model

In working through the various steps of the conflict-managing model, there are a number of facilitation practices, most of which were covered in previous chapters, that have broad-based applicability here. These fundamentals are the foundation for successfully managing conflict. Before moving ahead to examine the elements of the conflict-managing model, let's briefly review the foundation practices.

Before taking steps to resolve the conflict, write-out, clarify, and post the desired outcome(s) (Chapter 5). When an obvious difference exists that is pertinent to the subject under consideration, but that cannot be postponed or resolved quickly, you must acknowledge this situation and propose the desired outcome(s) linked to the resolution of the dispute. The desired outcome(s) should explicitly state what is to be accomplished at the conclusion of processing the conflict. However, the desired outcome(s) offered by you and written on the flip chart is only a proposal. It must be tested against the group like all desired outcomes to allow members to modify it if necessary, and above all, to gain their commitment. This activity is essential but needs to be done quickly. For example, you could say:

> Wearing my facilitator's hat, I'd like to remind the group that before we can properly tackle the controversy that has cropped up, we need to have a desired outcome. Based on what I'm hearing regarding the differences over the structure of our Personnel Operations Council, I submit that the desired outcome of working through our difference would be: To reach consensus on the mission, support goals, and operating principles of our Council. [The scribe notes this desired outcome on a flip chart.] How does this outcome statement strike everyone?

Process aroused feelings using flip charts. Emotional disturbances often accompany the effort to manage substantive conflict. However, feelings are prone to arise as the group engages in Step 1, clarifying existing positions and associated interests; Step 3, defining the areas of difference; and Step 5, resolving the difference. Regardless of when emotional conflict springs forth, it must be dealt with, not ignored, bulldozed over, or belittled. Processing means recognizing what is taking place and tending to it by providing group members with appropriate outlets for venting their emotions.

The facilitator needs to bear in mind several guiding principles when processing feelings as they become entwined with the management of substantive differences. All feelings need to be accepted as legitimate and real. They need to be understood, rather than evaluated. They need to be encouraged so that the group members can obtain psychological release through the simple process of expounding on their grievances. Letting off steam makes it easier for people to talk rationally later on and thus permits the processing of differences to move back to substantive issues and into the facts and solutions phases. Finally, to make it clear that emotions are not being ignored and to record what may be invaluable information for use later on, you should ensure that the feelings data are captured on flip charts and posted in full view of everyone.

State issues and problems situationally, not behaviorally. Constantly be on the lookout for ways to word problems or issues in situational terms, rather than in behavioral terms—especially accusatory or judgmental terms. To say "My assumptions are different from yours" is far removed from saying "Your assumptions are stupid." The former is a fact; the latter is a judgment.

Using flip chart pages to list and post the desired outcome as well as any "feeling" information greatly enhances depersonalization of the existing differences. What this activity does is shift attention away from the personalities involved to the posted information.

Use the task behaviors of seeking information and opinions, testing comprehension, summarizing, plus the process behavior of gate-opening (Chapter 6). Practicing these interpersonal behaviors will assist: the generation, clarification, and understanding of information related to people's points of view on the issues, the scoping of the areas of agreements and disagreement, and the growth of win/win solutions to revolve the issues.

No group is likely to resolve differences if it doesn't get to the core of the matter. Complete and accurate information is indispensable for the management of disputes. Since complete and accurate information is rarely presented spontaneously in a conflict situation, the information has to be "dug out of the heads" of the participants. This takes probing, reflective statements, and summaries.

Make use of the maintenance behaviors of encouraging, harmonizing, and tension relieving (Chapter 6). Focusing on these behaviors will strengthen the group's ability to stay together and mutually tear into the difference, as opposed to dividing into camps and tearing into each other.

Move swiftly to facilitate so that disagreement does not escalate into personal attacks (Chapter 6).   Personal attacks never can be tolerated when managing conflict. At all times, the task behavior of disagreement must remain confined to the issues and must not be permitted to turn into a personal attack-defend-counterattack spiral. Since these spirals are often the genesis for a great deal of destructive conflict that suddenly disables a group session, at the first sign of a spiral you must intervene at once. For example:

Max:

Well, I guess I shouldn't be surprised. That's the typical, narrow-minded, bean-counter approach you financial types are constantly stuffing down our throats.

Jim:

That proves how much you know, you're so ignorant . . .

Gail:

Hold it! Max, Jim, you're both getting personal and starting to attack each other. Let's stick to the issue of proposing ways to reduce variable costs in our advertising agency.

FACILITATING THE COLLABORATIVE APPROACH TO MANAGING CONFLICT: FIVE STEPS TO SUCCESS

Remember, the five steps for managing conflict are contained within two phases: differentiation and integration (see Figure 9–1). Let's now examine what you will need to do to facilitate each of the five steps that compose our conflict-managing sequence. Remember, the first three steps come under the umbrella of differentiation: understanding the nature of the conflict.

Clarify Existing Positions and Associated Interests

The initial task to be performed is to solicit responses and clarify the existing positions and associated interests held relative to the controversial topic by individual group members or by coalitions of members. Let's look at how this is accomplished.

Clarify existing positions.   As facilitator you need to solicit and record each person's current position on the subject. To prepare the group for the position-sharing process, you should allow the members a few minutes to collect their thoughts and write down, *in a dozen words or less*, their position statements. Imposing a limit of 12 words will prevent long-winded, rambling monologues during the position-sharing portion of the process.

With the pump primed, draw a line down the center of a flip chart page and head the left-hand column *"Positions"*—the right-hand column is not labeled at this time. Then, after handing the marker to the session's scribe so that the responses can be recorded, go around the table round-robin fashion, asking each person to state his or her position.

As each position is offered, the scribe gives it a number, records it, and, when necessary, checks back with the originator to be certain that the information written on the flip chart is accurate. Specific clarifications of any information being written down are processed immediately to ensure mutual understanding. This is strictly an information-sharing activity. As facilitator, you need to move the process swiftly and you must take action to gate-close any type of debate, analysis, or discussion of positions. Switching hats from facilitator to group manager affords you the chance to add your input to the list of positions being generated.

Each group member need not present a new or unique position statement. An individual may pass or, by acknowledging a previous item as being representative of his or her sentiments, can ask the scribe to place a check mark beside the chosen item, indicating support. You can have as many different positions as there are members in the whole group; however, the more common occurrence is to have diversity among a few subgroups, with possibly one or two people not aligned with any position.

Clarify interests behind the positions.   Your next task is to get at the interests behind each of the positions noted previously. That is, you must seek information regarding what the parties wish to accomplish, given their positions on the issue.

The manager or chairperson, acting as facilitator, gives the group participants a few minutes to reflect on their positions and, in 25 words or less, to note specifically what they hope to achieve, given those positions. When everyone is finished, you write *"interests"* at the top of the right-hand side of the flip chart pages partially completed earlier. Next, going round-robin in the same order as before, you have each person provide an "interests statement" to coincide with his or her previous "position statement." In doing this, you must make it clear, as the facilitator, that you are not seeking a justification of positions, but rather an understanding of the needs and desires that are the underpinnings of the positions. As interests are given, the scribe records them in the right-hand column across from each individual's position. However, names, initials, or other identifying marks must be excluded from the information captured on both sides of the flip chart.

Getting the interests recorded and posted for all to see is integral to understanding the true nature of the conflict and then reconciling it.

The importance of clarifying interests is underscored by R. Fisher and W. Ury:

> Interests define the problem. The basic problem lies not in conflicting positions, but in the conflict between each side's needs, desires, concerns, and fears. . . . Such desires and needs are interests. Interests motivate people; they are the silent movers behind the hubbub of positions. Your interests are what caused you to so decide.[11]

Keep people separate from positions and interests.   As mentioned earlier, when building the positions and interests flip chart pages, the scribe should not put initials or other identifying marks by the various responses. This is crucial because the objective at this stage is to uncover and understand positions and interests as a pool of information generated by the whole group, on behalf of the whole group, to be processed by the whole group.

Obviously, some people will remember who said what relative to the flip chart material. However, visually reinforcing this identification by writing and displaying names only increases the strength of the bond linking group members to their own positions and interests. It puts a major stumbling block on the path leading to the resolution of the conflict. People often interpret criticism of their position and/or interests as criticism of themselves. They react defensively and, in turn, attack the positions and interests of others. This defending and attacking substantially increases people's ego involvement with their original point of view and makes it less and less likely that a solution can be found to reconcile the parties' differences.

Numbering or lettering the flip chart items, for reference purposes only, helps make the psychological break between group members and their positions and interests. You can increase the power of this separation process by refraining from referring to an item as "Rachel's position" or "Jorge's requirements." Instead, reference them as "one of our positions" or "one of our interests."

A delightful illustration highlighting the importance of clarifying both the positions held and the interests behind those positions is given by Fisher and Ury:

> Consider the story of two men quarreling in a library. One wants the window open and the other wants it closed. They bicker back and forth about how much to leave it open: a crack, halfway, three quarters of the way. No solution satisfies them both.
>
> Enter the librarian. She asks one why he wants the window open: "To get some fresh air." She asks the other why he wants it closed: "To avoid the draft." After thinking a minute she opens wide a window in the next room, bringing in fresh air without a draft.
>
> This story is typical of many negotiations. Since the parties' problem appears to be a conflict of positions, and since their goal is to agree on a position,

they naturally tend to think about positions—and in the process often reach an impasse.[12]

The positions in this conflict were clear. One wanted the window open; the other wanted it closed. Only when the librarian got behind the two positions and identified the *interests* of the two men by asking what each one wished to accomplish was she able to come up with a solution that fulfilled both of their interests—fresh air without a draft. Clearly a win/win solution.

A vivid, practical example of the critical nature of interests in the managing of conflict is provided by D. Ertel:

> An engineer who had developed an innovative stamping tool was preparing to retire. He demanded a 3 percent royalty from his former employer for its use. The company, after carefully analyzing the value added to the production process by the tool, and on the advice of its accountants and investment bankers, extended a firm offer of 1.5 percent. After months of haggling they were no closer.
>
> With some work, a facilitator learned that the engineer had sought 3 percent as a means of insuring himself should he be held personally liable for a young shop worker sustaining injuries from the high-speed stamping tool. After further discussions, the facilitator discovered that the company could bring the engineer under its corporate liability policy, at nominal cost to the company. The company had never offered to do so because it did not understand the interest underlying the engineer's bargaining position. The engineer, upon learning that his retirement could be protected against the unlikely but catastrophic event, was quite satisfied to accept a royalty of around 1 percent.[13]

For anyone attempting to manage conflict within a group, comprehending the fundamental points about positions and interests cannot be overemphasized.

Define the Areas of Agreement

The basics. You next ask the group members to read all of the information on positions and interests that was recorded and posted during the previous step. Then the participants are asked to examine the interests column and *"itemize the areas where we have shared interests."* As members highlight areas of agreement, you can circle the statements or have the scribe record these points on a clean flip chart page.

The agreement definition activity does several important things at this stage of the conflict-managing process:

> > This task shifts the group's perspective from neutral to positive—from one of stating and clarifying individual positions and interests to one of collaborating in the search for similarities and agreements among these positions and interests.

> The task itself—involving the entire group in noting *"our"* areas of agreement—acts as a unifying force within the group.

> The task demonstrates to the group that the situation is not hopeless. Quite often this step reveals that more interests are allied than are disparate.

> The task provides positive momentum going into Step 3—defining areas of disagreement.

In general, the function of Step 2 is to visually display and emphasize that while there may be differences among group members, a pattern of agreement has been established. This base of shared and compatible interests becomes the foundation upon which to build further agreement.

A case study: But I just wanna have a friend over.

The example that follows will be familiar to many readers. While elementary, it nevertheless provides a light-hearted means for examining each of the five steps in our conflict-managing model. At the end of this chapter, another case will be presented to further increase the reader's comprehension of the process for facilitating group differences.

Getting off the school bus, Chad, 10 years old, hurries up the driveway and rushes into the kitchen through the side door. As the door bangs shut, Chad yells, "Hey, Mom, can I have a friend over this afternoon?"

Carol, 35 years old, has her afternoon already mapped out for shopping that has been put off too long. "Honey, we have to go to the mall this afternoon. I promise, tomorrow you can have a friend over."

Chad, obviously displeased, throws his jacket on the floor, kicks at it, and starts to cry. "But I just wanna have a friend over; I never get to have any fun," he wails.

After soothing him, Carol says, "Let's see if we can't work this out together.

In collaboration, Carol and Chad create the information shown on the tablet page in Figure 9–2. Besides clarifying both positions and interests, Chad's and Carol's efforts clearly indicate an area of agreement: both want to have an enjoyable afternoon. This area of agreement was noted on the tablet by circling the compatible interests as shown.

Define the Areas of Difference

The basics. With positions and interests clarified and agreements delineated, the third and final step in *the differentiation phase of understanding the nature of the conflict* is defining the areas of dispute—in other words, clarifying the essence of the difference. Unless the differ-

FIGURE 9–2
Positions and Interests Chart

Our Positions (what we want)	Our Interests (why we want it)
1. Go shopping this afternoon.	A. Save money on Chad's school shoes -- sale ends today at 5:00 PM
	B. Have a good time.
	C. Buy gift for Daddy for our anniversary tomorrow.
	D. Have Chad along for company and to try on new shoes.
2. Have a friend over this afternoon.	A. Play with a friend.
	B. It's my turn to play. I went shopping with you last week.
	C. Shopping is boring.
	D. Have fun.

ences are first brought into focus, group members are not likely to reach an outcome that truly resolves the conflict and leaves everyone satisfied.

The facilitation process for accomplishing Step 3 is straightforward. You ask all group members to review the chart of uncircled interests from the previous step and to identify points of contention among these items. The scribe compiles a list of the areas of difference as the group develops it. Recognition should be given to individuals who demonstrate clear thinking during this activity.

As an aid to defining and clarifying the areas of difference, the following framework can be used. My experience indicates that in many instances the conflict can best be understood by assessing the dispute in terms of goals, roles, procedures, relationships, limits, timing, information, or values.

> *Goals:* Is there conflict over what end result(s) the group is trying to accomplish?

> *Roles:* Is there conflict over who can or should do what?

> *Procedures:* Is there conflict over the methods, strategies, or tactics used for doing something (accomplishing a goal, resolving an issue, solving a problem, making a decision, etc.)?

> *Relationships:* Is there conflict over how the people will relate to each other?

> *Limits:* Is there conflict over what is or is not possible or what the group's authority really is?

> *Timing:* Is there conflict over when things should be accomplished or decided?

> *Information:* Is there conflict over the facts, figures, or data being discussed?

> *Values:* Is there conflict over what is right, wrong, fair, ethical, or moral?

By utilizing this framework, you quite often can help the group members discover that all of their points of contention can be consolidated into one, two, or, at most, three of these eight categories. Helping the group members see the bare bones of the conflict makes it easier for them to collaboratively resolve it. However, since no framework can cover all contingencies, the group might have to create other categories to account for disagreements and differences that fall outside the eight presented here. Still, there is no better place to start than with this framework.

The implication of Step 3 is that it is essential for you to facilitate, as quickly and accurately as possible, an understanding of the areas of conflict. The longer the contending parties remain unclear as to their areas of difference, the more arguments are prolonged, confusion is increased, and the heat of the verbal exchanges intensifies. The probability of maintaining conflict at a constructive level to achieve a win/win outcome will increase as the manager, in the role of facilitator, helps the group crystallize the nature of the dispute.

For example, after facilitating through Step 3 regarding a conflict over creating an in-house attitude survey questionnaire versus purchasing a canned (standardized) questionnaire from a consulting firm, the human resources manager summarizes the areas of difference by saying:

All of our differences are rooted in three areas: procedures, limits, and information. Regarding procedures, there is substantial disagreement over how best to evaluate our two alternatives. As to limits, we have a dispute over whether we have the knowledge and skills in-house to create a reliable and valid attitude survey questionnaire. Finally, with respect to information, we are arguing—without any evidence one way or the other—whether or not it would be possible to add 8 to 10 questions of our choosing to a canned survey questionnaire.

Jointly defining places where interests conflict is not to be taken lightly. It is value added to the overall conflict-managing process, for a number of reasons:

> The entire matter is made clearer; everyone can see the essence of the difference.

> The difference can be viewed more objectively by moving it out of the arena of feelings, subjectivity, and emotion.

> Defining the areas of difference shifts the conflict from the realm of something that seems unmanageable to the realm of something manageable.

> Even though disagreements and differences are being spot-lighted, the experience is positive, constructive, and collaborative.

But I just wanna . . . (continued).   Moving the tablet closer to Chad so he can get a better view of it, Carol says: "Well now, let's review what we've talked about so far. We are having a conflict over what we want to do today; we want to do two different things. However, no matter what we decide to do this afternoon, we both are in agreement that it should be fun. Is that right?"

Chad replies, "Right."

Carol says, "OK. Then let's look at our tablet and see if we can just pick out what we don't agree on."

Together they review the uncircled items on the tablet. Chad, looking over the list, offers the first thought. "I don't want to go shopping now because it's boring, but you have to buy my shoes this afternoon to save money." Carol writes that down and says, "I'm interested in having you along as company and to try on the shoes but you are interested in playing with a friend this afternoon." Chad interjects, "Plus, Mom, it's my turn to play; I went shopping with you last week." Carol notes that point and adds, "I also must buy Daddy's present for our anniversary tomorrow or he will be disappointed."

As Carol writes the points of contention on the tablet, she categorizes them along the lines of the eight-category framework discussed earlier. This brings the conflict into focus and clearly defines the areas of difference. Carol's and Chad's mutual effort produces the tablet page shown in Figure 9–3.

Carol summarizes: "If we look at this page, it's pretty clear that we have different goals; also, we have different ways of wanting to reach our goals. These differences are what our problem is all about."

Orient the Group to View the Areas of Conflict as Shared Problems to Be Solved Mutually

With the first three steps completed, the differentiation phase is finished. The nature of the conflict should be understood. The group process

FIGURE 9–3
Differences Chart

Our Differences

Goals:
- Mom interested in shopping to buy shoes on sale and to buy present for tomorrow's anniversary.
- Chad interested in playing with a friend and avoiding a boring shopping trip.

Procedures:
- Take Chad along for company and to try on new shoes.
- Chad stays home because it's his turn, went shopping last week.

---

now enters the second phase—integration. It's time to start harnessing the synergy of the group. At this point, the manager or chairperson needs to orient the group members to recognize that the conflict is a problem shared by the group, to be resolved by the group.

Use words and pictures. This portion of our conflict-managing sequence consumes very little time, yet is vitally important. It is the point of transition between understanding the conflict and taking measures to resolve it. This intermediate step gives you a chance to make certain that the group is properly oriented and mentally in sync before proceeding to the fifth—and final—step. At this juncture, the facilitation role requires you to emphasize two points. First, the existing differences are the reality of the here-and-now. They must not be regarded as barriers, dividing and isolating group members; rather, they need to be recognized, and then reduced or eliminated collaboratively. Second, working collaboratively means a side-by-side integrative relationship in which the full force of the group's energy assaults the identified differences instead of being dissipated in assaults on each other.

Achieving the intent of Step 4 is speeded if the words are accompanied by the two flip chart drawings shown in Figure 9–4.

This symbolic representation brings the words to life and dramatically increases the impact of the message. Also, if possible, seating group members in a semicircle around the flip chart provides additional reinforcement for the side-by-side assault on the differences. By doing these things, the proper mind-set is established among group members just before confronting the most challenging step of all—resolving the conflict through the relentless pursuit of teamwork and collaboration.

But I just wanna . . . (continued). Let's rejoin Carol and Chad. With the nature of the conflict understood, but before looking for a way out of their present dilemma, Carol says: ''Our problem may be a tough one, but it is not too tough for us if we put on our thinking caps and think of ways for both of us to have a pleasant afternoon.'' As she talks,

FIGURE 9-4
Differences as Barriers and Targets Chart

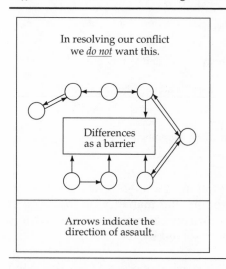

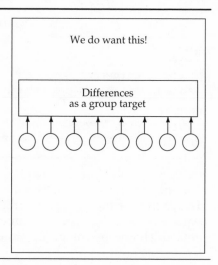

Carol draws a picture of two stick figures arguing with each other as they stand on opposite sides of a rectangle with words *our differences* printed inside its boundaries. "We don't want this to prevent us from working together, do we?" Carol asks while pointing to the rectangle.

"No," Chad replies.

Carol draws a second picture showing the two stick figures working side-by-side pushing the *differences* rectangle off the page. As she draws this picture, Carol says, "We need to be a team and work together to see if we can come up with some way for both of us to meet our goals and have fun at the same time. How does that sound?"

"Good," Chad declares.

Take Measures to Resolve the Areas of Conflict

With the nature of the conflict understood, and the group oriented to view the conflict as a shared problem to be solved mutually, resolution of the identified differences is the final step of the model. It is also the crux of the integration phase. You need to facilitate two separate activities. The first integration activity is leading the group in the *joint search for options* to overcome the differences; the second is *evaluation and selection of a win/win option* that resolves the differences. These two actions are similar to the third and fourth stages of the problem-solving process to be covered in Chapter 12 and 13.

Joint search for options.   Your objectives in facilitating this portion of the conflict resolution step are to help the group generate as many options for mutual gain as possible, to ensure that no idea is overlooked, to make certain that no group member feels neglected, and to safeguard all ideas from evaluation.

You begin the option generation phase by reviewing quickly the "positions and interests" flip chart pages created earlier, as well as the ones noting the areas of difference. (Refer to Figures 9–2 and 9–3 of our "I Just Wanna . . ." example.) This refreshes everyone's memory relative to the various positions and the differing interests behind those positions, as well as the points of conflict that are the target of resolution.

Next, focus the group members on the task at hand by reminding them that they all need to concentrate on coming up with as many potential solutions as they can that will reconcile part or all of the differing interests noted on the flip chart pages during Step 3.

Finally, you'll need to facilitate the actual generation of alternatives. This is the "thinking up" phase. It should be fun and stimulating for the entire group. It is a time for creativity and originality. My experience indicates that either free-wheel or round-robin brainstorming (see Chapter 10) is the most useful technique to mine the gold nugget ideas buried in the minds of the members. Brainstorming is appropriate because it is simple to facilitate, is energizing, and works well with small and large groups (over 15 participants). The manager, practicing the art of excellent facilitation, simply asks the group members to use the task behaviors of proposing and building to offer as many options for mutual gain as quickly as they can come up with them. As ideas are brought forth, the scribe records them all on flip chart pages.

Once the joint search for options is concluded, questions of clarification about particular items are handled, and the list is refined and consolidated to eliminate duplications and overlaps among the proposed solutions. Then, in the role of facilitator, you focus the group on the final phase in this collaborative process, finding a win/win outcome.

Joint evaluation and selection of win/win option(s) for resolving identified differences. Joint evaluation of the recorded options and the selection of one(s) that all group members either agree with or agree to support concludes our collaborative approach to managing conflict. As a prelude to undertaking this phase, you need to remind the group that its task is twofold: (1) evaluate all of the options proposed in the previous phase, and (2) select one or more that will satisfy the interests of all parties in conflict.

There are three segments to be facilitated at this point in the process.

Reduce the range of options to the significant few. As described in Chapter 10, use weighted voting to take the initial, unprocessed list of options and reduce it to the top three to six alternatives. By using weighted voting, the focus is on uncovering good and acceptable solutions, rather than on eliminating those thought to be bad and unacceptable. With weighted voting, each participant is given a set number of votes (say, 12) to distribute across the list of items (say, 8). The basic ground rules are: no more than one-third of a person's votes can be applied to any one item, all votes must be allocated, and no fractional votes. Concentrating on the significant few solutions considered most acceptable is a positive approach and is less likely to elicit defensive behavior. Also, this process eliminates wasting time processing obviously inadequate solutions not supported by any group member and, at the same time, avoids the devisive effect of majority rule.

Evaluate the short list of "significant few" options by developing a "likes and concerns" list.   You now facilitate an evaluation of the "significant few" options that remain from the previous step. This is done by asking the group members to present their "likes" and "concerns" for each of the proposed alternatives. However, *two ground rules for this process are: (1) Before a group member can voice a concern about a solution option, the person must first say what he or she likes about the option, and (2) when a person does raise a concern, he or she must also offer a suggestion for overcoming the concern.* All of the information associated with each option is recorded by the scribe.

This approach organizes the evaluation process. It assures a balanced examination of each of the significant few proposals for reconciling the existing differences. It provides you with a means to help the group guard against the normal human tendency to think only of objections without trying to figure out how they can be overcome. It also eliminates the tendency of people to take a black-and-white position either for or against each option without realistically trying to weigh alternatives. In essence, this evaluation process forces group members to "turn their individual kaleidoscopes." When they have to look for the good in all of the stated options, group members are forced to break away from fixed positions and proprietary interests and, instead, to consider several different viewpoints.

Reach consensus on mutually acceptable solution(s) to resolve the differing interests.   Usually when all of the significant few alternatives have been examined by the likes and concerns analysis, one or two will emerge as most acceptable to all group members. That is, *all* group members will either agree with, or agree to support, one or two of the proposed solutions for resolving the contrary interests. In that case, consensus, and thus commitment to a set of actions, will have been achieved.

While consensus is often achieved using the collaborative approach to managing conflict, it is not guaranteed. Fortunately, the manager, acting as facilitator, can employ a number of techniques in those instances when reaching consensus becomes difficult. The portion of Chapter 8 titled "The Realities of Forging Consensus: Some Tips and

FIGURE 9–5
Differences Resolution Brainstorm List

Our Ideas

---

1. Chad goes to friend's house while Mom goes shopping.
2. Chad takes a friend along on shopping trip.
3. Mom and Chad go shopping, then pick up a friend to play later and stay for supper.
4. Get a babysitter to watch Chad and friend while Mom goes shopping.

Techniques" is highly relevant to the task of facilitating the selection of a win/win option. You are encouraged to restudy that portion of Chapter 8 and take note of the points most applicable here.

But I just wanna . . . (conclusion). Let's return to the interaction between Carol and Chad for the last time. Carol says: "Before we move along, let's review what we've accomplished. First, we've found out that both of us want to have fun this afternoon. Second, I'm interested in doing the shopping that must get done this afternoon and having you along as company. I also want you along to try on the shoes. You're interested in playing with a friend and avoiding a boring shopping trip, plus you feel since you went shopping last week, it's your turn to stay home. Third, we've decided to solve this problem together. Am I right?"

Chad reads the tablet pages and replies, "Yeah, that's right."

Carol then moves to the next step. "What we need to do now is put our heads together and see if we can come up with several ideas that would allow *both of us* to do what we are interested in doing." After arranging the previous pages on the table for both to see, she turns to a new page and writes *Our Ideas* at the top. "Any ideas?" Carol asks.

"I have an idea," Chad exclaims. "You can do your shopping and I could go to a friend's house."

"Good," Carol says as she writes it on the page. "How about this idea? Since you want to be with a friend, we could go shopping together and you could bring a friend," Carol proposes.

Chad builds on this proposal by replying excitedly, "And then shopping wouldn't be boring."

The brainstorming process yields the results shown in Figure 9–5. Carol and Chad review the list. They agree that while all are good ideas, Number 1 and Number 4 do not satisfy Carol's interest of having Chad along for company and to try on the shoes. After a little more discussion around this topic, Chad makes a proposal combining Number 2 and Number 3. "Mom, how about it if I go shopping with you and we take a friend along. Then, when we get back, have him stay for supper."

After reflecting on Chad's idea Carol replies, "OK, that will be fine. However, one thing is very important. You're both going to have to listen to me. Remember, we want this afternoon to be fun for everyone."

"Don't worry, I'll listen. I'm going to call Todd first, and if he can go, I'll tell him he has to listen to you." As Chad dashes to the phone he exclaims, "Boy, Mom, this is going to be a great afternoon."

The five-step model just presented is designed to produce win/win, consensus outcomes. The actions decided upon to resolve the differences will be of high quality and have the full commitment of those involved in the implementation.

Consensus will be the rule rather than the exception when the five-step model for resolving conflict is utilized. The group is facilitated through a planned sequence of steps designed to generate authentic collaboration each step of the way. The whole group is used as a resource for resolving its disputes, rather than being told to accept the limited alternatives developed by the manager, other individuals, or subgroups.

THE PRISON GUARDS' UNIFORMS: A FINAL CASE OF MANAGING CONFLICT

Alan Filley provides an account of a group session held to decide on prison reforms in Wisconsin. His case description provides us an opportunity to close out this chapter with a final demonstration of the practical application of the collaborative model for managing conflict.

Nine of the state's top prison officials met to design an ideal correctional institution. In the course of the discussion, one group member proposed that uniforms traditionally worn by prison guards be eliminated. The group then began a lengthy argument about whether or not uniforms should be worn. One group member suggested that the issue be resolved democratically by vote. As a result, six people voted against uniforms and three voted in favor of them. The winning members looked pleased, while the losing members either got angry or withdrew from further discussion.

A group consultant present at the time suggested that the members take another look at the situation. Then he asked those in favor of uniforms to clarify why they favored them. Those officials stated that part of the rehabilitative process in correctional institutions is teaching people to deal constructively with authority, and they saw uniforms as a means for achieving that goal. When asked to clarify why they opposed uniforms, the other group members said that uniforms created such a stigma that guards had an additional difficulty laying to rest the stereotypes held by inmates before they could deal with them on a one-to-one basis. The group consultant then asked the group what ways might be appropriate to meet the combined goals, namely, teaching people to deal with authority and avoiding the difficulty of stereotypes held about traditional uniforms. While working on the problem, the group generated 10 possible solutions, including identification of prison personnel by name tags, by color-coded casual dress, or by uniforms for guard supervisors but not for guards in constant contact with prisoners. After discussing the various alternatives, the group decided upon the third solution.[14]

Let's analyze this case by contrasting the two processes used to handle the differences over uniforms. In the first situation, the group engaged in clear-cut conflict, which was only partially resolved by vote. In the second situation, the consultant facilitated the group in a true resolution of the conflict by following the process model advocated here.

PRISON GUARDS' UNIFORMS ANALYSIS: UNDERSTAND THE NATURE OF THE CONFLICT

Clarify Existing Positions and Associated Interests

The consultant asked those who held the position of maintaining uniforms to clarify their interests by *specifying why* they favored retaining the guards' uniforms. Then those who held the position of eliminating uniforms were asked to clarify their interests by *stating why* they opposed guards' uniforms.

Define the Areas of Agreement

The whole group was in agreement on their overall desired outcome— to design an ideal correctional institution.

Define the Areas of Difference

The consultant helped the group members define their disagreement as one of differing interests over *goals*. Those holding the position favoring the retention of uniforms held the goal of wanting to teach the prisoners to deal with authority; those holding the position favoring the elimination of uniforms had a goal of wanting to avoid the difficulty of stereotypes and interpersonal relationships that traditional uniforms fostered.

PRISON GUARDS' UNIFORM ANALYSIS: ORIENT THE GROUP AND RESOLVE

Orient the Group to View Areas of Difference as a Shared Problem to Be Solved Mutually

The consultant shifted the focus from one where members were opposing each other to one where they were united in opposing the issue and mutually resolving the difference. This was accomplished by asking the group members to collaborate in searching for a way to meet the combined interests of both coalitions, namely, teaching people to deal with authority while, at the same time, avoiding the difficulty of stereotypes held about traditional uniforms.

Facilitate Resolution of the Areas of Difference

By helping the group to generate a list of 10 potential solutions, to evaluate this list, and to select a solution that met the interests of both coalitions, the consultant facilitated a win/win agreement.

A CLOSING SUMMARY

Conflict itself is neither good nor bad. Conflict is the natural outgrowth of group interaction. It should not be swept under the rug; rather, it should be properly managed. Conflict falls into two categories: substantive and personal. Substantive conflict occurs when participants are at odds over the content, or substance, of the matter being processed. Personal conflict arises from the emotional clashes that occur during the struggle to resolve the matter at hand. This chapter focuses on methods for handling substantive conflict even in situations where feelings come forth and make management of the conflict more difficult.

A primary facilitation activity when dealing with conflict is to ensure that the discussion stays focused on the issues and does not turn into a network of personal attacks among group members. At the first sign of personal attacks, the manager in the role of facilitator must swiftly step in, halt the attacks, and reorient the group members to concentrate on the issues.

There are five techniques for managing conflict:

1. Avoiding: "Leave well enough alone."
2. Smoothing: "Hey, don't worry! Everything is OK."
3. Compromising: "Let's split the difference."
4. Forcing: "It will be done my way."
5. Collaborating: "Let's use the synergy of whole group to develop a win/win resolution."

All five of these methods have their time and place. However, the behavioral science literature presents a great deal of research which suggests that proper application of the collaborating approach offers the greatest probability of producing results that are of the highest quality and that give the most enduring satisfaction to the parties involved. If mutual need satisfaction is of paramount concern to the parties, and the collaborating strategy is harnessed to satisfy these needs, then both the substance of the differences and the relationship of the parties will benefit.

This chapter advocates a five-step collaborative approach to managing conflict whereby group members' energies are focused on defeating the differences, rather than defeating each other. Facilitating the collaborative sequence means helping the group search for outcomes that achieve the interests of the contending parties and are acceptable to everyone. The five steps—the basic components—for collaboratively managing conflict are summarized at the conclusion of this section.

Two cases—"But I Just Wanna Have a Friend Over" and "The Prison Guards' Uniforms"—were used to demonstrate the practical application of the conflict-managing model in two diverse settings.

In essence, the challenge to you as a practicing facilitator is to encourage diversity without encouraging personal conflict—to harness the constructive power of differences without igniting its destructive power. The tips, techniques, and processes presented in this chapter are all aimed at helping you meet this challenge.

The Collaborative Approach to Managing Conflict

Differentiation: Understand the Nature of the Conflict

1. Clarify existing positions and associated interests:
  > Clarify existing positions.
  > Clarify interests behind the positions.
  > Keep people separate from positions and interests.
2. Define the areas of agreement.
3. Define the areas of disagreement.

Integration: Orient the Group and Resolve

4. Orient the group to view the areas of conflict as shared problems to be resolved mutually.
5. Take measures to resolve the areas of conflict:
  > Search for joint options.
  > Joint evaluation and selection of win/win options for resolving identified differences.

NOTES WORKSHEET: DEVELOP WRITTEN RESPONSES TO THE TWO ITEMS LISTED BELOW

What Do You Feel Are the Main Learning Points from Chapter 9?	Elaborate on Why You Feel These Points Are Key

NOTES

1. For a detailed treatment on how to handle emotional clashes, see T. A. Kayser, *Mining Group Gold* (El Segundo, CA: Serif Publishing, 1990), Chap. 6, "Keeping the Gold Mine Productive in the Face of Emotion: Feelings, Facts, Solutions," pp. 103–19.

2. R. R. Blake, H. A. Shepard, and J. S. Mouton, *Managing Intergroup Conflict in Industry* (Houston: Gulf Publishing Company, 1964); P. R. Lawrence and J. W. Lorsch, *Organization and Environment* (Homewood, IL: Irwin, 1969); and, K. Thomas, "Conflict and Conflict Management," in M. D. Dunnette, ed., *Handbook of Industrial and Organizational Psychology* (Chicago: Rand McNally, 1976), among others, have identified five basic approaches to managing conflict. While terminology may differ among various authors, the behavioral aspects are remarkably similar.

3. M. Sashkin, *Conflict Styles Inventory Guide* (Bryn Mawr, PA: Organization Design and Development, 1986), p. 1.

4. L. D. Eigen and J. P. Siegel, *The Manager's Book of Quotations* (New York: Amacom, 1989), p. 76.

5. Lorsch and Lawrence, *Organization and Environment*, pp. 78–83.

6. G. L. Lippitt, *Organization Renewal: A Holistic Approach to Organization Development* (Englewood Cliffs, NJ: Prentice-Hall, 1982), p. 152.

7. M. Sashkin and W. C. Morris, *Organizational Behavior: Concepts and Experiences* (Reston, VA: Reston Publishing Company, 1984), pp. 326–27.

8. D. W. Johnson and R. T. Johnson, *Cooperation and Conflict: Theory and Research* (Edina, MN: Interaction Book Company, 1989), p. 172.

9. D. Tjosvold, *Teamwork for Customers: Building Organizations That Take Pride in Serving* (San Francisco: Jossey-Bass, 1993), p. 7.

10. R. E. Walton, *Managing Conflict: Interpersonal Dialogue and Third-Party Roles*, 2nd ed. (Reading, MA: Addison-Wesley Publishing, 1987), p. 92.

11. R. Fisher and W. Ury, *Getting to YES* (New York: Penguin Books, 1983), p. 42.

12. Ibid., p. 41.

13. D. Ertel, "How to Design a Conflict Management Procedure That Fits Your Dispute," *Sloan Management Review*, Summer 1991, p. 31.

14. A. C. Filley, *Interpersonal Conflict Resolution* (Glenview, IL: Scott, Foresman and Company, 1975), p. 33.

Chapter 10

List Management
Facilitating Divergent and Convergent Thinking

Chapter Objectives

> To demonstrate the vital role that orderly list management plays in successful group facilitation.

> To provide an integrated set of practical techniques, tips, and illustrations that will strengthen your ability to properly facilitate divergent and convergent thinking in group settings.

INTRODUCTION

The story is told that Harry S. Truman became quite frustrated with his cautious economic advisors. He stopped one session with them by yelling that he was tired of their wishy-washy, "two-handed" analysis. "On one hand this, but on the other hand that." Truman, thoroughly agitated, exclaimed, "Would someone please find me a good one-armed economist!"

This anecdote has direct application to list management. Once a list of items is generated by a group, its members often waste untold hours going through a "two-armed" debate on the consolidation and prioritization of the items—"on one hand this, but on the other hand that." When all is said and done, plenty has been said but little done.

The core of exemplary facilitation is the controlled management of information—both verbal and written. Since many group sessions involve the generation of a list of ideas (divergent thinking), coupled with the consolidation and refinement of the items on that list (convergent thinking), mastering the simple four-step process shown in Figure 10–1 will be of immense value when you are required to perform this crucial facilitation activity. The model will help you become a one-armed

FIGURE 10–1
The Four Steps of List Management

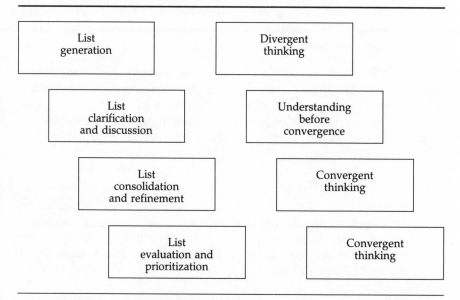

facilitator of list management by showing you how to eliminate rambling, unproductive, circular two-handed encounters.

Let's now examine each step of the Figure 10–1 model and use a case study as the means for explaining and integrating the four steps.

STEP ONE: LIST GENERATION

During many meetings, especially those concerned with problem solving, the group often finds itself faced with the need to generate a list of ideas around a particular subject. For example:

> The group may need to develop a list of potential solutions in response to the problem statement, "How can we reduce the gap between our current state of consuming an average of 100,000 kilowatts of electricity each month and our desired state of consuming an average of 90,000 kilowatts?"

> The meeting attendees may need to generate a list of positive forces and negative forces impacting the achievement of a particular goal by responding to the question, "What are the opportunities and risks associated with making our sales plan for this year?"

> The team may need to create a set of contingency options to a certain action like, "What alternatives do we have available if we can't lease all of the office space we need?"

> The group may need to establish a list of problems from which it will choose one to solve by responding to the question, "What problems—currently hindering our job performance—do we believe we have the necessary time, talent, resources, and influence to solve?"

During list generation, your task as facilitator is to ensure that the group is on a path of divergent thinking. Divergent thinking is an uninhibited process aimed at producing as many ideas as possible.

We will now explore three processes that you can use to build lists of ideas in a free and open manner—in short, to create divergent thinking.

Brainstorming

Brainstorming is an idea-generating technique pioneered by Alex Osborn,[1] an advertising executive. A group of people throw out their ideas as they think of them, so that each has an opportunity to build on the ideas of others. As Oliver Wendell Holmes said, "Many ideas grow better when transplanted into a mind different from the one where they spring up."

As facilitator, you must maintain the integrity of the brainstorming process by adhering to five fundamental principles.

1. *Stop initial judgment or premature evaluation of proposed ideas.* Thoughts are delicate and need to be protected and nurtured. Both criticisms and approvals of newborn ideas must be banned at this juncture. Your role is to encourage people to turn off their evaluators and turn on their imagination. There will be plenty of time for evaluation later.

2. *Be relentless in building a list.* Don't allow the group to stop brainstorming and start processing the first proposal that seems acceptable.

3. *Go for quantity, not quality.* At the outset, get as many ideas as possible brought forward, even incomplete or wild ones.

4. *Encourage hitchhiking.* Support use of the task behavior of building; remind participants to use ideas already written down as a springboard for a new idea.

5. *Don't overlook yourself.* By switching to your manager's hat, you should offer your ideas along with everyone else.

The process of brainstorming is straightforward. You write out on a flip chart page the subject about which a variety of alternatives or ideas are sought and note the allotted time for the brainstorming session. The wording of the situational statement should encourage specific, tangible ideas, not abstract ideas or opinions. You must make certain that the group members understand the situation, the desired outcomes of the brainstorming session, and the process to be followed:

> The desired outcome for this portion of our PTA executive committee meeting is to generate a list of potential fund-raising activities for us to sponsor this school year. We will brainstorm for 10 minutes using the round-robin method. Take a few seconds to collect your thoughts. I'll be starting with Cosmo.

There are two methods of brainstorming.

Freewheeling. This is the most familiar approach. With this method, the group members call out their ideas spontaneously and the scribe records all of them on the flip chart as quickly as possible and without question. If the group is large, 12 or more, two scribes may be needed to make certain all ideas are recorded as quickly as possible. Momentum is critical during a freewheeling brainstorming session.

Round-robin. With this process, you will go around the room asking each person in turn for an idea. The ideas are recorded on a flip chart as in freewheeling. One cycle around the room is considered one round. A group member may pass on any round. The activity continues until all members have passed during a round. As with all processes, even though you are the facilitator, you should contribute ideas (or pass) when your turn comes up. Passing in a given round does *not* preclude persons from contributing an idea on the next round or any succeeding round. Ideas presented in one round tend to spark ideas in subsequent rounds.

W. R. Daniels provides a fitting close to our brainstorming discussion with these remarks.

> The act of brainstorming simply separates two distinct intellectual functions— (1) quantitative generation of ideas, and (2) evaluation of the quality of ideas. It has been found that creativity and quantity of ideas are most easily generated in an environment that is safe from evaluation or criticism. Once a large volume of raw ideas is available, the evaluative process will usually yield a higher-quality final decision.[2]

Figure 10–2 presents a balance sheet on the freewheeling and round-robin methods.

Index Card Technique

As with brainstorming, the manager begins the process by recording on a flip chart the task statement for which ideas are sought. As facilitator, you would hand out two index cards to each group member (yourself

FIGURE 10–2
Brainstorming Balance Sheet

Plus (+)	Minus (−)
Freewheeling	
• Very spontaneous.	• Strong individuals may dominate the session.
• Tends to be creative.	
• Easy to build on other's ideas.	• Confusion sets in; ideas may be lost when too many talk at once.
• Energizing.	
	• Scribe can be overwhelmed by the quantity of simultaneous information to be recorded.
Round-robin	
• Difficult for one individual to dominate.	• Difficult to wait one's turn.
	• Some loss of energy and momentum.
• Process tends to be more focused.	• Reluctance to pass.
• Everyone is encouraged to take part.	• Long winded, rambling ideas presented since person "owns" the floor.
• Easy to build on other's ideas.	

included) and ask the members to silently and independently generate two ideas and write each idea on a separate card. Depending on the complexity of the task statement, sufficient time should be allowed to give members a chance to collect their thoughts and write them down.

Assume the task statement for the PTA executive committee reads: "What are some fund-raising events that this executive committee would be capable of sponsoring during the upcoming school year?" On her first card Juanita writes "car wash." On her second card she writes "rummage sale."

Next, all cards are placed face down in the center of the table. Someone other than the manager or committee chairperson collects the cards, shuffles them to preserve anonymity, and gives one-half of the deck to another member. Taking turns, the two members read exactly what is written on each card. The scribe numbers each item and records the stated information on flip chart pages. Completed pages are posted for all to see.

Once all the information is recorded and posted, you would hand out two more index cards to each individual. The participants are asked to review the flip chart material and see if any items trigger new ideas or extensions of existing ones. Additional ideas are written on separate index cards and placed in the middle of the table. The shuffling and recording process is carried out as before. A key process point for this and succeeding rounds is for members to turn in any blank cards each time so that everyone always hands in two cards. This round-by-round process continues until all the cards submitted are blank.

Figure 10–3 highlights the balance sheet on the index card technique.

FIGURE 10–3
Index Card Balance Sheet

Index Card Technique	
Plus (+)	*Minus (−)*
• Separates personalities from ideas.	• Some ideas may not be legible, understandable.
• Anonymity allows sensitive topics to surface.	• Slow.
• Avoids premature focusing on single ideas.	• Some participants may think it is overly structured.
• Avoids interrupting each other's thinking.	• Spontaneity and buzz of energy throughout the room are significantly reduced.
• Eliminates dominance by high-status, aggressive members.	• Some participants may get bored after a round or two.
• Provides strong task orientation that some groups may need to keep them focused.	• Easy to be a nonparticipant by turning in blank cards each round.
• Gives time to members to think and reflect.	
• Virtually eliminates pressure to group conformity.	

STEP TWO: LIST CLARIFICATION AND DISCUSSION

Once a raw list of items has been produced using one of the three methods previously noted, these ideas need to be clarified and discussed since at this stage the information most likely will be subject to multiple interpretations and misunderstandings. You will need to ensure a common understanding of the individual flip chart items if Step 3, consolidation and refinement of the list, and Step 4, evaluation and prioritization, are to be successful.

Regarding the proper processing of the clarification-and-discussion step, W. M. Fox offers some helpful guidelines:

> The purpose of the discussion phase is to provide an opportunity for anyone to seek or give clarification as to what an item means, and to give reasons why he or she is for or against an item. All other activity is ruled out.

> Participants may seek explanation from a presenter as to how his or her ideas would deal with a particular need or difficulty, and they may ask for more background or an example to clarify an idea; however, it is not our purpose to formally debate the merits of an item, reach agreement about an item, or persuade others to adopt our viewpoint through speech making or repetition.

> There will be no obligation to discuss any item, only the assured opportunity.

> At any time, a person may return to a previous item for further discussion, as long as the total discussion time on that item does not exceed any set limit.[3]

With a short list, *15 items or less,* the processing can be done serially. Each idea listed on the flip chart is taken in order and a short period of time is allocated for its clarification and discussion. You would point to Item 1, read it aloud, and say something like: "Does anyone wish to seek or provide further clarification about what Item 1 means, or does anyone want to make any statements for or against this item? Remember, this discussion time is not for bickering back and forth or attempting to reach total agreement on this item."

You would facilitate any discussion of the first item to ensure a full understanding, then you would move the group along to Item 2, Item 3, and so forth. In each case your goal is the same: Keep each discussion focused without wasting time, and maintain a free and open discussion climate.

If the list is a long one, *16 items or more,* the entire list is divided into quarters, with each quarter being treated as a block of ideas.

For example, given 32 items, the list would be divided into four blocks of 8 items each. Then, pointing to the eight items in the first block, you would say something like: "Given the eight items comprising the first block, does anyone have any pro or con comments, questions of clarification, or examples to offer with respect to any of these eight items." After this discussion is concluded, you would move the group along to the second block, the third, and so on. Experience shows that several items in a given block typically consume most of the discussion. Furthermore, once the group fully understands the process, much of the discussion is routine, requiring little intervention on your part.

Regarding list clarification and discussion, A. L. Delbec, A. H. Van deVen, and H. Gustafson provide additional insight:

The purpose of serial discussion is to enhance clarification while minimizing influence based on verbal prominence or status. To accomplish these dual objectives, the leader should "pace" the discussion, i.e., he or she should not allow the discussion to: (1) unduly focus on any particular idea, or (2) degenerate into argumentation. Suppose, for example, Member X feels that Item 7 is very important, and Member Y feels that Item 7 is specious. The role of the leader is to allow both points of view to be aired, but then to move the group on to a discussion of Item 8, since the purpose of serial discussion (either item-by-item or block-by-block) is to disclose thinking and analysis, not to resolve differences of opinion. Differences of opinion will be handled in the voting procedure.[4]

If an argument should begin to simmer, you should bring it under control by testing comprehension of the two points of view and make sure the scribe notes them on a flip chart:

> Fran, your point is that a 1950s Sock Hop would be a good activity for the PTA to sponsor because it is novel, has never been tried here before, and would involve parents, teachers, and students, right? . . . Fine, Bill, please note Fran's thoughts on our "key points" flip chart. Dale, your belief is that a 50s Sock Hop would be a poor activity for us to sponsor because the students won't relate to the early rock and roll songs and won't want to wear their parents' old-fashioned 1950s clothes, correct? OK, Bill, please record Dale's views on our flip chart. . . . Good job, Bill, now let's move along to the ideas comprising Block 2.

In summary, the clarification and discussion phase of list management is intended to illuminate all options as fully as possible, not to become a soapbox for lobbying, aggressive interaction, digressions, or hard-sell attempts to browbeat others into agreement.

STEP THREE: LIST CONSOLIDATION AND REFINEMENT

After the original list has been reviewed and processed, the next step in list management centers on combining similar items into a single reworded statement, eliminating duplicate items, and categorizing closely related items under a common headline. The purpose of this step is to make certain that the list contains a set of unique, differentiated items so that the final step—evaluation and prioritization—is not confounded by duplications, overlaps, and highly related but uncategorized ideas.

The list refinement step is a whole-group activity. As facilitator, the manager or chairperson asks all group members to review the list just discussed in Step 2 and to make proposals for items that could be combined, rewritten, or categorized. My own experience repeatedly indicates that groups get involved with this task and, through the synergy of the group, produce a consolidated list superior to what the manager could do alone. The give-and-take in modifying the list is energizing for the whole group and creates a collaborative commitment to the final version.

There are two guidelines for making this a successful activity:

> Ask group members to give the logic and rationale for their consolidation proposals so that everyone can better understand them.

> If two or more people cannot support a suggested change after a brief discussion, the modification is not made. Members should not be allowed to disagree with prolonged argumentation.

FIGURE 10–4
Brainstormed List and Consolidated List of Fund-Raising Ideas

Brainstormed Fund-Raising Ideas	Consolidated List of Fund-Raising Ideas
1. Car wash.	1. Car wash.
2. White elephant sale.	2. Rummage sale.
3. Candy sale.	3. Sweets sale:
4. Spring carnival.	• Candy.
5. Rummage sale.	• Baked goods.
6. School play.	4. Major school event:
7. Local merchants' ads in yearbook.	• Play.
8. 1950s sock hop.	• Variety show.
9. Clothing sale.	• Band concert.
10. School "garage sale."	• Spring carnival.
11. Variety show.	5. Dance:
12. Local merchants' ads in football program.	• Christmas formal.
	• 1950s sock hop.
13. Raffle.	• Valentine's Day dance.
14. Auction.	6. Local merchants' ads in school publications.
15. Band concert.	
16. Student/faculty basketball game.	7. Raffle.
17. Christmas formal.	8. Auction.
18. Bake sale.	9. Student/faculty basketball game.
19. Local merchants' ads in school newspaper.	
20. Valentine's Day dance.	

The PTA Executive Committee Meeting

Let's continue with our PTA example. The left column of Figure 10–4 shows the initial list of brainstormed and clarified fund-raising ideas. The consolidated and refined master list completed at the end of Step 3 is shown on the right.

In consolidating, the PTA decided that the white elephant sale, clothing sale, and school garage sale were all duplicates of the rummage sale concept. So they only listed rummage sale since this could include the sale of clothes and unwanted household articles. The three items suggesting the sale of advertising space to local merchants were consolidated into one statement, "local merchants' ads in school publications." The candy and bake sale activities were categorized under a single heading, "sweets sale." Four items—school play, variety show, band concert, and spring carnival—were lumped together under "major school events." Finally, the Christmas formal, 1950s sock hop, and Valentine's Day dance were placed together in the "dance" category. The consolidation task reduced the first list from a mixture of 20 items, some of which were duplicates, overlapping, or similar, to 9 unique, distinct items.

STEP FOUR: LIST EVALUATION AND PRIORITIZATION

With a consolidated list of discrete items displayed for everyone to see, you are prepared to move the group into the fourth, and final, step of list management—evaluation and prioritization. There are three primary processes for reducing a list to the significant few ideas of greatest merit, or, said differently, for promoting convergent thinking. The three processes are weighted voting, paired comparisons, and multivoting. They can be used independently or in combination. We'll look at each one in detail.

Weighted Voting

Weighted voting is a simple way to rank-order the positions and preferences of group members. Group members make individual judgments about the highest-priority ideas on the master list created in Step 3, and then express these judgments quantitatively to indicate their relative preferences.

The procedure for conducting weighted voting is summarized by four ground rules. All four ground rules must be adhered to if the weighted voting method is to function properly.

1. *The number of votes given to each team member for allocation among the items on the master list equals $1\frac{1}{2}$ times the number of items on the list.* For example, if the master list has 16 options, each participant would be allocated 24 votes for distribution across the sixteen items ($1\frac{1}{2} \times 16 = 24$). For all lists of 33 ideas or more, a maximum of 50 votes is assigned to each person. Thus, given a list of 44 items, each person still would be allocated only 50 votes. (Anytime the master list contains an odd number of items fewer than 33, use the "plus one" technique to greatly facilitate the computation of votes to assign to group members. With the plus one technique, add one point to the total list number, then multiply by $1\frac{1}{2}$. For example, with 25 items on the master list, plus 1 = 26, and $1\frac{1}{2} \times 26 = 39$. Thirty-nine becomes the number of votes given to each team member for distribution among the 25 items on the master list.)

2. *Team members cannot place more than one-third of their total votes on any single idea.* This rule makes all group members vote for at least three options and prevents someone from unduly influencing the proceedings by dumping all of his or her votes on one item. In our first example above, no member can place more than eight votes on any single item ($24 \times \frac{1}{3} = 8$). In our second example, no one can place more than thirteen votes on an

idea (39 × ⅓ = 13). Group members are always free to place less than the maximum number of votes on any item.

3. *All assigned votes must be used.* Each person must use all of his or her assigned votes. That is, no member can distribute only 20 of the 24 allocated votes, or 31 of the 39 assigned votes, across the items.

4. *All votes are cast as whole numbers.* Group members cannot split single votes among two or more items. For instance, it is not permissible to put 3½ votes on one option and 4½ votes on another. Only whole numbers are accepted as legitimate votes.

Facilitation of weighted voting is not difficult if you follow these few simple guidelines.

Rewrite the master list.   To commence the process, you should instruct the scribe to rewrite the master list (created in Step 3) onto a clean flip chart page using only the main item headings. These items are numbered consecutively. For instance, looking at the right-hand example in Figure 10–4, there are nine main item headings. This rewritten page will be used for recording votes. The original master list remains displayed in full.

Explain ground rules.   The four procedural ground rules covered earlier are carefully explained to the group. Time should be allowed to answer questions and provide examples to make certain everyone understands the process.

Hand out and review voting sheets.   You need to give a voting sheet to each member. After they are passed out, it is a good idea to illustrate how to use the sheet. Figure 10–5 shows a simple format for a sheet along with an example of how a member might fill it out. If voting sheets have not been made up in advance, it is easy to draw the format on a flip chart page and have everyone duplicate it on a sheet of notebook paper.

Conduct the voting.   Before the actual voting begins, you should go to a flip chart and write in big block numerals the number of votes each person has (15 votes for our PTA example) and the amount of time to do the voting (e.g., three minutes). As you write these numbers call everyone's attention to them. The voting process is normally completed in five minutes or less.

Next, ask the participants to carefully review all the items on the master list before distributing their votes. There is no conversation during this phase. If a few individuals require more time than the original

FIGURE 10–5
Sample Weighted Voting Sheets: Blank and Filled-In

Weighted Voting Sheet		Weighted Voting Sheet	
List Item Numbers	*List Votes Allocated*	*List Item Numbers*	*List Votes Allocated*
		#1	4 votes
		#3	1 vote
		#6	5 votes
		#8	3 votes
		#9	2 votes

amount set aside, give it to them. Don't rush people. During this time period, you also would complete a voting sheet.

Hold a process check. After everyone finishes voting, but *before* the voting sheets are collected, you need to do a process check by asking the group members to review their sheets and double-check to make certain that: they are filled out properly, all writing is legible, and the total number of votes used is exactly the same as the number originally allocated to everyone.

Collect and tally the votes. Collect the voting sheets from everyone and give them to another person to read aloud. The scribe records all votes on the rewritten master sheet in full view of the group so that everyone can see the ranking results unfold.

Second round of voting, if necessary. If there aren't two, three, or four alternatives that clearly "break away from the pack," a second round of voting may be required. In this case, you would review the entire list of items that received votes and eliminate the bottom 50 percent (i.e., the 50 percent with the least number of assigned votes). All items with zero votes are automatically eliminated.

Next, you would have the scribe write out on a clean flip chart page all of the items making up the top 50 percent. Then you would conduct a second round of voting. Except for the smaller number of votes given out to correspond to the shorter list, the weighted voting process utilized in round 2 is exactly the same as that used in round 1.

The PTA Executive Committee Meeting (Continued)

Let's go back to our PTA executive committee meeting. Assume that eight people are present, including the committee chairperson, and that the group wants to utilize the weighted voting process.

FIGURE 10–6
Results of PTA's Weighted Voting

Fund-Raising Ideas								
1. Car wash.	1	2	2	3	4	2		(14)
2. Rummage sale.	3	2	1	1				(7)
3. Sweets sale.	1	1	1	2				(5)
4. Major school event.	4	5	4	3	4	5	3	(28)
5. Dance.	2	3	1	3				(9)
6. Merchant's ads.	5	1	5	4	2	4	5	(26)
7. Raffle.	2	1	1					(4)
8. Auction.	2	5	4	5	3	2		(21)
9. Student/faculty basketball game.	1	1	1	2	1			(6)

After the consolidation process was carried out in Step 3, nine activities made the master list. This list was read aloud by the chairperson. Then, since nine is an odd number, the chairperson used the "plus one" technique and gave each person, including herself, 15 votes to spread across the nine options (9 items + 1 = 10; 10 × 1½ = 15 total votes per person). Based on the tally results and a short "final thoughts" discussion of the top four items, the executive committee decided to implement the two highest preferred ideas: hold a "major school event" (28 votes), and sell advertising space in school publications to local merchants (26 votes). However, since the "major school event" category had four options within it, the committee decided that the choice of which of the four proposed major school events to sponsor would be made at its next session using the paired comparisons method.

A review of the committee's voting, shown in Figure 10–6, clearly displays both the breadth and the strength of the member's preferences. Seven of the eight people preferred the activity of sponsoring a "major school event" (breadth) and all of those felt strongly about it as indicated by the weight of their votes (strength)—all votes were three points or above. The selling of advertising space also was preferred by seven of the eight participants, but two of them showed lesser interest than the others by assigning only one vote and two votes, respectively.

The attractiveness of weighted voting is that it produces a rank-ordered list of options that allows each member's vote to influence the final outcome while avoiding status, authority, power, and conformity pressures.

FIGURE 10–7
Number of Paired Comparisons Required for Lists of Varying Length

Number of Options on the List	Number of Required Comparisons	Number of Options on the List	Number of Required Comparisons
2	1	7	21
3	3	8	28
4	6	9	36
5	10	10	45
6	15	11	55
		12	66

Paired Comparisons

Like weighted voting, using paired comparisons will help a group quantify the preferences of its members. Each item on the list goes head-to-head against every other option. In each face-off, members vote for the option they prefer. Votes are recorded and totaled after all possible comparisons have been made.

Because the number of required comparisons accelerates rapidly for each additional item added to the list, it is best to *use paired comparisons when the group is evaluating a list of eight options or fewer.* Figure 10–7 presents a table showing the steep increase in required comparisons for each one unit increase in options.

The basic facilitation steps for conducting the paired comparisons process are outlined here. We will use our PTA executive committee example to demonstrate the process.

Rewrite the master list of items to be compared. Using the master list from Step 3 as the source, you should have the scribe write down all of the items to be compared on a clean sheet of paper. The items must be numbered consecutively. The rewritten sheet will be the working document for conducting the varied comparisons. The original master list remains displayed in full view.

Explain the process. Next, you would review how the paired comparisons process operates. If need be, set up a simple three-item comparison sequence to illustrate the technique. Use the graphic on the next page.

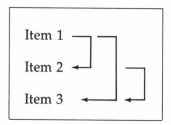

With three items, there are three comparisons required to have every item face-off against all other alternatives. First, Item 1 is compared to Item 2; then, Item 1 is compared to Item 3; and finally, Item 2 is compared to Item 3.

Solicit questions about the mechanics of the process to make certain everyone is clear on how it works.

Conduct the comparisons.   Acting as a facilitator, you would conduct the comparisons and tally the votes in full view of the group.

The PTA Executive Committee Meeting (Continued)

Let us now return to our PTA executive committee meeting. It is two weeks later, their next session. Recall that the committee previously had decided to use the paired comparisons technique to choose which one of the four proposed activities under the general heading "major school event" would be pursued during the upcoming year. The four proposals were:

1. School play.
2. Variety show.
3. Band concert.
4. Spring carnival.

Since every item must be compared to every other item on the list, a systematic procedure must be followed. The paired comparisons procedure for the PTA is to take alternative 1 (school play) and, one-by-one, compare it with each of the three items below it. Then option 2 (variety show) is compared, one-by-one, with the two options below it. Finally, Item 3 (band concert) is compared to the lone item below it. At that point all items will have squared off against each other.

During each paired comparison, each group member—including the manager or chairperson—has one, and only one, vote. He or she must decide which alternative is better. The number of votes cast in any comparison must equal the number in the group. Everyone must cast a vote

FIGURE 10–8
Paired Comparisons Voting Results

	Paired Comparisons Voting				
1. School play.	3	7	4	=	⑭
2. Variety show.	5	7	8	=	⑳
3. Band concert.	1	1	2	=	④
4. Spring carnival.	4	0	6	=	⑩

in each comparison, even if neither choice is very appealing. Votes are cast by raising one's hand.

Let's eavesdrop on our PTA executive committee chairperson as she conducts the actual paired comparisons process. Remember, there are eight people in attendance, including the chairperson.

> Now that we have discussed and clarified all four activities and understand what's involved with each of them, it's time to conduct the paired comparisons process. As you can see, I've neatly listed the alternatives 1 through 4 on a clean flip chart.
>
> For our first comparison, if our choice of a major school event was limited to sponsoring either a school play or a variety show, how many of you would prefer we hold a school play? Raise your hand if you think a school play is the way to go. Remember, everyone, if you don't raise your hand, you are automatically voting for the variety show.
>
> Let's see, three hands are up, including my own. So, next to "school play" on the flip chart I'll write the number 3 and, because the rest of you did not raise your hands, I'll write a 5 next to "variety show."
>
> All right, for our second comparison, if our choice of a major school event was limited to sponsoring either a school play or a band concert, how many of you would prefer that we hold a school play? Raise your hand to vote for a school play. Seven hands are up. OK, I'll note a 7 next to school play and a 1 next to band concert. [So it would go, until the last comparison.]
>
> Finally, if our choice of a major school event was limited to sponsoring a band concert or a spring carnival, how many of you would prefer that we hold a band concert? Raise your hand if you prefer a band concert over a spring carnival.
>
> Well, let's see two hands are up. Fine, I'll put a 2 next to "band concert" and a 6 next to "spring carnival."
>
> Let's now look over our flip chart and add up the paired comparisons vote for each event. [Figure 10–8 shows the final tabulated results.]
>
> Well, our process highlights the fact that when compared to all other potential activities, we prefer to sponsor a variety show over anything else.

Reviewing the voting on a comparison-by-comparison basis underscores the mechanics of this technique.

> Comparison 1: School play (3 votes) versus variety show (5 votes).

> Comparison 2: School play (7 votes) versus band concert (1 vote).

> Comparison 3: School play (4 votes) versus spring carnival (4 votes).

> Comparison 4: Variety show (7 votes) versus band concert (1 vote).

> Comparison 5: Variety show (8 votes) versus spring carnival (0 votes).

> Comparison 6: Band concert (2 votes) versus spring carnival (6 votes).

Also, given four items to compare, the table in Figure 10-7 indicates that six comparisons are required, and as you can see, the PTA executive committee made six comparisons to arrive at its outcome.

The power of paired comparisons comes from the choices it forces group members to make. Even when two alternatives seem equal, members must choose one or the other. Having to make difficult choices often leads people to see advantages or disadvantages they may not have noticed before.

Multivoting

Multivoting is a convergent thinking technique for quickly and easily reducing a long list of items or ideas (16 or more) to a manageable number (3 to 6). The process of multivoting is very simple to facilitate. Unlike weighted voting and paired comparisons, multivoting does not produce a rank-ordered, priority listing of alternatives. Instead, through several voting iterations, the multivoting process narrows a large—even seemingly unmanageable—list of options down to a pool of the significant few. Once multivoting has identified a small set of prime items, then paired comparisons, weighted voting, or consensus can be brought into play to rank-order this short list.

Rewrite the master list.   Like weighted voting and paired comparisons, multivoting is not utilized until the first three steps of the list management model have been completed and a consolidated master list of ideas is established. You would ask the scribe to rewrite the consolidated master list, consecutively numbering the ideas. This chart will be used as a worksheet for tallying votes.

First vote.   One index card is handed out to everyone. Each member votes privately on as many items as desired, but only once per

FIGURE 10–9
Multivoting Example

Round 1 Multivoting	
#2	#8
#3	#9
#4	
#6	

item. The voting process is best conducted by having the participants—including the manager—list each item number being voted for. (See Figure 10–9).

In the role of facilitator, you would collect the cards from everyone, shuffle them, and give the stack to another person who reads off the individual voting results. The scribe puts hash marks (卌 I) next to each item on the rewritten master list as it receives votes. The items which receive a relatively higher number of votes than the others are circled and remain for the second round of voting.

Second and subsequent votes. Let's assume that the original master list contained 23 items and, after the first round of voting, 16 items received a relatively higher number of votes (i.e., the other 7 received very few votes). For the second round, each member is given a number of votes *equal to one-half the number of items remaining*—in this case, 8. In other words, in the second round of voting, each participant now can vote for only 8 of the 16 remaining items.

Index cards are passed out, each person is asked to list eight items on the card in the same manner as round one. The cards are collected, shuffled, and given to another to read. All votes are tallied on the same chart used in the first round. The items which receive a relatively higher number of votes than the others are circled and remain for the third round of voting.

In this instance, if the second round of multivoting reduced the list from 16 to 7 items, then, using the plus one technique for odd numbers of items, each person would be given four votes to use during round three voting (7 items plus $1 = 8$; $8 \div \frac{1}{2} = 4$ votes for next round). The goal of multivoting is to reduce the original list down to three to six items. Having participants vote for one-half of the remaining items in all rounds after round 1 really forces people to carefully consider how to spend their votes, and it keeps shortening the original list each round.

The PTA Executive Committee Meeting (Concluded)

Let's revisit our PTA example. Figure 10–10 illustrates how the eight committee members might have voted on the nine fund-raising activities using the steps of multivoting.

FIGURE 10–10
Example of Round-by-Round Voting Using the Multivoting Process

			1st Vote		2nd Vote		3rd Vote
Activities							
1. Car wash.	卌 I	(6)	卌	(5)	I	1	
2. Rummage sale.	卌 I	(6)	II	2			
3. Sweets sale.	卌	(5)	II	2			
4. Major school event.	卌 III	(8)	卌 III	(8)	卌	(5)	
5. Dance.	卌 I	(6)	III	3			
6. Local merchants' ads in school publications.	卌 III	(8)	卌 I	(6)	卌	(5)	
7. Raffle.	II	2					
8. Auction.	卌 I	(6)	卌	(5)	卌	(5)	
9. Student/faculty basketball game.	卌	(5)	I	1			

Fund-Raising Ideas

With the first vote, where the participants could vote for an un-restricted number of items on the master list, only one item (7) was well below the others. The majority of items received five or six votes, with two others receiving eight. All but number 7 are circled as preparation for the second vote.

In the second round, with eight items remaining, each participant was allocated four votes—equating to one-half of the total items. This meant the entire group of eight members had a total of 32 votes to distribute across the list. The second column of Figure 10–10 shows how these votes were applied. When tallied, Items 1, 4, 6, and 8 received a relatively higher number of votes than the others. These four items were circled to indicate that they are the ones left for a third vote.

The voting process for round three is the same as for the previous two. Since four items remained entering the third vote, each member was given two votes. The team, then, had a total of sixteen votes to distribute across the four items. Figure 10–10 shows the outcome of the third vote. Items 4, 6, and 8 all received five votes and would be selected for further discussions and then rank-ordered using either paired comparisons or consensus.

Combinations

The three list reduction techniques just presented, along with consensus, can be exercised singly or in combination. Our PTA example showed two ways for using these methods in combination. In the first situation, weighted voting was used to rank-order the nine fund-raising options.

The weighted voting process revealed that holding a "major school event" was the number 1 choice of the group. The paired comparisons method was then employed to determine priorities among the four proposals within the "major school event" general category.

In the second example, multivoting was applied to the consolidated brainstormed list of nine fund-raising alternatives. After three rounds of multivoting, the top three items were identified. As mentioned then, these three activities would be chosen for further discussion and be rank-ordered using either the paired comparisons or the consensus approach.

Consensus and its facilitation were covered extensively in Chapter 8. At this juncture, a brief refresher on consensus and its role in list management and convergent thinking is all that is required. R. Barra captures the spirit of consensus by noting:

> Convergence by consensus is a form of decision making by which all team members have equal opportunity to express opinions. It is a process for making full use of available brain power and for resolving conflicts creatively. Complete agreement is not the goal—it is rarely achieved. When each member is able to accept/support the team rankings on the basis of logic and feasibility, you have reached consensus.[5]

Consensus should be used to set priorities in situations where the alternatives being considered are four or fewer. Therefore, whenever it is chosen as a tool for list management, consensus will always be exercised only after one or more of the other techniques have been used to pare a much longer list down to the elite two, three, or four options. If the final four alternatives are controversial, emotional, or complex, consensus may be the most appropriate way to rank final items. In many other situations, several rounds of multivoting or weighted voting, in conjunction with paired comparisons, may be all that is needed for a group to determine and commit to the significant few priorities from a much longer master list.

A CLOSING SUMMARY

The power of the list management model presented here lies in the way that it is segmented and sequenced. The process combines divergent thinking techniques—the generation of a large number of creative ideas—with convergent thinking techniques: the evaluation, prioritization, and selection of the significant few ideas from the many that were conceived during divergent thinking. While divergent and convergent thinking are integral to our list management model, they are distinct steps.

The critical importance of keeping divergent thinking (Step 1) independent from convergent thinking (Steps 3 and 4) is beautifully summarized by N. R. F. Maier:

The idea-getting process should be separated from the idea-evaluation process because the latter inhibits the former. When an idea is suggested, other group members tend to pass judgment on it. As a consequence, there is a reduced tendency to generate additional alternatives because the pros and cons of the first idea are being explored. Further, the person who generates ideas tends to be placed on the defensive and consequently hesitates to reveal ideas likely to be criticized. Some innovative and original ideas are unusual (hence the most questioned); don't let evaluation stifle creativity.[6]

Step 2, list clarification and discussion, also plays a major role in our list management model. This is the transition point between the divergent and convergent thinking. It ensures that no final choices (convergent thinking) will be made until all items have been clarified and understood. Everyone is given an equal opportunity to state their views and to influence the other group members. As a result, participants feel genuinely involved and fairly treated. Therefore, they are more likely to accept and support the final prioritization and decisions made, regardless of whether their ideas are included.

Step 3, list consolidation and refinement, and Step 4, list evaluation and prioritization, are pure convergence steps. Used singly or in combination, weighted voting, paired comparisons, and multivoting will provide structured processes for separating the wheat from the chaff. With a very short list, consensus is a useful approach for gaining wholesale commitment to one or two alternatives.

In conclusion, the value of our four-step model is that it brings structured discipline and simple facilitation requirements to what typically is a misunderstood and poorly implemented process.

NOTES WORKSHEET: DEVELOP WRITTEN RESPONSES TO THE TWO ITEMS LISTED BELOW

What Do You Feel Are the Main Learning Points from Chapter 10?	Elaborate on Why You Feel These Points Are Key

NOTES

1. A. F. Osborn, *Applied Imagination: Principles and Procedures of Creative Problem Solving* (New York: Scribner, 1963).

2. W. R. Daniels, *Group Power: A Manager's Guide to Using Meetings* (San Diego, CA: University Associates, 1986), p. 30.

3. W. M. Fox, *Effective Group Problem Solving: How to Broaden Participation, Improve Decision Making, and Increase Commitment to Action* (San Francisco, CA: Jossey-Bass, 1988), pp. 57–58.

4. A. L. Delbecq, A. H. Van de Ven, and D. H. Gustafson, *Group Techniques for Program Planning* (Glenview, IL: Scott, Foresman, and Company, 1975), pp. 52–53.

5. R. Barra, *Tips and Techniques for Team Effectiveness: A Quick Reference Guide for Creative Problem Solving and More Effective Meetings* (Lawrenceville, NJ: Barra International, 1987), p. 10.

6. N. R. F. Maier and G. C. Verser, *Psychology in Industrial Organizations*, 5th ed. (Boston: Houghton Mifflin, 1982), p. 609.

Chapter 11

Analytical Tools
Facilitating Seven Structured Processes for Displaying and Analyzing Data and Information

---

Chapter Objectives

> To present the techniques for constructing and using a set of tools for *displaying information graphically:* time charts, bar charts, and pie charts.

> To present the techniques for constructing and using a set of *graphic analytical tools* for problem solving: flow charts, cause-and-effect diagrams, Pareto analysis charts, and force field diagrams.

INTRODUCTION

One of the Japanese experts on quality and employee involvement compares the need for patience and discipline in learning to use basic analytical tools to that of the bamboo farmer. Once the bamboo seed is planted, the farmer must water it every day. He must do this for *four years* before the tree breaks ground! But when it does, it grows 60 feet in 90 days!

That's true of analytical tools; it takes time to learn and apply them, it takes nurturing, it takes practice, and it takes discipline. But once understood and applied properly, they will rapidly increase your analytical power.

The next two chapters will take you through the practices necessary to facilitate systematic, collaborative problem solving. As you will see, the second step of the problem-solving process is "analyze the problem." The tools presented in this chapter are the means to concrete problem analysis. While a little study and practice may be required for you to get comfortable using these tools, the time required is not too great.

The beauty of the analytic tools presented in this chapter is their broad application and ease of use. You don't have to be in the second step of a formal problem-solving activity to take advantage of them. You can apply them quickly and easily to many situations. You can use them to organize and clarify data and information, make a key point more effectively, lend credibility to your argument, stimulate thoughts in others, or bring critical thinking into the group. You should get comfortable using the tools routinely under a variety of circumstances to promote communications and understanding. These tools are your bamboo seeds; nurture their use and they will grow to be an integral part of your facilitation repertoire.

Before reviewing the various tools, I would like to extend my appreciation to Mike Haravich and Tim Gilbert of the Xerox Corporate Quality Office for their insights and comments on this chapter. Mike and Tim are true quality improvement gurus. Few people use these tools on a routine basis better than they do.

TOOLS FOR DISPLAYING INFORMATION GRAPHICALLY

If you or a subgroup have collected data through interviews, surveys, observations, benchmarking, library research, or some other means, displaying the results to the whole team is particularly important. During analysis and decision making, trends and sequences are often more evident, and comparisons more easily made, from graphic representations of data. Three common tools used for displaying data graphically are time charts, bar charts, and pie charts. These graphics are among the simplest and best formats for communicating data.

Time Charts

Use a time chart to display and summarize changes over time. Use the bottom, or horizontal axis, to show the time intervals, and the left side, or vertical axis, for your number scale indicating frequency. The plotted points are connected by a solid line. If the same time period is used, several sets of data can be shown on one chart. (See Figure 11-1.)

Bar Charts

Use bar charts to show a comparison of quantities of like items (lost customers by region, defects by shift, students by grade level, etc.). The different quantities are indicated by the length of the parallel bars used to represent them. Bars may run vertically or horizontally. To construct a vertical bar chart, use the horizontal axis to show the different regions, shifts, grade levels, or whatever factor you are working with. Use the

FIGURE 11–1

Time Chart Displaying the Number of Active Quality Improvement Teams for the First Half of the Year in Engineering, Sales, and Manufacturing

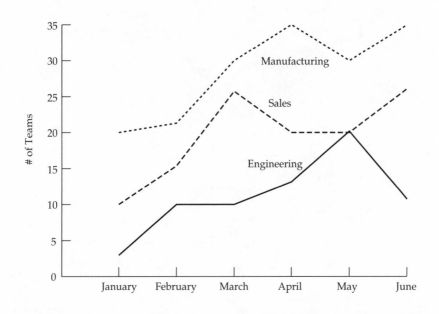

vertical axis for your number scale. To create a horizontal bar chart, reverse the axes. (See Figure 11-2.)

Pie Charts

Use a pie chart to show the relationship of parts of a whole to each other, and of each part to the whole. Show comparisons among quantities by dividing a circle into wedges (like pieces of pie). The whole "pie" equals 100 percent so the parts of the pie must add to 100 percent. The size of each wedge should be proportional to its percentage of the whole. Pie charts are easily interpreted and can present data effectively and efficiently. (See Figure 11-3.)

TOOLS FOR ANALYZING INFORMATION GRAPHICALLY

The tools described next are used to analyze data, as well as to display it. That is, the creation of these graphic displays is itself an analytic process.

FIGURE 11-2

Bar Chart Displaying the Number of Students (K–6) at Thornell Road Grade School

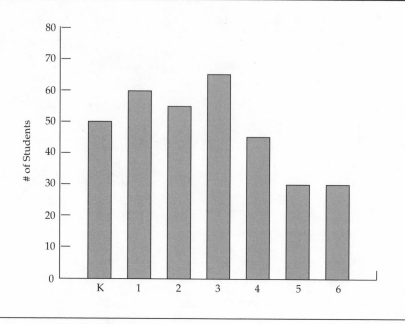

The Flow Chart

If I had only one tool to use for analyzing problems—the one I would give up last—it would be the flow chart. The reason is that in my experience, a flow chart will clear up roughly 30 percent of your problem-solving issues, especially work process issues, without any further activity.

A flow chart's construction does not have to be terribly complicated. It only has to make sense to the people who are creating and using it. A flow chart is nothing more than a pictorial representation of the steps leading to some output—it documents a work process.

When doing a flow chart, you must depict the function as it operates in reality, not how you believe the boss thinks it operates, or how the team would like it to operate. The best chance to obtain the *reality* of the process being charted is to make certain that someone who is intimately involved in the process is a member of the group. If it means bringing in an outsider or two to provide the requisite information, then do it!

Don't bring in the person who designed the original process. Don't bring in the theoretical expert on this process. Don't get someone who knows how the process should be run. It is imperative that you find and utilize the person(s) who actually lives with the process because that individual is the only one who knows how the process really func-

FIGURE 11–3
Investment Portfolio Displaying Various Investment Components

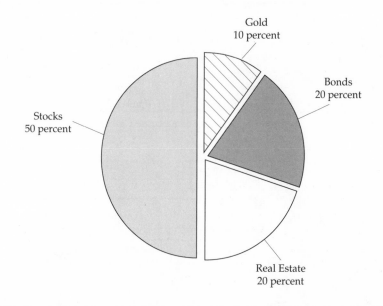

Gold
10 percent

Bonds
20 percent

Stocks
50 percent

Real Estate
20 percent

tions. This person is your "eyes and ears to reality." For a complicated process you may need a whole team of people from several functions to create a correct flow chart.

As Figure 11–4 shows, flow charting uses universal symbols—ovals, rectangles, diamonds, and arrows—to depict what is going on.

The value of flow charting is that it identifies improvement possibilities, unnecessary steps, unclear decision points, not enough decision points, too many movement steps, bottlenecks, pressure points, and so forth.

Flow charts can be applied to anything, from the travels of an invoice to the flow of materials, from the steps in making a sale to the steps in servicing a product.

Constructing a flow chart. The simplest way to start a flow chart is to tape a couple of pieces of flip chart paper on the wall either vertically (one above the other) or horizontally (side by side). Next, get agreement on the output (e.g., report published), write it on a self-stick note, then stick it to the bottom of the flip chart paper if your chart will flow top to bottom. If the chart will flow horizontally, place the output statement to the far right. Once placed, draw an oval around your output statement. Use round-robin brainstorming to solicit the critical process

FIGURE 11–4
Flow Chart Basics

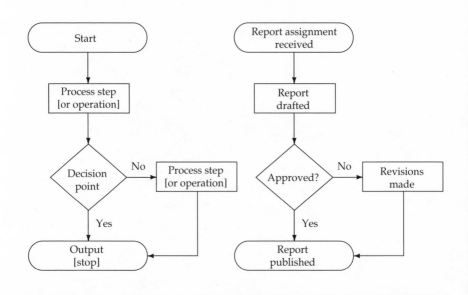

steps and decision points from the process experts. Stick these either above (or to the left) of the output statement, depending on format. Don't draw anything around them yet.

As facilitator, help the group add, delete, modify, and rearrange the self-stick notes until a consensus is reached on the sequence of process steps and decision points being charted relative to the predefined output. Remember, this sequence must reflect a consensus on how the process actually works—for better or worse—in reality. During all of the self-stick note writing and rearranging, if you are very familiar with the realities of the process, switch hats and add your perspectives and viewpoints. Finally, with all of the self-stick notes sequenced properly on the flip chart paper, draw your ovals, rectangles, and diamonds around the appropriate self-stick notes. Then finish off the flow chart by drawing the connecting arrows and writing in the yes/no notations.

Figure 11–5 is an example of a completed flow chart. By looking at the chart, all team members can visually review and then discuss the expense reporting system as it currently operates. The arrows that double back to earlier steps require special scrutiny because they often are signs of potential waste in the process. For example, does the next higher level manager have to review every expense report? In the spirit of shared power, maybe the manager only needs to sign-off on expense reports over $1,000. If that can occur, a wasteful rework step has been knocked out.

FIGURE 11–5

Completed Flow Chart for Departmental Expense Reporting Process

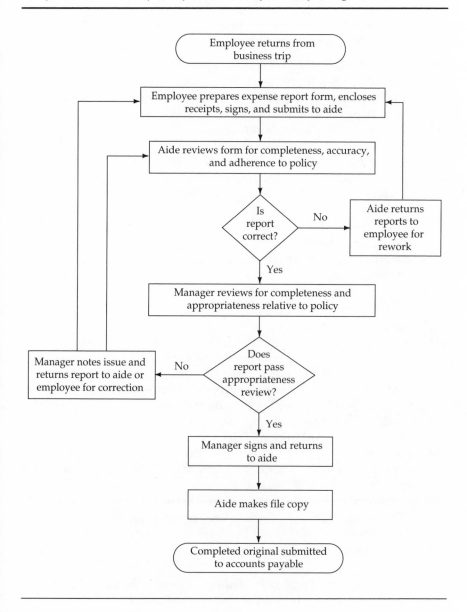

One tip for sharpening your analysis using flow charts is to draw two of them. *After you have developed a chart depicting reality,* draw a second one illustrating how the process *should* operate. Then, by comparing and contrasting the current situation (reality) with the desired situation (goal), pinch points and problem areas in the process often are easier to isolate and understand.

The Cause-and-Effect Diagram

The cause-and-effect diagram has two other common names. It also is referred to in the literature as: (1) the Ishikawa diagram (because it is based on a method developed by Dr. Kaoru Ishikawa—teacher, expert, and author of several books in the field of quality control), or (2) the fishbone diagram (because, when developed, it looks like a fish skeleton).

Cause-and-effect analysis is a powerful technique for triggering ideas, recording brainstormed ideas, and systematically examining an effect and the various causes that create or contribute to the effect.

Constructing a cause-and-effect diagram.   Facilitating the creation of a cause-and-effect diagram is fairly straightforward. Remember, for every effect there are likely to be several major causes and a number of subcauses.

Get consensus on the effect.   In many instances this may be a no-brainer. However, don't assume everyone sees the effect the same way. Ask for a proposal, or in your role as group member, suggest one yourself. Note it on a flip chart and test for consensus to make sure everyone is on board. If not, work with the group to modify the proposed statement until you get a consensus. My experience over many situations is that this is usually a routine, noncontroversial step.

Let's take an example and trace through the construction of a cause-and-effect diagram. At Pittsford TeleCom, interviews, surveys, and informal feedback throughout all levels of the company indicate a significant decrease of interest in, and commitment to, Pittsford's two-year-old Employee Involvement Program. The cross-functional team picked to address this situation has just concurred that the effect statement should read: *"Formal and informal feedback demonstrates a significant erosion of interest and commitment relative to our Employee Involvement Program across all levels of the company."*

Draw a spine of the "fish" and enter effect at the head.   The result of this activity would produce the drawings shown in Figure 11–6. For practical purposes, the wording at the head of the fish is an abbreviated version of the consensus statement developed by the group.

Show the primary causes as ribs coming from the spine.   Often it is difficult to work out a way of classifying primary causes. There are

FIGURE 11–6
Spine and Head of a Cause-and-Effect Diagram

> Feedback shows significant erosion of interest and commitment regarding our EI program.

---

three sets of universal causes that will serve your classification needs the vast majority of time.

4Ms	*4Ps*	*GRRP*
• Manpower.	• Policies.	• Goals
• Machines.	• Procedures.	• Roles.
• Methods.	• People.	• Relationships.
• Materials.	• Plant.	• Procedures.

The 4Ms are the most widely used, the 4Ps are most helpful when examining administrative areas, and GRRP is a valuable classification set when looking at the internal functioning or operations of a team of people. There is one other generic item—the Big E, *Environment*—that is helpful and can be used as a fifth category with any of the major groupings. The most important thing to keep in mind here is that the categories presented are only suggestions. Any major category that emerges or helps people think creatively is value added to the process. Encourage people to suggest a major category they feel strongly about. However, try to keep the major classification list in the range of three to six items so that the whole process does not get out of control. Also, don't be afraid to mix items from all three sets or mix some of your classifications with the standard ones if that's what is needed to best understand the cause-and-effect relationships. Nothing here is carved in stone.

For purposes of its analysis, the Pittsford TeleCom team took three categories from the 4Ps and added one of its own. (See Figure 11–7.)

Facilitate the generation of causes and their placement on the appropriate ribs.   The easiest process of building this piece of the cause-and-effect diagram is to do the following:

> Take each of the major cause categories one by one and lead a round-robin brainstorming activity to generate the possible causes. For example: "What, in our procedures, is causing the

FIGURE 11–7
Basic Structure of a Cause-and-Effect Diagram

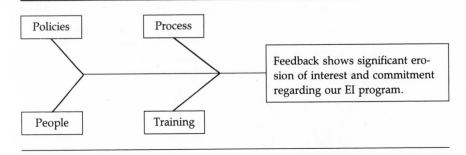

erosion of interest in and commitment to EI?'' or ''What, in
our policies, is causing . . .''

> Write each brainstormed cause in as few words as possible on
a self-stick note. Stick each note next to the appropriate major
category rib. For example, next to the major rib for ''Training,''
stick the note ''Training an irritation.''

> For each cause ask, Why does this happen? For example, ''Why
is training an irritation?'' Place this answer on a self-stick note
and show it as a subcause branch off the cause being worked. For
example, Why is training an irritation? ''It's perceived as extra
work.'' Keep probing each subcause by asking why.

Facilitate a consensus on the most likely root causes.   Now it
is time to look for the significant few key causes which are at the root
of the effect. Like the other steps, this facilitation activity is not difficult.

> Have the group scan the diagram and highlight any causes or
subcauses that appear repeatedly; circle them. These are always strong candidates for root cause selection.

> With repeated causes highlighted, ask group members to iden-
tify other root causes and explain why they feel that way. Encourage an open discussion. Keep in mind that a potential root
cause is any cause that has no subcauses linked to it, or is the
final subcause for a particular item on the diagram.

> Once the discussion is completed for a potential key cause, ask
the members to raise their hands if they believe it is a root
cause. If a simple majority is achieved (more than 50 percent of
the members raise their hands), circle the item.

> With all circled items now serving as the set of choices, lead
the group in either a weighted voting or multivoting activity

FIGURE 11–8
Completed Cause-and-Effect Diagram

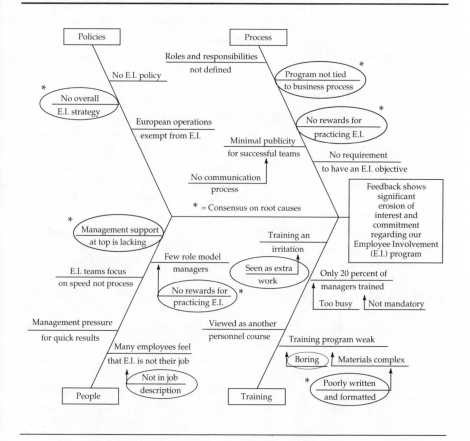

(see Chapter 10) to carve out the significant few (three to five) root causes.

> Next, with the significant few identified, test consensus to make certain everyone is together in their agreement or support for these items. Designate the chosen root causes with an asterisk.

> Finally, the root causes selected must be validated by collecting supporting data and information on them. Should any of the identified root causes prove to be invalid, you and the team should return to the cause-and-effect diagram and dig out several other, less-obvious root causes on this second go-around by repeating the process just described.

Figure 11–8 shows the final cause-and-effect diagram that was completed by the Pittsford TeleCom group.

The cause-and-effect diagram can be linked directly to a flow chart in the following way. Once you've identified a bottleneck, an unclear decision point, a pressure point, and the like, with your flow chart, you can write the identified bottleneck as an effect statement. Then you can work through a cause-and-effect analysis as just described and unearth the root causes of the bottleneck.

Pareto Analysis

A Pareto analysis, displayed as a Pareto chart, rank-orders data and shows which factors in a situation occur most frequently. This ranking is useful in determining which aspects of a problem or situation would yield the greatest payback for the time, money, or effort invested. The data is displayed on a chart like a bar chart but arrayed in descending order. Pareto analysis is a technique that separates the vital few from the trivial many.

Vilfredo Pareto, a 19th century Italian economist, displayed data about income this way. He wanted to show that the majority of wealth was held by a very few people—that wealth was unequally distributed. The familiar 80–20 rule (80 percent of the wealth is held by 20 percent of the people) is an example of Pareto analysis. A Pareto analysis often is used to rank-order quality problems and put them in perspective according to their magnitude or prevalence. For each problem type, the number of occurrences is recorded on a check sheet for a sample of items over a given time period. The results, depicted in a bar graph, are ranked in descending order of incidence. (See Figure 11–9).

By its steepness, the curve of cumulative percentages always visually emphasizes the importance of each item. Pareto diagrams can aid decision making by demonstrating where to begin quality improvement activities or how to allocate limited resources to a quality improvement program. You can see in Figure 11-9 that 80 percent of customer complaints about service quality result from slow response time and from the failure of equipment to stay fixed. Concentrating resources to fix these two areas will eliminate 80 percent of the service quality problem.

Constructing a Pareto chart.   Pareto charts can be built by one person or a team of people. Following a number of programmed steps will do the trick.

> Use a checklist to collect the frequency of events occurring across a set of different categories for some defined period of time (e.g., eight hours, two weeks, one month).

> Arrange the raw data (frequency of occurrence) in order from largest category to smallest.

> Calculate the total number of occurrences.

FIGURE 11-9
Pareto Analysis of Customer Complaints Regarding Quality of Service

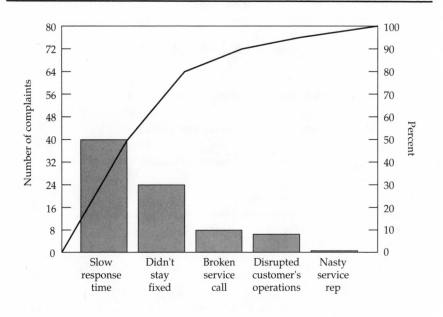

> Compute the cumulative percent.

> Draw horizontal and vertical axes on graph paper.

> Scale the left-hand vertical axis for frequency (0 to the total number of occurrences) and scale the right hand vertical axis for cumulative percent (0 percent to 100 percent). Note: Make sure that the two axes are drawn to a common scale, e.g., 100 percent is opposite the total frequency; 50 percent is opposite the halfway point in this raw data, and so on (Figure 11-9).

> Working from left to right, construct a bar for each category, with height indicating frequency. Start with the largest category and add the rest in descending order (Figure 11-9).

> Plot the cumulative percent line (Figure 11-9).

Instead of frequency on the left-hand axis, Pareto charts are often built using dollars as the standard of measurement. Real power can be generated if you use two Pareto charts for analysis. Develop one showing frequency and one showing dollars. This allows you to link the two and the analysis may uncover some eye-popping data. You may find, for example, that some problem occurring frequently is costing you $1,000 per month, while a problem occurring half as often is costing you $10,000

FIGURE 11–10
Model of a Force Field Analysis

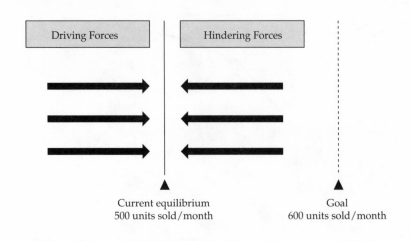

per month. Whenever possible, do a Pareto analysis for both dollars and frequency to extend the incisiveness of your analytical process.

Force Field Analysis

This technique, introduced into management theory by Kurt Lewin, is logical and easy to comprehend, even for people who have never constructed a force field before. Another virtue of the force field is its applicability to a wide variety of problem-solving situations. The basic structure of a force field analysis is represented in Figure 11–10.

Lewin looked upon a level of performance within an organizational setting (production, sales, customer satisfaction, defects, trust, collaboration, etc.) not as a static habit or custom but rather as a dynamic balance of forces working in opposite directions. *Driving forces* were seen to be facilitating and powering the situation to change to a higher equilibrium point. *Hindering forces* were seen to be countering the driving forces by restricting and restraining movement to a higher equilibrium point. Therefore, the present state of affairs for a given situation is in equilibrium because it is being maintained by a variety of offsetting forces that "keep things the way they are" or "keep me behaving in my customary ways."

Regarding problem solving, force field analysis holds that a problem arises out of the stationary product of driving forces and hindering forces. Thus the two sets of forces working against each other are causing a problem because there is a gap between our current state, where we

FIGURE 11–11
Completed Force Field Analysis

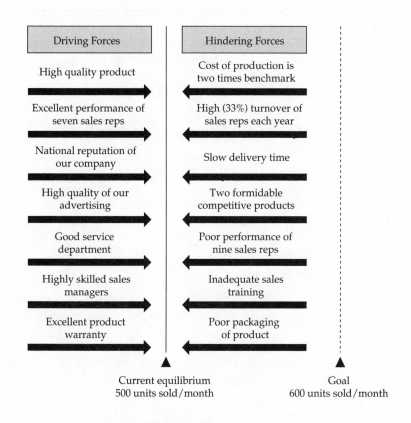

Driving Forces	Hindering Forces
High quality product	Cost of production is two times benchmark
Excellent performance of seven sales reps	High (33%) turnover of sales reps each year
National reputation of our company	Slow delivery time
High quality of our advertising	Two formidable competitive products
Good service department	Poor performance of nine sales reps
Highly skilled sales managers	Inadequate sales training
Excellent product warranty	Poor packaging of product

Current equilibrium
500 units sold/month

Goal
600 units sold/month

are, and our desired future state, where we want to be. Figure 11–11 presents a completed force field for your review.

Constructing a force field chart.   The steps to construct a force field chart are explained in detail in the following sections.

Define the situation.   Facilitate a group discussion that produces two very concise statements (6–10 words each) declaring the "current equilibrium" situation and the "goal" situation. Draw the framework and write the two statements in place, as shown in Figure 11–11.

Identify driving and hindering forces.   Lead a brainstorming session to get a list of forces. As each idea is given, write it on a self-stick note and stick it on the appropriate side of the *current equilibrium* line. Review both sides of the chart and, as a team, discuss, refine, and consolidate both the driving and hindering forces lists. Don't be afraid to move forces from one side of the chart to the other. Often the discussion of the forces produces new insight to warrant a change in several forces from hindering to driving or vice versa. Don't rush this activity. You're finished when the group has reached a consensus on all the forces on each side of the *current equilibrium* line (i.e., those forces creating the *now* situation).

Decide which forces to focus on for change.   According to force field analysis, it is important that you look at both sides of the issue. If you tackle problems only by trying to decrease some hindering forces, or only by trying to increase some driving forces, you are less likely to improve performance than if you analyze both sides of the situation simultaneously.

Facilitate a discussion around the following questions as you examine hindering forces you might reduce or eliminate:

> Which will be the hardest to eliminate or reduce? Why?

> Which will be the easiest? Why?

> How long will it take?

> Can this hindering force be turned into a driving force?

> What consequences might we expect from changing this force? What results?

For the driving forces you might strengthen or build from, facilitate a discussion around these questions.

> Is this force being utilized fully?

> Could this force be applied in other ways?

> Are there helping forces not listed?

> How much control do we have over this force?

> What consequences might we expect from changing this force? What results?

Zero-in on the forces to change.   Facilitate a convergence of thinking, using weighted voting or multivoting, to reduce the list to the top three or four on each side. Then use the paired comparisons process to prioritize the few selected forces on each side. This allows the group to develop strategies in the most appropriate sequence to maximize the chosen driving forces and minimize the chosen hindering forces.

Extending the Figure 11–11 example.   In our example, if you only tried to decrease the hindering effect of nine poor performing sales reps by getting rid of them, you would run the risk of alienating some of the better performers and you might end up still selling only 500 units a month. Or if you increase one of the driving forces, you might well run into increased resistance from one of the hindering forces. The result of such one-sided analysis could be increased tension in the system, but no upward movement in performance.

As you examine your force field, look for combinations from both sides as sets of linked forces to be altered simultaneously. For example, in this illustration you might see the opportunity to take the skills of selected sales managers and use them more creatively by having these people work more intensely with several of the poorly performing sales reps to increase their skills. Another combination, linking and working two opposite forces in tandem, would be to improve the quality of the sales-training effort (a hindering force) by using the skills of your seven best sales reps (a driving force) as trainers for the rest of the staff. Force field analysis is powerful because once a group completes the task of agreeing on what actually are the hindering and driving forces, the solutions often become quite obvious.

Keep these analytical tools in mind. They will be referred to in Chapter 13 and will be used in the case example at the end of that chapter.

A CLOSING SUMMARY

This chapter presented the techniques for facilitating seven simple, structured processes for displaying and analyzing data and information. The beauty of the analytical tools presented in this chapter is their broad application and ease of use. These tools are not tied exclusively to a specific step in a formal problem-solving process. While they fit nicely into formal problem solving, you can routinely use them to organize and clarify data and information, to build a stronger case for ideas, to help sharpen the critical thinking of the group, to avoid jumping directly from problem definition to problem solution, to stimulate group thought and discussion, and to use "pictures" to represent a thousand words.

The tools are classified into two broad categories: those that display data graphically and those that help analyze data as well as display it. Each of the seven tools covered in the chapter will be highlighted here for easy reference.

Graphic display tools.

Time charts display changes in a particular event over time; they are useful for showing fluctuations or growth of a particular event.

Bar charts display a comparison of quantities of like items (e.g., sales volume per store or number of people trained in basic statistics per department).

Pie charts show the relationship of parts of a whole to each other, and of each part to the whole.

Graphic analytic tools.

Flow charts document work processes and help reveal bottlenecks and pinch points.

Cause-and-effect diagrams provide a systematic way of looking at an effect and the causes contributing to that effect. By looking for sub-causes within the main causes, root causes of the effect often can be uncovered.

Pareto analysis, displayed as a Pareto chart, rank-orders data showing which factors in a situation occur most frequently. The data is shown on a chart like a bar chart, but arrayed in descending order. Pareto analysis is a technique that separates the vital few from the trivial many.

Force field analysis identifies the forces that both help and hinder closing the gap between the current equilibrium point and the new, desired goal.

NOTES WORKSHEET: DEVELOP WRITTEN RESPONSES TO THE TWO ITEMS LISTED BELOW

What Do You Feel Are the Main Learning Points from Chapter 11?	Elaborate on Why You Feel These Points Are Key

Chapter 12

Group Problem Solving I
An Orientation to Systematic, Collaborative Problem Solving

Chapter Objectives

> To provide a set of facilitation behaviors that are key to creating and maintaining collaborative problem-solving teams.

> To examine the pitfalls to be avoided and the benefits to be gained through the application of systematic, collaborative problem solving.

> To highlight the role of problem sensing as the precursor to problem solving.

INTRODUCTION

The professor had just handed out the final exam papers to his students when his graduate assistant rushed up to the lectern in a panic. "Professor Sharkey, you've made a terrible mistake. This is the same test you gave last year; everyone will know the answers!"

"Not to worry," replied the professor. "The answers are different this year."

So it is with problem solving. The steps in the process, the questions you ask, may be the same, but the answers—the solutions—will vary greatly from application to application. Because of the full bloom and acceptance of employee involvement teams, work group and cross-functional problem-solving teams, self-managed work groups, and quality improvement teams within American business, education, and government, collaborative problem solving has skyrocketed as a mainline organizational activity. This acceptance, in turn, has created an unrelenting need for managers at all levels, task force chairpersons, problem-solving team leaders, and committee heads to learn the fundamental how-to's of a consistent, organizationwide, problem-solving process capable of helping groups collaborate in identifying, analyzing, and solving business and organizational problems.

As a matter of fact, facilitating others in collaborative problem-solving ventures is becoming an essential skill expected of managers and individual contributors alike, at all levels, and across all functions of the enlightened and progressive organizations leading the way into the 21st century. Progressive companies are unleashing the collective genius of their organizations to improve quality, increase customer satisfaction, improve their return on assets (ROA), and recapture market share. Group problem solving is at the core of their strategy for success, and it is making the difference between establishing a climate of vigorous growth or existing in a state of stagnated survival, or even worse, going out of business.

This latter point is vividly demonstrated by the following story. Three retail establishments in Akron, Ohio, were located next to each other on Main Street. On Monday, the store on the left—tired of losing business to the other two—put up a sign in its window: SALE—ROCK BOTTOM PRICES, EVERYTHING AT LEAST 50 PERCENT OFF. On Tuesday, the store on the right retaliated with this sign: SALE—LOWEST PRICES IN TOWN. WE WILL NOT BE UNDERSOLD. On Wednesday, thrown by these aggressive maneuvers and feeling the crunch from both sides, the manager of the middle store held a collaborative problem-solving meeting with his staff. Shortly thereafter they put up their sign which simply proclaimed: MAIN ENTRANCE FOR ALL THESE BARGAINS. The middle store thrived and the other two stores, starved for customers, went out of business.

BASIC FACILITATION BEHAVIORS FOR SYSTEMATIC, COLLABORATIVE PROBLEM SOLVING

Before getting on with the details of a specific problem-solving process, we need to review several behavioral principles that will be of immense help to you when conducting group problem solving. These principles define a set of guidelines that will help you properly plan and facilitate problem-solving meetings. They are the foundation for the systematic process that will be detailed in the next chapter and should not be taken lightly.

Clearly State and Post the Purpose and Desired Outcomes of Every Problem-Solving Session

Nothing is more fundamental to mining group gold than writing, posting, and clarifying the purpose and desired outcomes for each problem-solving meeting you facilitate. As emphasized in Chapter 5, the purpose and desired outcomes are the "compass settings" for the entire session. They keep the meeting focused, on track, and provide a benchmark against which you and the team can measure the session's actual outcomes.

In some cases, a problem can be satisfactorily solved in just one meeting; in other instances, a series of meetings will be needed. That means a session may be focused on just one facet of the problem-solving process. For example, for a complex problem requiring many meetings, the third session in the sequence may have a desired outcome stated as "Potential solutions brainstormed." The fourth meeting may have a different outcome noted as "Brainstormed solutions from previous meeting evaluated."

Ensure that the Right People Attend Each Problem-Solving Session

After developing the purpose and desired outcomes, you must reflect on this information and use it to help screen attendees. Although you may consider including a number of people, only those deemed essential to the attainment and implementation of that session's desired outcomes are invited. Nonessential people at problem-solving sessions are useless. Unless you have a solid reason for inviting a person to a session, the invitation should not be extended.

Each meeting needs to be viewed as a unique event, and people should be selected accordingly. Especially with sessions that are part of a sequence of meetings dealing with a complex problem, don't get in the habit of inviting the same people to every session. Circumstances and needs do change considerably as progress is made over time.[1]

Clarify that You Expect Everyone in Attendance to Share Responsibility for a Successful Session

A successful group problem-solving effort is not the sole responsibility of the manager or task force chairperson. As the leader and primary facilitator of a problem-solving team—be it your own direct reports or a cross-functional group of people—you need to make it clear from the outset that you expect all participants to share responsibility for a successful problem-solving activity. No single individual (even if you are the manager or chairperson) can prevent the group process from breaking down if the other members are intent on ignoring the purpose, desired outcomes, and agenda as well as resisting any process discipline, making no effort to listen and understand each other, and trampling on each other to see who can control the session. *Shared responsibility is created when the primary facilitator designates all others in attendance as secondary facilitators.*

By recognizing and stating that problem solving is a collaborative group effort to which all members contribute, you are helping to develop a sense of teamwork and group cohesion. Initiating a shared responsibility for facilitation goes a long way toward ensuring that all group resources will be used productively.

Set the Stage, Then Wait, to Avoid Becoming a Promotional Leader

If you are conducting a *group* problem-solving session—or series of sessions—it must mean you need and want the thoughts, ideas, perspectives, and synergy of the group members in order to solve the problem. Therefore, your goal from the outset is to initiate an open, collaborative climate within the group. If your mind is already made up regarding the definition, analysis, and solution to the problem, don't play manipulative, self-serving games by giving team members a feeling of participation and collaboration. Instead, announce your decision along with your reasoning for it and get on with the implementation.

However, when you see the group members as a resource and genuinely want to mine their gold nuggets of wisdom in order to solve a problem, the following guidelines will help you initiate the open, collaborative climate that is essential to group problem solving.[2]

Present the problem so the focus is on the situation, not behaviors. Behaviorial statements tend to be judgmental and to immediately lock in on a limited and biased perspective—the people are at fault. On the other hand, situational statements are descriptive and impersonal—they produce a wider view of the problem and seek to generate collaboration among group members, including the manager.

Present the problem situation so it encompasses common interests. Making the problem situation appealing means showing group members what they will gain from taking a critical look at it and spending the necessary time to solve it. There are at least three powerful ways to present a problem situation so that it conveys mutual interests:

> Help the members realize that they have what it takes to solve the problem or, at the very least, to develop a set of recommendations that will be given full attention by higher management. Either approach absolutely will increase the members' motivation to tackle it. Having control over one's destiny is a significant motivator.

> State the problem situation so that it stresses the development of processes and procedures that are fair to everyone concerned. For example: "As you all know, in six weeks we move

across the river to our new building. While that facility is more plush, it offers us less space than we have now. So, what would be a fair process to determine who gets what space?"

> Set forth the problem situation so that personal goals are easily aligned with organizational goals. This is a prime technique for creating common interest. For example, offering the staff development administrators within a school district the opportunity to revise a narrow and outdated training curriculum that they have been dissatisfied with for several years meshes common interests. The district wants the curriculum revised, and the staff development administrators want to revise it because they are dissatisfied with the status quo.

Initially share only primary information.   Another ingredient in building an open, collaborative climate is for you to share whatever relevant knowledge and situational facts you have regarding the problem situation. Properly supplying essential information involves several considerations.

> You provide background information in a descriptive, nonevaluative manner.

> You present only what is needed to clarify and understand the problem situation.

> You set forth your expectations.

> You delineate the range of freedom the group has in solving the problem—you note any boundary conditions limiting its activities.

Be succinct.   Less is better. Use no more than five minutes to present the information called for in the three previous steps. Remember, this is just the beginning of the problem-solving activity. More detailed information can be introduced later in the process as the need arises. This guideline prevents overwhelming the group with too much too soon.

Wait!   After the stage has been set by carrying out the first four principles, to initiate a truly collaborative atmosphere you must resist the temptation to immediately influence the group by interpreting the information you have provided, suggesting how it should be used, or, worst of all, jumping directly to a solution and telling everyone what "the answer" is.

It is imperative that you avoid becoming a promotional leader who, after outlining the situation, rushes forth and says, "Here's how I define the problem, here's what we need to do to fix the problem, and here's my strategy for fixing it . . ." before the others have a chance to offer their views and insights. Nothing else will do more to squash the discussion and stamp out candor. "Now that we know what the boss wants to do, let's deliver it. Who are we to challenge the wonderful, creative ideas of our boss?"

Therefore, the fifth principle for initiating an open collaborative problem-solving climate requires that you stop, "bite your tongue," and hold back your thoughts, perspectives, value judgments, and favored actions. Keep the door open for members to freely explore the problem, rather than restricting the information processing by imposing a specific direction to the exploration. You can sprinkle your thoughts throughout the discussion as it unfolds.

Remember that Problem Solving Is as Much an Emotional Process as It Is Rational

As you read this chapter and the next, do not make the classic mistake of believing that a systematic, logical, and orderly process will make problem solving a piece of cake. It won't! Thinking so overlooks the fact that people are rational *and* emotional. Even though systematic, logical, and orderly approaches to decision making are helpful, you can never completely divorce emotions from the process of problem solving. Often the dynamics of defining a problem, analyzing it, generating potential solutions, and selecting and planning a solution are as much psychological and emotional as they are logical.

Keep in mind this simple sequence to group productivity: *feelings, facts, solutions.* Anytime a group slides into the feelings phase, you need to encourage individuals to express their emotions, process them in an organized manner, and move into phase 2—facts. If this is not done, the session will get bogged down in a directionless, emotional confrontation. Processing feelings means that you, wearing your facilitator's hat, must stay neutral (by *accepting* other's feelings as real and by *encouraging* people to express their feelings) and you must understand rather than evaluate any expressed feelings (by *probing* with nonevaluative questions and by being *sensitive* to nonverbal cues). As feelings are expressed, write them on flip charts so all participants can see in black and white that they are being heard and understood correctly. Post this information for use throughout the remainder of the problem-solving session.[3]

AN ORIENTATION TO SYSTEMATIC, COLLABORATIVE PROBLEM SOLVING

The problem-solving process shown in Figure 12–1 is a marvelous one. No matter what your problem is, this process makes it go away. "You

FIGURE 12–1
The Ideal Model

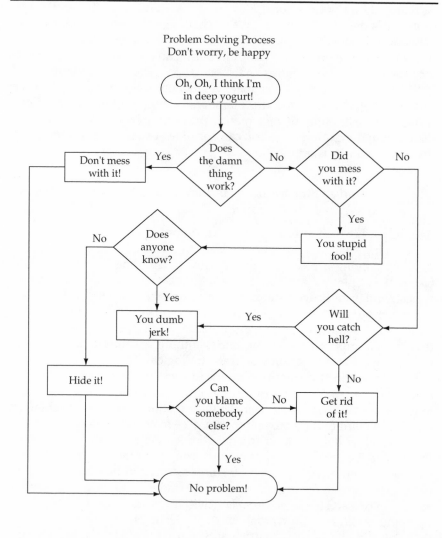

Problem Solving Process
Don't worry, be happy

don't have to worry, you can always be happy!'' If only life were that simple. Obviously problems are not solved so neatly. In the real world, working through tough problems is a time-consuming and often frustrating experience.

Most problem-solving situations consume an extended period of time, from several hours to several months or more. No manager, chairperson, or administrator can escape for very long the task of having to facilitate a group through a problem-solving meeting or, very often, a series of meetings. Whenever that occasion arises, you need to be able to routinely activate and facilitate a systematic, collaborative process that will help you be a successful "miner of group gold." The six-step problem-solving process introduced in Figure 12-2 and examined in detail in the next chapter is the pathway to your success. The six steps around the wheel are the same ones Xerox has chosen as its generic, corporationwide problem-solving process. I have built upon those steps by adding the problem-sensing portion. I have found problem sensing to be a critical phase that individuals or teams have to work through along their journey to collaborative problem solving.

Pitfalls Avoided

Using the six-step model advocated here, you will be in a much stronger position to help your team avoid the pitfalls of ineffective problem solving, such as:

> Jumping to a solution before effectively analyzing the true nature and dynamics of the problem under consideration.

> Failing to gather critical data, about either the problem or proposed solutions.

> Tackling problems that are beyond the control or influence of group members.

> Working on problems that are too general, too large, or not well defined.

> Allowing habit and past experience to restrict mental flexibility in generating and evaluating potential solutions.

> Failing to plan adequately how to implement and evaluate recommended solutions.

The Facilitation Benefits Gained

As facilitator, your job is made easier when you apply the six-step, collaborative problem-solving wheel shown in Figure 12-2 because:

> It provides a common process and language that all team members can learn and use.

> It arranges your group's problem-solving activities in a logical, sequential order so that everyone is following the same steps in the same order.

> It focuses everyone's attention on what needs to be done at each step of the process.

FIGURE 12–2
The Six-Step Collaborative Problem-Solving Model

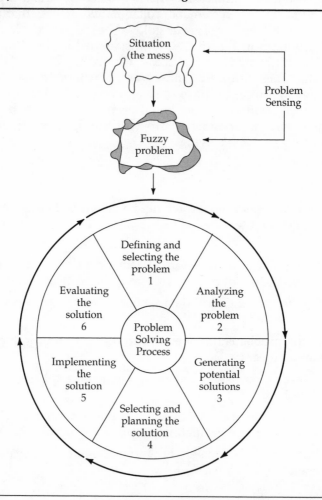

Source: The six-step wheel reprinted with permission of the Xerox Corporation.

> It helps you and your team members recognize the potential pitfalls mentioned earlier by asking critical questions at each step of the problem-solving process.

> It helps you and your team members decide the right time to move on to the next problem-solving step.

It is best to think of this problem-solving method as your guide, or a kind of road map, for facilitating collaborative problem-solving efforts. This process provides structure and direction to your facilitation activity. It points the way for addressing difficult problems in a thorough, step-by-step manner. The more complex a problem, the more useful a systematic, collaborative process becomes. The specifics of the full process will be covered in the next chapter.

PROBLEM SENSING: THE PRECURSOR TO PROBLEM SOLVING

Closely allied with problem solving—but antecedent to it—is problem sensing. Problems typically do not come to a group neatly packaged with a big bow and a flashing neon sign reading Problem. Most of the time the true problem is either unknown, disguised, ill-defined, buried in a mass of data, or some combination of these conditions. All that exists is a feeling held by an individual or group of individuals that some state of affairs is unsatisfactory.

W. G. Dyer clarifies the problem-sensing cycle that is often a precursor to the problem-solving process:

> [In sensing] the manager begins not with a problem but with a concern or feeling of unease that perhaps there are areas that should be improved. With this concern as the motivating influence, the manager begins to gather data by talking to people, asking questions, perhaps initiating a questionnaire or survey. The focus of all this is to find out if there are any conditions that are keeping people from being as effective as they could be in their jobs. Having gathered data, the manager then analyzes the information to see if there is enough evidence to decide that there is, in fact, a problem or problems that should be solved.[4]

Problem sensing is no small task because the problems you face—regardless of your role, responsibilities, and formal position in the organization—are really clusters of information and observations from which meaning must be extracted. The volume, variety, and constant disruptive elements in the stream of information you receive each day make problem sensing an activity worthy of your concentration.

Stressing the disruptive elements in the reception and interpretation of messages, H. Wilensky describes the vagaries of problem sensing:

> Sources of failure are legion: even if the initial message is accurate, clear, timely, and relevant, it may be translated, condensed, or completely blocked by personnel standing between the sender and the receiver; it may get through in distorted form. If the receiver is in a position to use the message, [he or she] may screen it out because it does not fit with [his or her] preconceptions, because it has come through a suspicious or poorly regarded channel, because it is embedded in piles of inaccurate or useless messages [excessive noise in the channel], or, simply, because too many messages are [being] transmitted [information overload].[5]

Note Wilensky's comments and do your best to eliminate or reduce your susceptibility to these failures in the problem-sensing arena by keeping an open mind to the information you receive. Use the interpersonal skills of seeking information, seeking opinions, summarizing, and testing comprehension to help you understand, sort, organize, and interpret the information you receive.

You alone—or in conjunction with several others—processing the myriad information pieces received over time, may begin to feel vague dissatisfactions with particular aspects of how the total organization, department, bureau, agency, group, or task team is performing. What you are reacting to are the symptoms of a problem. Let's look at some examples:

> "I don't know what the problem is, all I know is our inventory control system is a mess. We don't have any idea what we have in our warehouse."

> "Our billing methods are all screwed up. We've got to do something. People are being billed three and four times for lab tests and medicines they've already paid for."

> "Look, school-based planning is not working. I don't know why. The whole thing is a mess."

> "Damn, our costs are way out of line. The Japanese can sell their units here in the States for less than what costs us to build ours."

In all four instances, the red light is blinking. A "mess," based on symptoms, is noted. *Problem sensing is taking place, not problem definition.* As you will see in the next chapter, correct problem definition does not involve symptoms.

At this point, either alone or in a small group if that is the forum, a broad statement that sets the stage for problem definition needs to be developed. Keep it general and brief. You are not trying to define the problem here; as Figure 12-2 illustrates, with problem sensing, you are simply trying to move from *your detection of "a mess"* to a *"fuzzy" problem-statement.* You're basically staking out the general boundaries within which the problem will be defined. Fuzzy statements include the following:

> "Why can't we get accurate, current, and easy to understand data about everything we have in our warehouse?"

> "Fifteen percent of the customer invoices we send out each month contain errors. Why can't we turn out 100 percent accurate bills every month?"

> "According to the minutes of the school-based planning team, three recommendations for improving teacher–student relations have been made. Yet nothing has been implemented. Why is this?"

> "Why can't we get our unit manufacturing costs in line with our competitors' costs?"

With these types of fuzzy statements, implied in the word *why* is a follow-up question: What can we do to fix the situation?

Other forms of fuzzy statements are ones representing a condition that, if improved, would increase the efficiency and effectiveness of the situation or function. Examples include:

> "How can we get our meetings to start on time?"

> "What can we do to cut down on the high absentee rate at our middle school?"

> "We've got a warehouse full of obsolete widgets—how can we best utilize them without throwing them away?"

> "Our customer satisfaction ratings are terrible—what needs to be done to improve them?"

Many groups get stuck at this point. They feel strongly motivated by sensing the mess and the fuzzy problem, but no one on the team, including the manager or chairperson, knows how to move forward. The felt need remains strong. However, without a systematic process capable of producing meaningful action to remove it, the group flails and struggles, with nothing to show for its efforts except an abundance of frustration, anger, and a cynical I-don't-give-a-damn outlook toward future group problem-solving initiatives. Or, if the group does move forward, it does so in the worst possible way. It takes the fuzzy problem-statement as "the" defined problem, skips the analysis, jumps immediately to concocting an ill-defined—and often incorrect—solution, implements the solution, then discovers that not only didn't the solution work, it caused other problems that made matters worse.

It does not have to be this way. Using the felt need of the mess and the fuzzy problem as the initial jumpstart, you can bring the power of the six-step problem-solving wheel into play to help you and your small group collaborate in solving or significantly reducing the impact of problem(s) being faced. In the next chapter we will look at each of the six steps individually and in detail so that you can see how to make the problem-solving process work for you.

A CLOSING SUMMARY

This chapter introduced you to five facilitation behaviors necessary for systematic, collaborative problem solving:

1. Clearly state and post the purpose and desired outcomes of every problem-solving session.

2. Make certain the right people are in attendance at each problem-solving session.

3. Clarify that you expect everyone in attendance to share responsibility for a successful session.

4. Set the stage, then wait, to avoid becoming a promotional leader:
    > Present the problem so that the focus is on the situation, not on behaviors.
    > Present the problem situation so it encompasses common interests.
    > Initially share only primary information.
    > Be succinct.
    > Wait!

5. Remember that problem solving is as much an emotional process as it is rational.

Next, the six-step, collaborative problem-solving model was introduced. In this chapter the emphasis was on the problem-sensing portion of the model. Problem sensing is the precursor to problem solving. It is a feeling held by an individual or group that some state of affairs is unsatisfactory. Problem sensing has two pieces: recognizing that some ill-defined *mess exists*, and clarifying the mess through the development of a *fuzzy problem-statement*.

The point that problem sensing *is not* problem solving was emphasized. Problem sensing sets the stage for problem solving. During problem sensing you are making a determination of whether or not a problem exists that is worth pursuing through implementation of the six-step, collaborative process. If the answer is yes, you go for it by following the guidelines presented in Chapter 13.

NOTES WORKSHEET: DEVELOP WRITTEN
RESPONSES TO THE TWO ITEMS LISTED BELOW

What Do You Feel Are the Main Learning Points from Chapter 12?	Elaborate on Why You Feel These Points Are Key

NOTES

1. For a more extensive treatment of who should attend, see Thomas A. Kayser, *Mining Group Gold: How to Cash In on the Collaborative Brain Power of a Group* (El Segundo, CA: Serif Publishing, 1990), pp. 31–36.

2. The subject of initiating an open, collaborative climate is given more detailed treatment in Kayser, *Mining Group Gold*, pp. 125–32.

3. For an in-depth discussion on the how-to's for facilitating feelings see Chapter 6, "Keeping the Gold Mine Productive in the Face of Emotion: Feelings, Facts, Solutions," Kayser, *Mining Group Gold*, pp. 103–17.

4. W. G. Dyer, *Contemporary Issues in Management and Organization Development* (Reading, MA: Addison-Wesley Publishing, 1983), p. 33.

5. H. Wilensky, *Organizational Intelligence: Knowledge and Policy in Government and Industry* (New York: Basic Books, 1967), p. 41.

Chapter 13

Group Problem Solving II
Facilitating Six Steps to
Problem-Solving Success

Chapter Objectives

> To present a practical six-step group approach to identifying, analyzing, and solving problems in a systematic, collaborative manner.

> To provide the how-to's for facilitating each step of this six-step model.

> To demonstrate the applied power of this six-step process through a business case study.

INTRODUCTION

Sally, the wife of a busy executive, complained to her friend Clare that she never saw her husband because he came home late every night, and she was bored staying home alone. Clare chimed in immediately and said, "Oh, poo, I have the perfect solution to your problem. You just need to get out and exercise a little. It'll keep you busy and relax you too. Here, take my bicycle and ride it 10 miles every night this week. You'll feel a whole lot better. Call me next week and tell me how you feel."

"Well, I don't know. Seven days of bicycling isn't something . . ."
"Sally, trust me. Do it! Now get along."

The next week Clare got a call from Sally. Clare excitedly asked, "Well, how do you feel now?" Sally said, "Lousy, terrible, worse than ever."

"My word," replied Clare. "Why?"

Sally, in a voice filled with exhaustion, said, "I'm tired, sore, hungry, and I'm 70 miles from home!"

I'm sure those weren't the results Clare expected. But if you look back at the dynamics of the problem-solving process that was used, then the results—while still humorous—aren't really surprising at all.

Far too many individuals and groups try to solve problems in a random, undisciplined, quick-and-dirty manner. A problem situation arises, a rambling, often argumentative discussion ensues, the problem definition is ignored, analysis is bypassed altogether, solution generation and selection turn out to be whatever the manager tells the group to do— or whatever the dominant coalition can once again railroad the group into doing. There is no time for discussion of the pros and cons of the solution or for a critical look at potential implementation problems. The solution is forced upon the group and implemented by a bunch of non-committed people. The results in most cases are disastrous. Not only isn't the problem solved, but matters are made worse. This, in turn, triggers a crisis, more pressure, and a more intense cycle of what happened previously.

The opening story, while involving only two people and not quite as extreme, well illustrates the point about poor problem-solving practices. But it doesn't have to be this way. Let's move ahead and begin to explore the power of facilitating systematic, collaborative problem solving.

SETTING THE STAGE

If you examine the behavioral science literature, you'll uncover a wide variety of problem-solving models in terms of the actual steps employed—most models fall within the range of four to nine steps. The basic process is the same; the models with fewer steps tend to consolidate several of the discrete steps that are spelled out in the longer models.

The six-step Xerox model, shown in Figure 13-1, is a generic process and that is its strength. The steps involved are applicable to any kind of problem-solving situation, whether it occurs in your head, in a two-person group, in a large committee, or in the total organization. As I detailed in Chapter 12, I have expanded the original wheel by adding the problem-sensing phase.

A generic, structured process provides a method that everyone can understand and use to greatly improve synergy among the parties involved. In any meeting, at any time, at any location, if someone says, ''I propose we use our problem-solving model to tackle this one,'' everyone around the table will understand exactly what steps and discipline are required.

Although the six steps are shown in Figure 13-1 as a wheel and numbered sequentially, a group seldom glides smoothly from Step 1 to Step 6 without having to make several loops back to revisit and revise information from earlier steps. The realities of problem solving are that it proceeds by fits and starts, both rationally and emotionally; however, the total pro-

FIGURE 13–1
The Six-Step Collaborative Problem-Solving Model

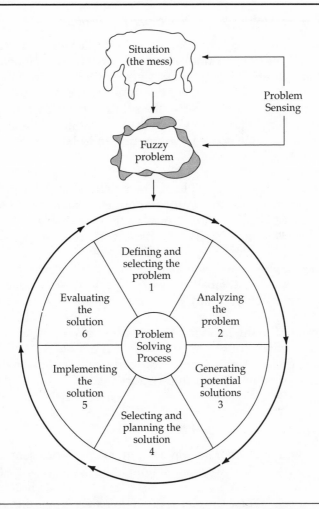

Source: The six-step wheel reprinted with permission of the Xerox Corporation.

cess does proceed through each of the six steps identified in our model. By moving a team around the wheel, you actually will be facilitating the group through a series of divergent and convergent thinking activities. Remember from Chapter 10, divergent thinking is used at idea-generating stages—like Steps 2 and 3, when the group is exploring the differences and creativity among members. Convergent thinking is used at idea-sorting and idea-selecting steps—like Step 4, when the group needs to evaluate solutions and agree on the best one(s) for implementation.

FACILITATING COLLABORATIVE PROBLEM SOLVING

Step 1: Defining and Selecting the Problem

The output of this step is the definition and selection of a problem for further problem-solving action. This is the most important and possibly the most difficult step in the process. Poor facilitation leads to the deadly trap of identifying and defining symptoms as the real problem. This, in turn, leads to the development of a solution for the wrong problem. There's an old saying: Nothing is as useless as the right answer to the wrong question. Time spent in attempting to isolate the real problem, therefore, is time well spent.

Remember where you are at this point. The fuzzy problem statement that identifies the general problem area may have been given to you by a higher authority and now you have pulled a small problem-solving group together to begin defining and tackling the problem. Or you may have had the original feelings of discomfort. Working alone, you developed the fuzzy problem statement that is now going to be addressed by a small group of appropriate people you have selected to collaborate with you in resolving it. Finally, the fuzzy problem statement may have been determined by you and your direct reports and now, together, that same group will attempt to solve the problem. What is important to keep in mind is the idea that the fuzzy problem may arrive at your doorstep in a variety of ways. However, it is not *the problem*. How you facilitate the group from this point forward will be critical to the overall success of your problem resolution effort.

Perceive Problems as Gaps

The most vivid and accurate way to understand a problem is to view it as a gap. An excellent working definition is: *"A problem exists anytime there is a difference between a current state (as is) and a desired future state (what should be)."* For example, a problem exists when our customers are buying only 500 units a month and our strategic plan forecasted 2,000 purchases a month. Or another example, a problem exists when you and your family are in London's Heathrow Airport without your luggage, when you and your family should be in Heathrow with your luggage. Writing a good problem statement means first defining the two conditions: the as-is condition, which describes the situation as it currently exists, and the desired-future-state condition, which describes the result if the problem is successfully solved. Finally, the problem statement itself is developed. *This statement always is written in terms of, How can we close the gap between the current and the desired state?* The following example will illustrate the problem definition process.

Current state: On average, 20 percent of all sports cards we produce each month are miscut.

Desired state: Beginning with this year's new line of football cards, on average, only 0.5 percent of all sports cards produced each month are miscut.

Problem statement: How can we close the gap between our current state of having, on average, 20 percent of all sports cards produced each month be miscut *and our desired future state* where, beginning with our new football cards, only 0.5 percent of all sports cards produced each month are miscut.

Facilitating the Development of the Current Situation Statement

Using one of the divergent thinking methods presented in Chapter 10 (freewheeling or round-robin brainstorming or the index card technique), a list of 5 to 10 as-is statements is generated by the group. All ideas are listed by the scribe on flip chart paper and posted for all to see. Each rough statement is discussed and clarified. The list is refined and consolidated to eliminate duplicate or overlapping items. Next, utilizing convergent thinking as outlined in Chapter 10, you choose one of the rough as-is statements. Quite often weighted voting or multivoting is exercised to first narrow the list; then paired comparisons or consensus is used to make the final selection.

Once the rough as-is statement has been chosen, you facilitate the group in refining and modifying this item into a polished statement acceptable to all.

Here are three guidelines for developing the current state piece of the problem statement:

Do specify the extent. Our as-is description clearly specifies the extent of the current situation—on average, 20 percent of all sports cards we produce each month are miscut.

Do not specify causes. Our as-is statement does not specify that "90 percent of all miscuts are made by people with less than six weeks' service working on the manual cutting machines." We don't know that yet.

Do not specify solutions. Our as-is statement does not specify that "we need to develop a one-day skills-training program for all cutters and then create teams of experienced and inexperienced cutters on all three shifts."

Our as-is statement is well written. It makes no assumptions about who or what caused the miscuts, what should be done about the miscuts, or how terrible it is that miscuts exist. The statement is a clean, succinct description of a current situation. As officer Joe Friday would say each week on the TV show "Dragnet," "Just the facts, ma'am."

The Desired State

This is a succinct description of what the future would look like if the current state is resolved. It is like a lighthouse beacon providing constant direction throughout the gap-closing transition. The desired state should be as objective as possible so it can serve as a meaningful benchmark against which to evaluate the effectiveness of the solution implementation. In our example, we will know we have solved the problem if, beginning with the new line of football cards, on average, only 0.5 percent of all cards produced each month are miscut.

The Problem Statement Itself

While this statement is straightforward, it must be written in terms of "gap closing" since closing the gap between the current and the desired state really is the problem facing the group. By following the sentence structure *"How can we close the gap between our current state of. . . . and our desired state where . . ."* an incisive problem statement easily can be crafted.

Defining Problems as Symptoms Is Eliminated

By defining problems following the method outlined here, you virtually eliminate the single most common problem-solving mistake—defining the problem in terms of symptoms. Symptoms are the surface side effects of the real problem. The true problem usually is buried underneath a pile of symptoms. It is a grave mistake to attempt to define the problem in relation to your first dissatisfactions. The reason is that these early dissatisfactions typically are reactions to the symptoms of an underlying problem, not to the problem itself.

Let your initial dissatisfactions and your fuzzy problem statement simply be the lead-in to Step 1 of your problem-solving effort. By systematically developing a succinct situational statement of the current condition (free from expressed or implied causes and solutions), along with an objective statement of the desired future condition (the result if the problem is successfully solved), you've set up your problem as a *gap-closing* activity. At that point, by writing a problem statement focused on closing the gap between the current state and the desired future state, you have eliminated the serious error of defining the problem in terms of symptoms.

E. Schein, writing on this subject, provides insight to another dimension of this situation. Defining the problem in terms of symptoms invariably leads the group to skip over the analysis phase and to jump directly to generating solutions:

> Let's take the example of sales falling off [which is a symptom]. . . . Manager X has called together his key subordinates and they sit down to discuss "the problem" of declining sales. If the manager is not sensitive to the issue [of proper problem definition], he may soon be in the midst of a discussion of whether the advertising budget should be raised or 10 more people should be sent into the field. But has he as yet defined the problem? . . . He doesn't know what he really should be working on.[1]

An old but true axiom applies to Step 1: A problem well defined is half solved.

Several Examples of Problem Statements

Each of the following examples shows weak aspects of problem definition, the reasons a particular segment is weak, and a proper restatement of the problem.

Example 1:

> *Current state (weak):* The time to give a car a lube job and oil change at our three service centers is too long.

This is not specific enough. How long is "too long"? A proper statement would be:

> *Current state:* 28 percent of all lube-and-oil-change jobs at our three service centers take 30 minutes or more.

> *Desired state:* The response time for all lube-and-oil-change jobs is 20 minutes or less.

> *Problem statement:* How can we close the gap between our current state of having 28 percent of all lube-and-oil-change jobs taking more than 30 minutes and our desired state where all lube-and-oil-change jobs are completed in 20 minutes or less?

Example 2:

> *Current state (weak):* People are not contributing as much to the United Way Campaign this year because the economy is in a recession.

This is a cause. An economic recession is only one among many possible causes for diminished United Way contributions this year—it's not the problem. Also, this statement is not specific as to how much campaign contributions are down. A proper statement would be:

Current state: With two months remaining in our annual campaign, the dollar amount of United Way contributions is down 25 percent versus last year.

Desired state: By the end of our campaign on April 30, United Way contributions will exceed last year's dollar amount by 15 percent.

Problem statement: How can we close the gap between our current state of United Way dollar contributions running 25 percent below last year, with two months remaining in our fund drive, and our desired state of exceeding last year's dollar amount by 15 percent at the campaign's close on April 30?

Example 3:

Current state (weak): We need to change the set of universities we are currently using to recruit our new college hires.

This isn't a problem, it's a solution. What's the problem? It might lead to a different solution. A proper restatement would be:

Current state: Fifty percent of our new college hires leave the company within 18 months of being hired.

Desired state: Retain 95 percent of our new college hires for at least five years.

Problem statement: How can we close the gap between our current state of having 50 percent of our new college hires leave within 18 months of being hired and our desired state of retaining 95 percent of our new college hires for at least five years?

As you can see, both the current elements and the desired-state elements of the general problem statement are based on specific information about the problem. We call this information data. Often when writing the problem statement, you and your group will discover that you do not have enough information to make the problem statement specific. If that is the case, move on to Step 2 and collect data about the extent and nature of the current-state situation. Then, with specific information in hand, move back to Step 1 and refine the problem statement.

The as-is element of the problem statement is the most difficult piece to define since it represents a condition that is going on right now. It is dynamic, it is happening, it is real! The desired-state part of the problem is merely a condition you would like to achieve in the future and, as such, it is easier to develop. The focus for Step 2 always will be on analyzing the here and now—the current situation.

Selecting a Problem

Sometimes the group may have identified and defined several problems in the course of working through this first step. Wearing your facilitator's hat, your job is one of leading a whole-group discussion to select the problem that the team will work on, or the one it will work on first. I have found that focusing the discussion around six criteria, while by no means an exhaustive list, is an immense help in selecting a problem if you are facing several choices. The six criteria along with a few words of clarification follow.

1. *Control:* "To what extent does the group have the influence and/or authority to bring about a closing of the gap between the current state and the desired future state?"

2. *Importance:* "How much does it matter whether this problem is solved?"

3. *Difficulty:* "What is the degree of group effort required to work this problem through to a solution?"

4. *Time:* "How long will it take to resolve this problem?"

5. *Return on investment:* "What is the approximate expected payoff from solving the problem?"

6. *Resources:* "To what extent are the necessary resources to solve the problem accessible to the group (people, money, equipment, etc.)?"

You and your team may want to add or substitute other criteria. This is fine. However, if you do include any other criteria, make certain everyone agrees with and understands them. The ones shown here are guidelines providing some structure for holding a meaningful discussion around problem selection. As facilitator, don't allow the group to get bogged down in nit-picking detail or into a destructive argument over applying precise measurements to the criteria. It is no crime to move on to Step 2 and do some analysis of a chosen problem and discover that you need to return to Step 1 and either redefine the problem or choose another one to work on. Hang loose; be flexible.

Step 2: Analyzing the Problem

After a problem has been defined and selected for further work, the next phase to be facilitated is analysis. The most important thing to keep in mind throughout the second step is *the focus of the facilitation effort is on analyzing the current state to uncover the cause or causes for what exists.* With this understanding, you then will be able to look for ways to eliminate the discrepancy between what exists and what is desired.

For some problems, what we know and/or what others know may provide more than enough information to do a superb job of analyzing the problem. The gold nuggets of wisdom, accumulated over the years in the heads of people, are a powerful source of information and understanding. However, many times personal knowledge is not enough. It can be subjective, slanted, and value laden. We need factual data to supplement our personal knowledge.

Three words best describe the group effort during the analysis phase: dig, dig, dig. Giving and seeking information and opinions, proposing, and building are important interpersonal skills to emphasize at this time. Feelings and emotions can be quite strong and they must be facilitated as described in the previous chapter. Facts will be critical to developing a meaningful analysis; they will often be intertwined with feelings. Facts need to be assembled and studied after people's feelings have been heard, understood, and accepted.

Some fundamental probing questions.   Rarely will you be able to assemble all of the information you would like to have to analyze the problem. Some data may be difficult or costly to secure. Time may limit the amount of information that can be gotten together. As part of your planning process, you will help the problem-solving effort if you think through what information is needed and in what priority.

The following questions, while short and to the point, are an effective "facilitation shovel" for the digging task that needs to occur to more thoroughly understand the current as-is state.

> What is happening with respect to the current situation?

> Where and when is it occurring?

> What evidence do we have of this? (For example, identify concrete instances or examples of events that support existence of the current situation?).

> What are the dimensions (size, scope, severity) of the current situation?

> What is affected? Who is affected?

> When was the current situation first recognized as being undesirable?

> Is the current condition a unique or recurring situation?

> What similar situations have occurred in the past?

> How relevant are those past experiences to this current situation? (Did similar conditions, objectives, or ground rules apply then?)

Remember, at this point you and the team are digging, probing, clarifying; you are working together to get a better handle on the details behind the as-is state. The old standby questions of who, what, where, when, and why, as well as how many, how big, how much, and the like, are invaluable at this point. Help the group identify cause-and-effect connections between events. While not a true brainstorming session, the atmosphere should be free, open, casual, and supportive. Get thoughts, ideas, perspectives out of people's heads and recorded on flip chart paper.

A process for facilitating the nine questions.   You can make this a very powerful and dynamic activity by having each of the previous nine questions written on a separate flip chart page and posted around the room prior to starting this activity. Then, taking each question in turn, have the group members give their views and have the scribe write them down. If someone makes a good point for flip chart page 8 (similar situations that occurred in the past), while you are gathering information for flip chart page 1 (what is happening with respect to the current situation), have the scribe note that point on flip chart page 8. Then refocus attention on the flip chart page 1. Keep the information flowing, stay loose, and get everyone involved. Open the gate for quiet members.

If you or the group members want to rewrite, eliminate, or add questions to the suggested list covered here, do it. In fact, this modification activity is quite good for pulling everyone into the process and generating team ownership of the analysis. Ask group members what questions need to be answered to build a complete picture of the problem.

After the information is assembled, on the flip charts, work with the group to organize it in a form that makes sense to best answer these questions: What does it all mean? How does it all tie together? Sometimes at this stage you may discover, based on the new inputs, that what was first defined as the problem is not a good definition. Other factors may have been uncovered which force a restatement of the problem. It may be necessary to return to the first step to redefine the gap in terms of the current and the desired state. This should be accepted as a normal aspect of effective group problem solving; it does not indicate failure on your part as facilitator.

Tools to facilitate problem analysis.   The cause-and-effect diagram, the force field diagram, and the Pareto chart, all of which can be reviewed in detail in Chapter 11, are especially useful tools for Step 2. All three are simple to facilitate and provide a structured process for analyzing the problem. They are most effectively employed after you've held the probing questions discussion to help everyone understand and get within the same frame of reference regarding the as-is condition. A brief reminder of the tools is included here.

> *Cause-and-effect diagram* (the fish bone) is a systematic way of looking at an effect and the causes that contribute to that effect. Similar causes are grouped together for clarity.

> *Force field analysis* identifies those factors that both help and hinder closing the gap between the current state and the desired state.

> *Pareto chart* is an excellent way to rank order, by frequency of occurrence, the identified root causes of a problem situation. It focuses the group on the significant few causes that are the biggest contributors to the problem.

If at some point the analysis gets bogged down, call a process check to see if missing information or data are causing the stagnation. Use the group to help identify what is missing and where the information or data might be located. If need be, stop your current session and appoint the appropriate people to go off and obtain what is required. Maybe a subject matter expert (a financial analyst, a strategic planner, a quality control specialist, a person from the local community, etc.) needs to be brought to the next session to share specialized information that you and the group require to properly analyze the problem. If so, identify who is needed and get them to the next meeting.

Two deadly traps: Nit-picking versus generic fluff.   Two common traps that ensnare and destroy groups during the analysis activity are the nit-picking trap and the generic fluff trap. With nit-picking, as the analysis unfolds, the group gets entangled in destructive arguments over irrelevant microdetails. At the other extreme, with generic fluff, the group analysis is so roundly worded and superficial that it is virtually useless.

Be attuned to these two traps. Even if you, as manager or task force chairperson, miss the signals, someone is sure to eventually call a process check and complain about the stalled analysis because ''we're fighting over the irrelevant nits'' or ''we're wasting our time going through the motions of an analysis with our superficial, meaningless dialogue.'' Regardless of the source of the discovery, your task as facilitator is to move the group out of whichever trap it is in. You have two opposing strategies that you can employ to make progress—*generalizing* and *exemplifying*.

If the group is fixated on nit-picking detail, use the strategy of generalizing. Get group members to broaden their thinking by saying things like, ''The details of changing our agencywide recognition event for superior performers is not as important at this stage as understanding the pros and cons of whether or not we should even hold the event. Let's stick with this broader question for now.'' Or: ''Fighting over the wording and format to improve our performance appraisal form isn't the issue we should be addressing now. Let's refocus on the more general question of root causes of employee dissatisfaction in the accounting department.''

If the group is on a shallow, insubstantial analytical journey, use the strategy of exemplifying to correct it. Bring the members down from the clouds and get them to be more incisive in their analysis by asking for specific examples. "What do you mean by 'funny things going on'? Give me some concrete examples of funny things." Or: "I keep hearing everyone talking about lack of help. Would each of you please describe a situation you personally were involved in that exemplifies a lack of help."

Keep the discussion shifting as required from the general to the specific or vice versa to make certain a complete examination of the problem takes place.

Step 3: Generating Potential Solutions

This is the fun part, the creative, imaginative, thinking-up stage of our problem-solving process. Once the key cause or causes have been isolated, we need to search for as many ways as possible to reduce or eliminate these root causes. Remember what was said earlier: "With a problem defined as a gap between what exists and what is desired, *problem solving involves the development of solutions to reduce or eliminate the causes of the defined gap so that this gap is closed."*

Since all identified root causes rarely can be resolved at once, attack the cause, or the significant few causes, accounting for most of the gap. If you haven't done so already, a Pareto analysis would be useful at this point. The concepts of divergent and convergent thinking, as presented in Chapter 10, will play a major role at this stage. Initially, the objective is to produce as many ways as possible—including some wild ideas—to solve the problem. Later these ideas will be screened and evaluated. Remember, it is far easier to tame a wild idea than to invigorate a timid one! Throughout the entire solution generation activity, support for ideas and for those proposing them needs to be high.

Tips for facilitating Step 3. The following steps will be most helpful.

Review the results from Steps 1 and 2. Before getting on with solution generation, review the problem statement from the first step and reexamine all the data collected and analyzed in the second problem-solving step. A careful review of previous work often leads to ideas in the search for solutions.

Use brainstorming to get ideas for solutions. Brainstorming was thoroughly covered in Chapter 10. The freewheeling method is most often used at this juncture. Your main task in the role of facilitator is to review the rules of brainstorming and then assure that the group adheres to them. The scribe should record the suggestions quickly and verbatim on a flip chart.

Draw from past experience.   If things get bogged down, ask the group to compare this problem to a similar one from the past. What actions were taken? Which were effective? What might be increased, decreased, reversed, substituted, rearranged, combined, or adapted from the solutions previously generated?

Bring in additional people for your group.   The solutions-generation step is a fine opportunity to involve people outside your group. Co-workers and managers can bring insights from their level in the organization. Resource people or functional experts can bring special expertise and additional perspectives when developing very specific or technical solutions.

Help your scribe.   Test comprehension on a proposal that is technical or complex to make sure it has been heard correctly. Also, by repeating what a person says, the scribe hears it twice and has an additional few seconds to write it down. Bring on an additional scribe to another flip chart if the pace gets too fast and the original scribe can't keep up.

Keep encouraging everyone, gate-open for quiet members.   Saying things like "OK, that's nine ideas, I'm sure we are not through yet," "We're really cooking now; let's keep going," or "We're doing fine; let's see if we can't come up with five more ideas" all produce and maintain energy and momentum. Watch body language and who is not involved. Bring them in. "Art, you've always got good ideas. Toss one up on the flip chart." Or, "Carrie I can see you have an idea on the tip of your tongue; what is it?"

When you finish, congratulate the group for its effort.   "Well done. 20 solutions is a lot for a tough problem like this one. Now we've got the raw ideas to lick it." Generating a list of potential solutions takes time and energy; the group should be publicly recognized for its effort.

Step 4: Selecting and Planning the Solution

Once the list of solutions is made, it is time to evaluate them, select the best solution or set of solutions, and plan for implementation. Combining some of the potential solutions into a set of solutions, mixing and matching for the best outcome should be done at this point. A basic set of evaluation criteria needs to be used to assure that each potential solution gets a fair hearing. Playing favorites at this point is counterproductive.

Selecting the solution.   The question at the forefront of this half of Step 4 is: What is the *best* way to close the gap between our current situation and our desired future state? Even though a particular solution may not work on its own, it may have elements that are good. Take the time to combine the good parts of various ideas; then each final alternative should be carefully, critically evaluated. As in Step 1, a simple, generic set of criteria can be used as the evaluation filter.

A word of caution: To avoid paralysis by analysis, don't agonize over very small differences between options, particularly if those differences are smaller than the group's ability to evaluate reliably.

At this point, wearing your facilitator's hat, your job is one of leading a whole group discussion on the criteria to be used in selecting the solution. Use the suggested set which follows as a starting point. While not exhaustive, this list has stood the test of time and experience as a worthy, meaningful set.

The six criteria, along with a few words of clarification, are shown here.

1. *Control:* "To what extent can implementation of this solution be managed or significantly influenced by the group?"

2. *Appropriateness:* "To what extent does this solution solve the problem by closing the gap between the current and desired state?"

3. *Resources:* "To what extent are the necessary resources to implement this solution (e.g., people, money, equipment) accessible to the group?"

4. *Time:* "How long will it take to implement this solution?"

5. *Acceptability:* "To what extent will the people impacted by this solution, buy into it?"

6. *Return on investment:* "What is the expected payoff from implementing this solution?"

Just as you might do with the problem selection criteria discussed earlier in this chapter, you and your team may want to add or substitute other criteria. This is perfectly acceptable. If you do include any other criteria, make certain there is a consensus around both their definition and the desire to include them as part of the decision process. The list provided here is a great foundation and can be used in most situations without any alterations. In any case, a simple set of criteria provides focus and structure to the solution selection discussion that is fundamental to any problem-solving process.

Step 4 (continued): Planning the Solution for Implementation

Unless the selected solution is converted into action, it has very little value. The second half of Step 4, therefore, is to plan how the solution should be put into effect and monitored.

The following guidelines will help you in your process of solution planning:

> Specify and clarify the tasks that must be done—this includes obtaining any approvals required from others outside the team to move ahead.

> Sequence those tasks—decide on the order in which they should be done.

> Assess the requirements for each task—who is needed to do what? How long should it take?

> Establish a schedule, with completion dates for each task or activity.

> Make sure everyone knows who is responsible for each task.

> Establish a control system—set up a simple monitoring system to track whether or not specific tasks are being performed or short-term targets are being achieved as planned.

> Use the desired future-state of the problem statement as the constant goal against which the effectiveness of the solution is always being measured.

Step 5: Implementing the Solution

This step consists of carrying out the action plan developed during the second phase of Step 4. To make sure the blueprint for implementation is adhered to, progress needs to be monitored. A useful checklist to help monitor implementation includes: (1) the tasks involved in implementing the solution, (2) resource assignments to the tasks, and (3) dates by which the tasks are to be accomplished. Also, the team needs to remember to collect the necessary data for evaluating the effectiveness of the solution.

Life in the real world, being as complex as it is, means sooner or later the implementation plan will need to be modified, and contingency plans set in motion, as unforeseen difficulties or opportunities appear. The experienced team expects this, does not get too upset when it happens, and gets on with whatever corrective actions are possible.

Step 6: Evaluating the Solution

Once the solution is in place, the team may think the problem-solving job is finished. Not true. The team is responsible for obtaining direct feedback on the implementation outcome in order to determine whether the proposed solution actually solved the problem.

The process is not complicated. As facilitator you need to help the team collect data on its results and compare this information with the desired-state portion of the problem statement created in Step 1. This comparison will indicate if the team has met its goal. In reality, most solutions are a mixed bag. They are neither tremendous flops nor stellar successes. Typically, some elements of the solution are implemented better than others; this is to be expected. However, knowing the condition of the implementation effort at all times enables the team to make improvements or modifications that will help solve the problem.

If the desired state is not satisfactorily achieved, then you may need to begin the problem-solving process over again (this is why the PSP is drawn as a continuous wheel). Even if the desired state has been met, you need to help the team continue to monitor the situation to make sure: (1) that the solution continues to work, and (2) no new problems are created by the solution itself. Finally, care must be taken in this step to avoid creating a bureaucratic nightmare or cumbersome systems for checking the checkers.

Step 6, then, closes the loop on the problem-solving wheel because it centers on evaluating the success of the solution and deciding whether or not further problem solving is necessary. Without evaluation, we have no objective way of knowing whether our solution was a success, to what extent it was a success, and whether or not it may have led to a new problem.

THE TELEPHONE OPERATORS: AN INTEGRATIVE CASE STUDY[2]

This case study demonstrates how the problem-solving process works. The case presented here is based on the initiatives of the manager of support services and her team of six telephone operators at the home office of a large insurance company. The six operators were divided into three pairs, with each pair located at one of three separate stations. Each station served a major division of the company, but they were all on the same floor of a sprawling office complex. Each operator handled roughly 100 calls per day, meaning the team handled approximately 600 calls per day. Besides simply answering the phone and routing calls, the operators were trained to answer many basic and recurring questions about the insurance products offered by the firm.

Customer satisfaction surveys administered by the insurance company indicated that customers tended to become angry when the phone was answered after the third ring, or when they were placed on hold for more than 30 seconds after the operator answered and attempted to route their call. These surveys also revealed that, on average, 18.5 percent of all customers calling on a given day (i.e., 111 callers) experienced at least one delay with their call. A delay was defined as either having one's call answered after the third ring, or being placed on hold for 30 seconds or more as the operator attempted to route the call to the appropriate party.

The survey results caught the manager of support services by surprise and thus acted as the problem-sensing stimulus. She thought, "We have a mess on our hands." In addition, because the telephone operators realized they often were making the all-important first impression on potential customers (as well as continued impressions on current customers), the whole team decided to use a systematic process to tackle the fuzzy problem—"Why do we keep customers waiting?" The support services manager, besides being an active participant in all discussions, also accepted the role of primary facilitator.

Step 1: Defining and Selecting the Problem

The team's initial meeting to define the problem resulted in the following statements:

Current state: Surveys show that, on average, 18.5 percent of all customers calling on a given day experience a telephone delay— customer call answered after the third ring, or customer placed on hold for 30 seconds or more while call is being routed.

Desired state: Only 3 percent of all customers calling on a given day experience a telephone delay.

Problem statement: How can we close the gap between our *current state* of having 18.5 percent of our customers calling on a given day experiencing a telephone delay and our *desired state* of having only 3 percent of our customers experiencing a telephone delay.

Once the problem statement was written, it became a motivating factor for the team. Now they all could see that solving this problem would bring about a *sixfold decrease* in angry, waiting customers.

Step 2: Analyzing the Problem

In another session, the support services manager facilitated the team in a discussion of the present system for answering and routing calls, and the potential reasons for making the customer wait. To do this, she facilitated a cause-and-effect analysis, brainstorming all possible causes. The result is shown in Figure 13–2.

Because the team of operators did not have information indicating which factors were the most likely causes, they devised checklists to record the number of delayed calls over a four-week period along with the reason for the delay. The most common causes of customers kept waiting were shown to be:

FIGURE 13–2
Cause-and-Effect Diagram of Telephone Delays That Keep Customers Waiting

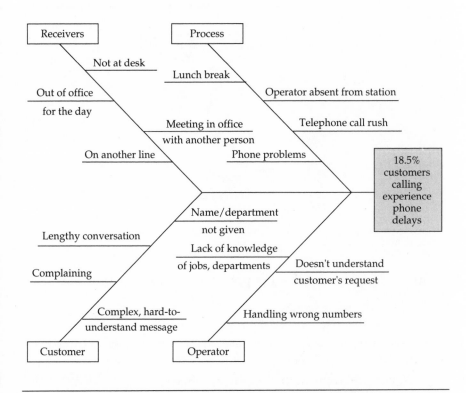

A. Only one operator at a given station instead of two.

B. Receiving party not available to take the call.

C. Department/name of the receiving party not known or given.

D. Telephone call rush.

E. Other.

This checklist data then was arranged in a Pareto chart to rank-order the causes in terms of significance. The chart in Figure 13–3 clearly indicates that one-half of the delays occurred when one of the two division operators was not on duty at her station.

Step 3: Generating Potential Solutions

At their third meeting, the support services manager led her team in a brainstorming exercise that generated a number of potential

FIGURE 13–3

Causes of Telephone Delays Ranked by Significance Before Action Plan Implementation

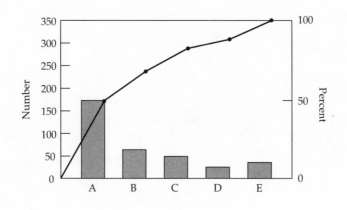

solutions designed to solve the primary causes of the problem. Their suggestions:

1. Set up and staff two new operator stations.

2. Make certain two operators are always on duty at all three stations.

3. Have employees notify operators when leaving desks or being out of earshot of ringing phone.

4. Teach operators how to politely cut off long-winded callers.

5. Get a new phone system with better features.

6. Eliminate all operator stations; give all employees a direct line.

7. Complete a directory of staff members, job titles, and phone numbers—update bimonthly.

Step 4: Selecting and Planning the Solution

As the fourth meeting began, the team was taking each of the seven potential solutions from the previous session and testing each one against six common criteria often used to help select solutions: team control, appropriateness, resources required, time required, acceptability, and return on investment.

At the conclusion of the exercise, the team reached a consensus on three actions to implement:

2. Two operators always on duty.

3. Employees notify operators when leaving desk.

7. Compile a directory and update bimonthly.

Next, to make their recommendations viable, the team set about developing an integrated action plan to smoothly implement the three solutions.

1. To ensure there were always two operators on duty at each station, the team developed a plan for a three-phase lunch break instead of the current two-phase break. This reduced, from three to two, the number of open switchboard positions requiring coverage during each lunch break phase. This made coverage easier since only two administrative staff members were needed at any one time to give lunch breaks.

2. To encourage employees to leave messages when they were to be away from their desks, their cooperation was requested at their regular staff meetings. Posters also were placed around the offices in each division to publicize the new practice.

3. Finally, the team took responsibility for the development and production of the initial directory, as well as responsibility for the bimonthly updates. The directory was designed especially to help the operators quickly and accurately locate the appropriate employee for a given incoming call.

Step 5: Implementing the Solution

The team's plan was approved by the senior staff and implemented as laid out.

Step 6: Evaluating the Solution

In order to evaluate their solution set, the team collected additional data regarding telephone delays three months after action plan implementation. The results are shown in the Pareto chart, Figure 13-4.

The total number of delayed calls was dramatically reduced to around 17–18 per day. This meant the desired state of 3 percent delays out of an average of 600 calls per day had been achieved! Furthermore, no other new problems arose as a result of implementing the current action plan. This case is an excellent example of having a work unit manager unleash the collective genius of her team to solve a critical business problem.

FIGURE 13–4
Cause of Telephone Delays Ranked by Significance after Implementation of Action Plan

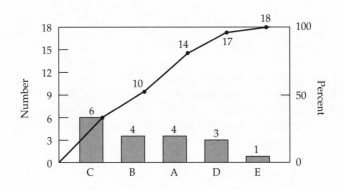

A CLOSING SUMMARY

As Figure 13–1 shows, the problem-solving process steps are in the shape of a wheel. This indicates the continuous flow of systematic, collaborative problem solving—the need often to cycle back to the beginning to refine and rework the original solution set after its initial implementation. A brief review of each step is provided here as a refresher.

Step 1: Defining and Selecting the Problem

During Step 1, the problem is first viewed as the difference between some current condition (as is) and some future condition (what should be). The problem statement defining the problem to be solved is written in terms of "How do we close the gap between our current state and our desired future state?"

Given a set of defined problems and the ability to tackle them only one at a time, commonly used selection criteria for choosing a problem are: control, importance, difficulty, time, return on investment, and resources. Step 1 is extremely important because through this process initial team member internalization, enthusiasm, and commitment to the problem are being secured.

Step 2: Analyzing the Problem

During this step, you and your team identify, collect, and analyze data to confirm that the identified problem is real. You work to verify that the key causes are supported by your data analysis. The same data may also indicate when and where the problem is most serious. Cause-and-effect diagrams, force field analysis, and Pareto charts are very useful tools of analysis at this stage.

Step 3: Generating Potential Solutions

This is the dynamic, energizing, fun part of problem solving. In Step 3, you facilitate the team in generating, building, and combining creative solutions through the process of brainstorming. The final list of potential solutions is reviewed and clarified so all members understand each one.

In your facilitation role, you need to concentrate on maintaining the rules of brainstorming, helping your scribe, encouraging people to participate, gate-opening for quiet members, and recognizing the group for its effort when the job is completed.

Step 4: Selecting and Planning the Solution

Step 4 begins with developing criteria for evaluating each potential solution. Experience has shown useful criteria to be: control, appropriateness, resource availability, time, acceptability, and return on investment. The criteria are used to judge each solution and help highlight the best solution(s). Finally, a plan is developed to implement the solution(s). Along with the steps for carrying out the solution(s), the plan should include a strategy for getting managerial approvals, contingency plans, and a way to measure the success of the solution in solving the problem.

Step 5: Implementation

During Step 5, the plan developed in the previous step is carried out. The progress of the plan is monitored, data for evaluating the effectiveness of the solution is collected, and contingency plans are implemented as required.

Step 6: Evaluating the Solution

In Step 6, the problem-solving wheel is completed by evaluating the solution and checking for new problems created by the solution. If any new problems arise, the problem-solving process needs to begin anew.

NOTES WORKSHEET: DEVELOP WRITTEN
RESPONSES TO THE TWO ITEMS LISTED BELOW

What Do You Feel Are the Main Learning Points from Chapter 13?	Elaborate on Why You Feel These Points Are Key

NOTES

1. E. Schien, *Process Consultation,* Vol. 1, *Its Role in Organization Development* (Reading, MA: Addison-Wesley Publishing, 1988), pp. 62–63.

2. The case study presented here is one I have adapted and expanded from a much shorter and simpler version found in "Statistical Quality Control Tools: An Overview for Managers," in *Effectiveness through Involvement Series* (internal publication, Xerox Corporation, Stamford, CT, July 1982), pp. 18–20. I have used my version of the case for many years to provide managers with a simple, concrete example of the six-step problem-solving process in action.

INTEGRATING WHAT'S BEEN LEARNED

Chapter 14

Human Resources Redeployment
An Integrative Case Study

Chapter Objectives

> To use a work example as a means for demonstrating the manager's use of a variety of facilitation tools, techniques, and processes presented throughout this book.

> To highlight the power of secondary facilitation in action.

INTRODUCTION

The case you are about to read is the transcript of a meeting involving Mel, a company president, and the seven individuals who report to him directly. The company is a small consumer electronics firm with an established name in the marketplace. This session has been called by Mel to decide how to handle nine surplus engineers who will be without a job in six weeks when their canceled project (Ramrod) shuts down. Ramrod was this firm's competitive response to the Sony Walkman.

The names and positions of the team members: Mel, company president; Tom, manager of engineering; Kate, manager of quality assurance; Bill, manager of manufacturing; Andrew, manager of finance; Randall, manager of strategic planning; Joanne, manager of marketing; and Deonne, manager of human resources.

As you read the case, pay particular attention to how Mel moves between his two roles of primary facilitator (focused on group process) and group member (focused on the session's content). Notice how he sets the stage for the discussion. Above all, be alert to how he uses the tools and processes described in this book. While he does a good job overall, he is not perfect; there are some things he could have done better. Also keep an eye on the other members of Mel's group and try to identify good examples of secondary facilitation where they help the group process as well as examples where they hinder and disrupt the group process.

Finally I have included my comments down the right-hand side of the page as a way to bridge back to the key learning points from the previous chapters. For your first or second reading of the case you may want to cover my comments and immerse yourself by making your own notes at various points throughout the dialogue. Have fun with this case. Pretend you are sitting in a corner watching the group operate. What do you see? What feedback would you give the group members regarding the things they did well? In order to improve, what would you challenge them to do differently next time?

"What to Do with Our Surplus Engineers, That Is the Question"

Mel: Okay. Well, I'm glad you all were able to make time for this important meeting. I know you are all busier than "one-armed paper hangers." [While flipping back a blank page to reveal a prewritten flip chart page, Mel points to the different items as he speaks.] The purpose of today's session is: to share and process information relative to redeploying nine surplus engineers from the canceled Ramrod project. The desired outcome is: consensus on which new jobs all nine engineers will be redeployed into when Ramrod shuts down in six weeks. Regarding roles, I'll be the primary facilitator for this session; the rest of you, of course, have the role of secondary facilitators. Bill, would you take the minutes and note any action items that arise.

An excellent beginning. The purpose, desired outcomes, and agenda all were prewritten, posted, and reviewed right upfront. He also used a nice mixture of two processes in setting roles. Mel selected a minute taker and asked for a volunteer to be the timekeeper. He also made it clear everyone was to act as secondary facilitators.

The one concern I have at this point is the feasibility of redeploying nine engineers in one 90 minute session. Mel may have underestimated the complexity and emotion of this issue.

Bill: Sure.

Giving information.

Mel: The meeting is scheduled for 90 minutes so we are going to need a timekeeper. Any volunteers?

Seeking information.

Joanne: I'd be happy to do that. I haven't been timekeeper for a while.

Giving information.

Mel: Good. Why don't you give us a time check with 60, 30, and 5 minutes to go.

Encouraging. Proposing.

Joanne: You've got it.

Agreeing.

Mel: Excellent! You'll see on the agenda the first five minutes are set aside for Tom to review the background and issues of the Ramrod cancellation. Then we have 75 minutes to process information as a whole group in reaching consensus on the jobs the engineers will move into. Finally, we'll use the last 10 minutes to review decisions, action items, and do a meeting evaluation. Any issues with the purpose, desired outcome, roles, or agenda for this session?

Checking back with the group to make sure everyone is on-board and committed to the meeting's direction. Anyone with a differing perspective has an opportunity to speak up.

All: Nope. Sounds fine to me. We need to do this. Let's get going.

No one questioned the feasibility of the desired outcome so let the proceedings begin.

Mel: You all got the memo I sent out yesterday officially canceling the Ramrod project. Engineering has been working ·behind the scenes with Human Resources for the past several days to lay some groundwork for this session. What I'd like to do now is give Tom his time to fill in everyone on the key particulars of the cancellation. Tom.

Giving information.

Gate-opening for Tom.

Tom: Thanks, Mel. Let me get right down to the nitty gritty. We have had to cancel the Ramrod project for three very good reasons. First, we had serious reliability problems with the product. Second, our unit manufacturing costs were 50 percent

Giving information.

The information giving has a hard-sell edge to it. But that would be natural since these are Tom's people and he cares about them.

higher than Sony's. Third, Magna-vox and Pioneer beat us to market and will unveil well-featured, com-petitively priced products next week at the Consumer Electronics Show-case in New Orleans. What this means is that there are now nine good engineers that no longer have a job on this project. And with the current dynamics of the engineering reorganization and the head count reductions, I cannot absorb these people in any of my on-going proj-ects. The best I could do is down-grade them and stick them in the en-gineering services unit, which is way beneath their skill level. All of these engineers are average to superior performers. My main concern right now is that we redeploy them as quickly as possible, with no reduc-tion in salary or grade level. Deonne has some thoughts to share based on our work yesterday. Deonne.

Gate-opening for Deonne.

Deonne: Okay. You all have the package I hand carried to each of you yesterday—the folder containing the personal histories of all nine engi-neers and the worksheet to help you rank-order the engineers according to your individual needs. I know most of you have openings so my idea is that I'd like to go around the table and see where we have matches.

Giving information.
Proposing.

The creation and distribution of prework by Deonne was a form of secondary facili-tation. The team members got to study the backgrounds of the engineers and make some initial selections before com-ing to the meeting. This saved precious in-session processing time.

Mel: Well, before we do that, let me put on my president's hat and re-mind you of the suitable openings we have within the other functions. We've got 3 positions in quality as-surance, 1 in finance, 2 in marketing, 8 in Seattle in the manufacturing

Good role modeling of "hat switching" from facilitator (process) to president/ group member (content).

Giving information.

area, and 10 here locally in the Minneapolis plant.

Kate: OK, of the three positions I have in quality assurance, two of them I haven't matched yet, but one of them is a sure fit with Dick Dutton. I've worked with him before; he's a strong performer with a statistical background and computer expertise. He's a natural for my QA project manager position. Also, I see from his personal history he has a developmental inkling that way. So mark me down for Dutton.

Giving information

A well thought-out selection.

Bill: Mel, I'm confused. Things are moving too quickly. I'd like to suggest to keep things clearer, Tom, could you record on the flip chart each function and the number of openings it has? Also leave room to write in names as each function selects someone.

Excellent example of secondary facilitation. Intervening to help the group process.

Tom: Good idea; I wish I had thought of that. Mel, will you give me the functions and number of openings again so I can record them?

Encouraging.
Seeking information.

Mel: Sure. [Mel repeats the earlier information while Tom records.]

Giving information.

Tom: Now, Kate, you said you wanted Dick Dutton for a QA project manager position, so I'll write his name next to one of your openings, OK?

Test comprehension.

Another nice piece of secondary facilitation to make certain the written information was correct.

Kate: Right on.

Giving information (confirming).

Joanne: Let me try something on you. I have two sales openings in the field and it occurs to me that a techni-

Proposing.
Giving information.

cal background is not a bad idea. It might be a very useful skill for selling some of our more sophisticated audio and video equipment. How about Ruth Walsh? I'd be willing to take her. And Jon English looks good to me.

Tom: Ruth Walsh and Jon English to fill the two sales slots. Great!

Summarizing.
Positive feelings.

Andrew: [Forcefully] Hey, wait a minute! The only person I could possibly use in finance is Jon English. In looking over his paperwork, I see he has an MBA. I've been looking for someone to slip into a financial analyst position. I think this guy would be perfect. I wouldn't have to spend forever retraining him.

Disagreeing.
Giving information.
Giving opinions.

Joanne: Fine. If you want English you can have him. This Bob Cline— he's that young guy from MIT right? I'd be willing to put a young, aggressive engineer on my sales force. Tom, make it Ruth Walsh and Bob Cline for me.

Giving information.

Swapping people around like they are interchangeable robots.

Tom: [As he writes on the flip chart] Let me see if I've got this straight. Finance will take Jon English and marketing will take Ruth Walsh and Bob Cline, right?

Secondary facilitation.
Testing comprehension.

Andrew and *Joanne:* [Together] Right.

Giving information (confirming).

Bill: That accounts for four of them. I'll take the other five. I'm desperate to fill four of my Seattle foreman openings. I could start these guys tomorrow if I could get them, and I have a key maintenance supervisor slot here in Minneapolis. I

Giving information.
Giving opinions.

think the engineering background for all of these positions will be super; it will really help the manufacturing line. It's a real job opportunity for most of them.

Randall: [Says nothing, but body language indicates frustration and disgust.]

Tom: Great! This is terrific, because that means we have been able to redeploy my nine engineers into these other organizations. And we did it in all of five minutes. I'm very pleased. I think this is one of the greatest accomplishments our group has made. We have been able to get through a very divisive issue with no conflict. I feel great. Thank you very much.

Positive feelings.
Encouraging.

Tom may feel terrific; however, the process was too easy. No critical thinking! This was a "cattle auction." It's a perfect example of groupthink. No thought has been given to the longer-term consequences of these decisions.

Deonne: Me too! It makes me feel good too! I don't often get the opportunity to see line managers working so enthusiastically on a personnel issue.

Encouraging.
Everything is "peaches and cream," or is it? Randall hasn't said a word yet. What is he feeling? Mel, as primary facilitator, should have picked up on this and gate-opened for Randall. Since he has obviously missed the boat on this key facilitation intervention, anyone as secondary facilitator could do it. The whole team is asleep at the switch.

Group: [In chorus, except for Randall] Yes! Who needs team building? Right! We are a team! Excellent teamwork!

Randall has now pushed away from the table and is aloof to the self-congratulatory hubbub. He is agitated and it's obvious he wants to say something but he remains quiet.

Mel: Now let me slip on my facilitator's hat and test my comprehension of this decision to make sure we have consensus. We've canceled the Ramrod project. We've got nine engineers to redeploy. Kate, you've taken Dick

Another good example of hat switching.

Summarizing on the way to testing comprehension.

Dutton. Joanne, you're going to take Jon English—no, that's not right, Jon is going to finance. Joanne, you're going to take Ruth Walsh and Bob Cline. The other five . . .

Joanne: Well, I'm wiling to give Cline a try.

Gate-closing Mel. Giving information. Qualifying her decision already.

Mel: Well, sure. And I think if he's as aggressive as his paperwork looks like, he probably can do the job there. Then we're going to slot the other five people into manufacturing—four in Seattle and one in the Minneapolis operation. Is that right?

Summarizing and testing comprehension used in combination; well done.

Group: [In unison, except for Randall] Yes. You're right. That's got it. We're done.

Agreement and harmony among all but one.

Mel: Good! Well, we've got consensus then. Why don't we wrap this up and get back to work. We've saved close to an hour and ten minutes.

Wow! A major blunder. Mel got caught in the hubbub trap of assumed consensus. He's sure he has consensus but Randall never said a word. You can only test for consensus one way—go around the table, one-by-one, and ask each person in turn to declare support or nonsupport for the course of action being decided.

If Randall doesn't gate-open for himself, the team has made a poorly thought-out, groupthink decision, by assumed consensus with one member totally noncommitted to the outcome. It indicates how easy it is to ignore the silent person.

Randall: [Angrily, with eyes darting around the table looking at everyone] Hold on! Time out! You people are all crazy! You're not thinking clearly about this thing. Don't break your arms patting yourselves on your backs. You've made a lousy decision and I won't be a party to it.

Performance checking. Disagreeing. Mild attacking. Giving opinions. Giving information. Asking rhetorical questions. Seeking information from Deonne via a direct question.

A powerful piece of critical thinking. *Randall had the courage to stand up to*

You're playing with people's careers and lives. You're making decisions about these people that—I don't know if the people would make these same decisions for themselves. [Now with passion] These are engineering people that have gone to school and gotten engineering degrees. They've gone into an engineering job and here we are making salesmen out of them, manufacturing people, quality assurance people. But the question is, What would they say? Have we involved the people in this process? We are talking about uprooting families, moving them halfway across the country. What would the people say? Deonne, have the people even had a chance to comment on this?

all the group members and challenge them. If he hadn't, the group would be revisiting the whole decision again under the emotional fire of those engineers who were not happy about their dictated fate. Randall confronted the team and forced it to think about the consequences now.

Not everyone will be as strong as Randall and challenge the group. That is why everyone must be alert to gate-open for quiet members throughout the discussion. Listen, understand what they are saying. Critical thinking is a precious group resource.

Deonne: [Caught off-guard, stammering] Well, uhm, not really, actually, a, ahem, no. I guess maybe we have gotten the cart before the horse. As human resources manager I certainly support including them in the process. I guess I didn't realize that everyone would pitch in and help and it would go as smoothly and easily as it did.

Giving information.

Tom: Well, Randall, you've made some excellent points. And now that you mention it, I think that we did jump to a quick solution like we are prone to do. Now I have serious reservations about the decision I agreed to just five minutes ago. Randall, I'm on your side.

Encouraging, supporting Randall.

Randall's critical thinking has changed Tom's view of the decision he thought was so wonderful a few minutes ago.

Randall: Good, good.

Supporting.

Joanne: Performance check, we have 60 minutes left on the clock.

Time check.

Mel: Thanks, Joanne.   *Supporting.*

Bill: [Exasperated, indignant] We   *Disagreeing.*
don't have time to redo this. I have   *Giving information.*
products I have to get out the door.
I need those four engineers in Seattle
just as I said. I could put them to
work tomorrow if I had them.

Kate: [Sarcastically, glaring at Ran-   *Disagreeing.*
dall] You want quality in your prod-   *Attacking.*
ucts? Come on, man, chill out. Dut-
ton is perfect.

Andrew: [Firmly.] As you're finan-   *Giving information. Showing support*
cial manager, I'd like to remind you   *for the original position.*
that having those people not quickly
redeployed, having them sitting
around after six weeks doing nothing, will cost us big bucks.

Kate: That's right!   *Agreement.*

Joanne: [Displeased, looking across   *Giving information.*
the table at Tom and Randall] Look,
I need my people now. I understand
where you two are coming from, but
we're talking about . . .

Mel: [In response to an excited side   *Primary facilitator handling disruptive*
conversation between Kate and Bill   *behavior. Keeping the group focused.*
about the stupidity of discussing this
further] We have two meetings go-   *Emotions are running high but no one is*
ing on. The subject is important   *getting vicious or personal. Mel is letting*
enough that we should all be paying   *the catharsis flow, allowing people to get*
attention to what is being said. Jo-   *their feelings out. Good strategic facilita-*
anne has the floor.   *tion.*

Joanne: Thank you, Mel. The point   *Giving information.*
I was making was we're talking
about a lot of sales available. If we   *Again hedging her bets with the new*
don't get these sales, someone else   *people. She says she understands the*
will. I understand what you're say-   *other side, but does she really?*
ing, but let's be reasonable. I need
these people now and I'm going to

hire them. If you want me to be help-ful—these are, with all due respect, kind of "iffy" performers. I'd be happy to give them a try. I'm trying to be a team player, but I can't wait for six weeks while you, Tom, daw-dle around shutting down Ramrod. [Tom just glares at Joanne, says nothing.]

Where did all the earlier harmony and cohesion go? Mel is going to have to in-tervene soon and facilitate through this conflict.

Bill: [Heatedly] I don't understand what the problem is. We as a com-pany pay their relocation costs; we pay for them and their family to go out and look for houses . . .

Feelings. Giving information to defend his position.

Tom: [Rankled and angry, slap-ping the table] You're looking at this as strictly a *business* decision! What about the people? You're wearing blinders. You're only looking at the business . . .

Gate-closing Bill. Feelings, countering Bill's defense. Starting to get a little per-sonal.

Bill: [Very worked up] This *is* a business! And if we don't start running it like a business and con-tinue to turn a profit, we're all going to be standing in the unem-ployment . . .

Gate-closing Tom. Feelings starting to get out of hand.

Mel: Hey, Bill, Tom. Let's hold it and see if we all can't get back on track. I've heard everything every-one has said. Speaking to you with my president's hat on, if it wasn't for Randall bringing us up short, we would have made a dumb decision. I share in what happened earlier—I facilitated us into a groupthink, as-sumed consensus, decision. The proof of the importance of Randall's critical thinking is the emotional con-frontation it has generated. I agree with Randall and Tom that we need to involve the people. We don't have

Productive gate-closing.

Performance check. Giving information. Owning up to his mistake in facilitating the earlier groupthink decision. Nothing will help build an open, collaborative cli-mate faster for everyone than the manag-er's admission that he or she made a mis-take. Mel also does a nice piece of hat switching to give his position on the involvement issue. We know where he stands, but it wasn't a dictate.

the right to make arbitrary decisions about people's lives and careers.

Now, let me switch to my facilitator's hat and summarize what I'm hearing after we strip away the emotional heat. What I hear developing are three very distinct camps. One camp, Randall, Tom, Deonne, and myself argue that we must involve the engineers in the decision about where they are redeployed. A second camp, Kate, Bill, Joanne, those who have openings, want people tomorrow because they are under the gun and shorthanded. They aren't willing to wait six weeks. A third camp is Andrew. As manager of finance, he reminds us that we've got a financial issue here, a cost problem; we can't afford to pay these people to be idle after Ramrod shuts down. We've got to have them relocated; we can't afford to have them on the payroll without producing.

Super hat switch back to facilitation. In his whole flow of comments, we know precisely when he was operating from his group member role and from his facilitator role.

Beautiful job of summarizing. The random unstructured arguments are brought into sharp relief. Mel sorts the problem into three parts and states each one in situational—not behavioral— terms. He could never have performed this valuable facilitation service if he wasn't hanging back, watching, listening, and monitoring the rather heated discussion.

Now, I'm not hearing any consensus coming together around here. Our task as a team is to quit fighting amongst ourselves and collaborate in searching for a solution that can accommodate all three camps.

With this commentary, Mel has facilitated the session from feelings into facts (with his three camps summary) and is now moving the group into the collaborative solutions phase.

Tom: [Emphatically] Right! We have six weeks to work with. We don't need to make a final decision today. Those six weeks are like money in the bank; they give us flexibility.

Giving information. Reviewing a fact and using it as the foundation for solutions. Good insight.

Bill: [Forcefully, but in a much calmer tone] I realize getting people tomorrow is out of the question. But I would hope I could get some of them before six weeks are up.

Bill has calmed down and tempers his viewpoint. Collaboration is beginning.

Joanne: I agree with Bill; I feel exactly the same way. I want to do right by the people, but we must set some limits to their involvement. We are running a business, don't forget.

Supporting. Acknowledges she has people's interests at heart, but reminds group about the business side of things.

Kate: I don't want to force someone to take a job they don't want; however, I can't let my QA positions go unfilled for eternity while employee involvement anarchy reigns.

Giving information. Uses exaggeration to make her point.

Tom: [In a friendly, teasing tone] I can see the movie billboard now. Three empty desks and chairs with cobwebs in the foreground and a dozen people beating on each other with micrometers, statistical notebooks, and rolled up control charts in the background. Then in big flaming red letters across the picture: "Don't miss it! QA positions go unfilled for eternity while employee involvement anarchy reigns."

Tension relieving. Picks up on Kate's exaggeration. Nicely placed, appropriate, well timed.

Group: Much laughter.

Tension release.

Andrew: [Poking Tom] You're in the wrong business; you should be working in Hollywood. Look, I believe in employee involvement. But let's face it—the process of involving employees in decision making can be very time-consuming. If you involve them in this instance, you're going to go beyond six weeks. I merely want to point out, when you go beyond six weeks, every month you have these people sitting around doing nothing is going to cost us in excess of $35,000.

A humorous retort. The tension has been fully broken. Andrew reiterates his point that for financial reasons the process can't go beyond six weeks.

Randall: I understand the business issues. All I'm saying, and Tom brought up the point earlier, is that

Giving information and building. He clarifies and extends the value of having time available to involve the engineers.

if we have six weeks, why not use part of the time to have them give us some input into their destiny and let's make this decision based on what they want to do. It may turn out that some of these decisions are correct and the people are happy. Why don't we ask them what they want to do? And let me be clear: I don't want the process to go beyond six weeks.

He also supports Andrew on not allowing the process to go beyond six weeks.

Tom: Neither do I.

Information giving, supporting Andrew and Randall. The group is coming together.

Deonne: I'm hearing something very interesting that I want to test with everyone. First, underneath our differing positions, we have agreement around the common interests of wanting to do right by the people while still making a good business decision. That's one point. Second, getting specific, Bill, Joanne, and Kate support employee involvement so long as they can start getting people before the six weeks are up. Randall, Tom, Mel, and myself are urging employee involvement but want a good business decision; we don't want this thing to go beyond six weeks. Andrew, citing the financial implications, supports employee involvement only if we can *guarantee* that everyone is placed before Ramrod terminates. Have I got it right?

Superb secondary facilitation. Harmonizing. This is the breakthrough statement of the entire session. Deonne draws from the managing differences model. She goes beyond positions by focusing on interests and summarizes the general areas of agreement that have formed. She also tests comprehension on the specific areas of agreement around common interests.

Deonne has crystallized the entire discussion at this point.

[Deonne tests her interpretation by going around the table and asking everyone if she has correctly stated their interests. Each person confirms she has hit the nail on the head.]

Explicit test of consensus.

Mel: Well that piece of secondary facilitation really brings everything into focus for me.

Encouraging, recognizing how Deonne has helped his own thinking.

Joanne, how much time is left?

Informaiton seeking.

Joanne: Thirty-five minutes.

Information giving.

Mel: Thanks. Speaking from my role as president, it's obvious we have a lot more than thirty-five minutes worth of work to do. Based on Deonne's observations and her confirmation of our common interests, I propose the following process. I'd like Bill, Randall, and Andrew to join with Deonne and work out a redeployment plan that meets three specific criteria:

1. The total plan must be 100 percent implementable within six weeks.

2. The plan must involve all nine engineers in the decision-making process for a portion of the six weeks. This will give them a chance to voice their ideas and concerns on when, where, and how they would like to be redeployed.

3. The initial roll-off of engineers must begin before six weeks, the sooner the better, so that Bill, Joanne, and Kate can start filling their critical vacancies ASAP. It may be that a few engineers won't be available until the full six weeks have elapsed. If that's the case, we'll just roll with it.

Hat switching again from facilitator to group manager. As manager, Mel makes a proposal to have a subgroup develop a plan that accommodates everyone's interests. The interests are stated as the three criteria for the plan. The group is now totally focused on a collaborative effort to achieve consensus. Mel also checks back with the group to see if anyone is dissatisfied with his proposal.

Also, notice that Mel—as manager—has taken charge and made decisions about how to proceed while still keeping a collaborative process intact. He made an autocratic decision on how to move forward—which is his right as the manager—but he certainly was heavily influenced by the group discussion over the past 55 minutes. Finally, Mel made certain that everyone's interests were accommodated in his proposal to ensure the group's commitment and emotional support to make it work.

Mel: Time is short. Today is Wednesday. I'd like to reconvene the whole group on Monday at 1:00 in this room. At that time, we'll all review and refine the subgroup's plan and collaborate to get consensus on a final course of action. Any questions or issues on the proposal?

A good example of using a committee from the whole group to do preliminary work and reach a consensus, then using the work and consensus of the small group as a springboard to consensus within the whole group.

Randall: It'll be tight but we can do it.

Support.

Deonne: I'm OK with it.

Support.

Andrew: We gotta do it.

Support.

Bill: Andrew, Deonne, Randall, and I represent all three positions and special interests. If we put our heads together, I'm certain we can come up with a solid plan that accommodates everyone, as outlined by your criteria. I'm looking forward to it.

Support.

Mel: Good. Even though this session had some major twists and turns, I think we made tremendous progress on a tough problem with many interrelated issues.

Encouraging during the wrap-up.

Kate: We actually went through three stages: groupthink and false harmony, conflict, and now collaboration.

A nice piece of information sharing that summarizes the dynamics of the session.

Mel: You're right. Oh, one last thing. Here is a copy of the "Group Session Effectiveness Evaluation" we have been using to critique our meetings. Fill it out and give it to Bill so he can put the results in our minutes. We'll review the results at our Monday meeting.

Closes with a written meeting process check.

This session was not all milk and honey. It had its ups and downs, its conflict and harmony, its feelings, facts, solutions transition, its mistakes, its strong primary and secondary facilitation, its tensions, and its humor.

Mel did an excellent job of switching hats to keep the group informed about the role he was operating from as he made transitions between the role of primary facilitator and group manager. Randall saved the team from a groupthink decision because he had the courage to speak up against the majority opinion (which in this case was everyone else but him). Not an easy thing to do, but he did it because he had strong convictions. Through everyone's collective efforts, a potentially explosive situation was turned into one that reached a productive conclusion. Mel, sorting out positions, and Deonne, clarifying the interests behind the positions, performed major pieces of facilitation. With that accomplished, getting the group members to focus their energies on reaching consensus on a strategic plan to accommodate the interests of all members was the final step. Mel did a unique thing when he defined the criteria for the strategic plan in terms of interests that emerged from the three positions. That was the art of excellent facilitation performed at its best.

There are other examples of facilitation hits and misses within this meeting that you may have marked. That is fine because this analysis was not meant to cover every nuance.

A CONCLUDING THOUGHT

There is an old story about three men fishing on a small lake. The owner of the boat watches in astonishment as his two companions, one after the other, climb out of the rowboat and walk across the water to the concession stand. Assuring himself that his faith is as great as theirs, the owner steps from his boat and promptly sinks. The first fisherman turns to the second and says, "Do you suppose we should have shown him where the rocks were?"

Like the story, facilitating collaboration is not a simple matter of getting out of an old rowboat, strolling across the water into a conference room, waving your arms, sprinkling magic fairy dust on everyone, and then sitting back to watch a beautiful meeting unfold. You need to know where the rocks are. That's what this book has been about. I've tried to show you where the rocks are so you can use them as stepping stones to *unleashing the collaborative genius of your work team.*

Index

CRM Films

CRM Films is a world leader in the production of organizational training videos. Its ever-expanding library is relied on by training professionals in business, education, government, and the military to elevate the insights, interpersonal skills, and workplace performance of hundreds of thousands of people every day.

For more information call
1-800-421-0833

CRM Films
2215 Faraday Avenue
Carlsbad, CA 92008

MINING GROUP GOLD BOOK
To order *Mining Group Gold: How to Cash-in on the Collaborative Brainpower of a Group,* call
1-800-762-4496

Other books of interest to you from Irwin Professional Publishing . . .

THE TEAM-BASED PROBLEM SOLVER
Joan P. Klubnik and Penny F. Greenwood

This unique book (with 3.5″ diskette included) makes it easy for teams to focus
on the specific steps of the problem-solving process and the skills necessary for
ensuring team success. Includes a real-world model that integrates the ideas
presented in the book with challenges faced in everyday team situations. (200
pages, includes diskette)
ISBN: 0-7863-0290-9

LEADING TEAMS
Mastering the New Role
John H. Zenger, Ed Musselwhite, Kathleen Hurson, and Craig Perrin

Shows how managers can successfully adjust to today's changing team-based
work environment. Includes several self-tests and quotes, stories, and advice
from successful team leaders. (275 pages)
ISBN: 1-55623-894-0

THE CREATIVE COMMUNICATOR
399 Tools to Communicate Commitment without Boring People to Death!
Barbara A. Glanz
Kaset International

Includes several models, guidelines, and fresh ideas for organizations that want
to communicate their quality commitment to employees and clients. (200 pages)
ISBN: 1-55623-832-0

Available at fine bookstores and libraries everywhere.